KANT ON FREEDOM, NATURE, AND JUDGMENT

Kant's *Critique of Judgment* seems not to be an obviously unified work. Unlike other attempts to comprehend it as a unity, which treat it as serving either practical or theoretical interests, Kristi Sweet's book posits it as examining a genuinely independent sphere of human life. In her in-depth account of Kant's critical philosophical system, Sweet argues that the *Critique* addresses the question: for what may I hope? The answer is given in Kant's account of 'territory,' a region of experience that both underlies and mediates between freedom and nature. Territory forms the context in which purposiveness without a purpose, the Ideal of Beauty, the sensus communis, genius and aesthetic ideas, and Kant's conception of life, and proof of God are best interpreted. Encounters in this sphere are shown to refer us to a larger, more cosmic sense of a whole to which both freedom and nature belong.

Kristi Sweet is Associate Professor of Philosophy at Texas A & M University. She is the author of *Kant on Practical Life: From Duty to History* (Cambridge, 2013), and numerous essays on Kant's practical philosophy and aesthetics.

KANT ON FREEDOM, NATURE, AND JUDGMENT

The Territory of the Third *Critique*

KRISTI SWEET

Texas A&M University

Shaftesbury Road, Cambridge CB2 8EA, United Kingdom

One Liberty Plaza, 20th Floor, New York, NY 10006, USA

477 Williamstown Road, Port Melbourne, VIC 3207, Australia

314–321, 3rd Floor, Plot 3, Splendor Forum, Jasola District Centre, New Delhi – 110025, India

103 Penang Road, #05–06/07, Visioncrest Commercial, Singapore 238467

Cambridge University Press is part of Cambridge University Press & Assessment, a department of the University of Cambridge.

We share the University's mission to contribute to society through the pursuit of education, learning and research at the highest international levels of excellence.

www.cambridge.org
Information on this title: www.cambridge.org/9781009005326

DOI: 10.1017/9781009036634

© Kristi Sweet 2023

This publication is in copyright. Subject to statutory exception and to the provisions of relevant collective licensing agreements, no reproduction of any part may take place without the written permission of Cambridge University Press & Assessment.

First published 2023
First paperback edition 2024

A catalogue record for this publication is available from the British Library

ISBN 978-1-316-51112-1 Hardback
ISBN 978-1-009-00532-6 Paperback

Cambridge University Press & Assessment has no responsibility for the persistence or accuracy of URLs for external or third-party internet websites referred to in this publication and does not guarantee that any content on such websites is, or will remain, accurate or appropriate.

For my teachers.

For nature is our problem, the text for our interpretations.
—Immanuel Kant (*R* 18:274)

Contents

Acknowledgments	*page* viii
List of Abbreviations	ix
Introduction: Out in the Territory	1
1 Reason, Hope, and Territory	20
2 Reflection, Purposiveness, Metaphysics	56
3 "Life" and the Ideal of Beauty	81
4 The Sensus Communis and the Ground of the Critical System	104
5 Genius, Aesthetic Ideas, and a Spiritualized Natural Order	131
Interlude: Transition to the Critique of Teleological Judgment	154
6 The Domain of Nature as System: Ends	157
7 Hope and Faith: God in the Critique of Teleological Judgment	182
Conclusion: To See What Good Is There	204
Bibliography	207
Index	214

Acknowledgments

Three chapters of this book are expanded and developed from earlier versions of ideas published elsewhere. Parts of Chapter 2 appear in "Kant, Figal, and the Logos of Appearance," in *Die Gegenständlichkeit der Welt: Festschrift für Günter Figal zum 70. Geburtstag* (Tübingen: Mohr Siebeck, 2019). An earlier version of Chapter 3 appears in "The Ideal of Beauty of the Meaning of 'Life' in Kant's Philosophy," in *Kant and the Feeling of Life* (Albany: State University of New York Press, 2022, forthcoming). Parts of Chapter 4 appear in "Kant on the Sensus Communis: On What We Have in Common and the Ground of the Critical System," in *International Yearbook for Hermeneutics/Internationales Jahrbuch für Hermeneutik* 19 (2020), 98–112.

Research for this manuscript on Kant's concept of "territory" was supported by the Glasscock Center for Humanities Research, which awarded me a faculty fellowship to pursue this line of inquiry.

Abbreviations

Anth	*Anthropologie in pragmatischer Hinsicht* / *Anthropology from a Pragmatic Point of View*, in *Anthropology, History, and Education*
Br	*Briefe* (AA 10–13) / *Correspondence*
G	*Grundlegung zur Metaphysik der Sitten* (AA 4) / *Groundwork for the Metaphysics of Morals*, in *Practical Philosophy*
GwS	*Gedanken von der wahren Schätzung der lebendigen Kräfte* (AA 1) / *Thoughts on the True Estimation of Living Forces*, in *Natural Science*
IaG	*Idee zu einer allgemein Geschichte in weltbürgerlicher Absicht* (AA 8) / *Idea for a Universal History with a Cosmopolitan Aim*, in *Anthropology, History, and Education*
KpV	*Kritik der praktischen Vernunft* (AA 5) / *Critique of Practical Reason*, in *Practical Philosophy*
KrV	*Kritik der reinen Vernunft* (cited by A/B pagination) / *Critique of Pure Reason*
KU	*Kritik der Urteilskraft* (AA 5) / *Critique of the Power of Judgment*
LJ	*Logik Jäsche* (AA 9) / *Jäsche Logic*, in *Lectures on Logic*
MAN	*Metaphysische Anfangsgründe der Naturwissenschaft* (AA 4) / *Metaphysical Foundations of Natural Science*, in *Theoretical Philosophy after 1781*
MC	*Moralphilosophie Collins* (AA 27) / *Moral Philosophy, Collins*, in *Lectures on Ethics*
MS	*Die Metaphysik der Sitten* (AA 6) / *The Metaphysics of Morals*, in *Practical Philosophy*
OP	*Opus postumum* (AA 21–22)
PG	*Physische Geographie* (AA 9) / *Physical Geography*, in *Natural Science*

Prol	*Prolegomena zu einer jeden künftigen Metaphysik die als Wissenschaft wird auftreten können* (AA 4) / *Prolegomena to Any Future Metaphysics That Will Be Able to Come Forward as Science*, in *Theoretical Philosophy after 1781*R
	Reflexionen (AA 14–19) / *Notes and Fragments*
SF	*Der Streit der Fakultäten* (AA 7) / *Conflict of the Faculties*, in *Religion and Rational Theology*
TG	*Träume eines Geistersehers, erläutert durch Träume der Metaphysik* (AA 2) / *Dreams of a Spirit-Seer Elucidated by Dream of Metaphysics*, in *Theoretical Philosophy 1755–1770*
TP	*Über den Gemeinspruch: Das mag in der Theorie richtig sein, taugt aber nicht für die Praxis* (AA 8) / *On the Common Saying: That May Be Correct in Theory but It Is of No Use in Practice*, in *Practical Philosophy*
zeFP	*Verkündigung des nahen Abschliss eines Traktaats zum ewigen Frieden in der Philosophie* (AA 8) / *Proclamation of the Imminent Conclusion of a Treaty of Perpetual Peace in Philosophy*, in *Theoretical Philosopher after 1781*

Introduction
Out in the Territory

At the end of the *Critique of Pure Reason*, and again in his *Logic* lectures, Kant lists his now famous four questions: "1. What can I know? 2. What should I do? 3. What may I hope?" (KrV A805/B833). A fourth question – "What is the human being?" – is constituted by the first three (LJ 9:25). The answers to the first two questions of knowing and doing are given explicitly in their own critical examinations, respectively: the *Critique of Pure Reason* and the *Critique of Practical Reason*. Moreover, both of those texts are decisively oriented by the question they seek to answer. It is not obvious, however, what the orienting question of the third *Critique* is. It is even less obvious that the *Critique of Judgment* may be found to answer to the remaining question of *hope*. One hardly finds the word (*die Hoffnung*) in the text, let alone as a dominant motif. Yet, while "hope" itself is not thematized in the text, the very problem that gives rise to the need for hope is announced in the Introduction as the guiding thread of the inquiry. We find it in Kant's articulation of the "gulf" between freedom and nature that must be bridged (KU 5:175–6). A need for hope is born of our concern for freedom's efficaciousness in the natural order and has as its object a nature that is reconceived in the context of this concern.

Even under the auspice of the announced concern for freedom's efficaciousness in the natural order, the text often remains unclear or underdeveloped with respect to how its arguments may speak to the concern. It is hard, too, to overstate the internal diversity and complexity of the text itself. In some sense, then, it is not hard to see why scholars have not settled on the proper interpretative key for the text as a whole, or, as the case may be, rejected such a possibility entirely. The complexity is apparent even in a brief survey of some of the things the text treats substantively: the power of judgment, reflection, the principle of purposiveness, beauty, art, the sublime, organisms, the system of natural laws, culture, and the existence of God. Organizing how these multiple topics form a coherent whole in the context of Kant's own intersecting and sometimes oblique concerns is, to say the least, a daunting challenge.

My aim in this book is to provide an account of the third *Critique* as a unified text. Crucial to this endeavor is developing what I take the interpretative master key of the text to be. My thesis is that the interpretative master key to the text is the problem of *hope* – hope forms the horizon for Kant's examination of the multiple and seemingly disparate judgments of reflection human beings make. Hope, for Kant, is about the relation of reason and nature – specifically, conceiving of a nature that accords with the demands of freedom. What one hopes for is that nature, which appears indifferent or hostile to human ends, is, in some way, actually hospitable for human life. We hope that nature is underwritten by a deeper law than what we find in our experience as constituted by the laws of the understanding. We further hope that this deeper law also allows nature's law to be fully intelligible to us. Hope, then, is about the fittingness of nature and the world for human beings; hope seeks some evidence that we have a place in the broader context in which we find ourselves, that nature is not alien to us. The answer to the question of hope provided by the third *Critique* is in its description of a new vision of nature – it suggests a cosmic sense of nature, a larger system of nature to which we *belong* and which is meaningful. I further argue that for Kant, we encounter this nature in what he names the *territory* of judgment – a distinctive sphere of human life that allows for the transition he announces as necessary between freedom and nature.

In arguing that the third *Critique* is meant to answer the question of hope, I argue that we understand the internal unity of the text by way of the role the book plays in Kant's philosophical system. That is, the systematic function of judgments of reflection is the key to understanding the text as a whole. I argue this because Kant clearly takes the task of the third *Critique* to find a bridge across the gulf between freedom and nature – the gulf that gives rise to the need for hope in the first place. The significance of this bridging, however, can only be grasped if we first come to understand the character of this gulf and what drives the need for a bridge in the first place. This is no easy task – the problem captured in Kant's brief articulation of it in the Introduction of his text is nothing less than reason's demands in its relation to nature, which stands as the central axis and motivating tension of his entire critical project. Reason ultimately has an interest in unity – even more than this, in rational unity. Reason desires for everything to be rational, that is, to be determined by and identical to itself; this would be the pinnacle of a world fit for us. However, this is not how we find the world we inhabit; we then must turn to the next best thing in a *system* that approximates unity. Reason's interest takes shape in numerous ways. Practically, we are concerned about reason's efficacy in the natural order – we need our freedom to be made real and concrete through our actions. In consequence, we thus also need to think nature's susceptibility to the work of freedom. Theoretically, we seek the absolute intelligibility of nature in a system of laws. While the practical dimension may be said to be existential – that is, it pertains to our existence and whether we are making a difference in the world or belong to it at all – there is a further lathe to the existential import of the problem of hope as well. Bridging the gulf between freedom and nature speaks not only to completing the system of philosophy but also, with this, to the system of human faculties. It is a question about the unity – or, rather, systematic and harmonious relations of – the faculties of the human soul. The third *Critique* speaks then to the vocation of the human being to fulfill the demands of freedom in transforming the natural order as well as the possibility of an integrated, holistic human subject.

Judgments of reflection – the proper subject matter of the *Critique of Judgment* – are what allow for freedom and nature to be related to each other as parts of a larger system, and thus ultimately answer to our deepest philosophical and existential concerns. As I will seek to show, Kant argues that judgments of reflection form a third independent sphere of human life that functions as both *transition between* and *ground of* freedom and nature. The introduction of this sphere – the region of reflection is what Kant names a territory – mediates between and allows freedom and nature to come into relation, thus giving rise to a *system*. Judgments of reflection will be seen to serve both as a kind of hidden ground of as well as a transitional or intermediary sphere between the domains of freedom and nature. For Kant, it is constitutive of his transcendental philosophy that freedom and nature remain interminably independent of each other; the unconditioned and the conditioned will always remain mired in dialectic.[1] Yet reason cannot abide the separation of the two spheres of human life. What I will show is that while judgments of reflection do not ultimately supply any kind of *unity* to freedom and nature, they will address reason's interests in part through their *referential relation* to such a unity. Judgments of

---

[1] I think it is important to note that this is not an oversight on Kant's part, but rather an explicit commitment. It was clearly available to him to find an inner unity to freedom and nature. His commitment to their independence from each other was based squarely on his transcendental methodology; his recognition of and philosophical grappling with the problems this generated for him did not lead him, however, to acquiesce to reason's own need for this unity.

reflection complete the critical system in their independence from both freedom and nature; yet they also *suggest* the possibility of freedom's efficacious in the natural order in virtue of their gesture toward *life* – Kant's name for the inner unity of freedom and nature that is foreclosed by the critical system.

It is the *gesture* toward unity that has troubled, excited, and confused many philosophers and scholars after Kant. It appears troubling because, as Kant himself makes clear, life – or, the inner unity of freedom and nature – is not admissible into the critical system. Kant then, it would seem, opens himself up to charges of inconsistency or even senility. It appears exciting because in *life*, reason's needs do seem finally to be met and there is no longer a remainder or anything outstanding under the purview of reason. Here, it is not only that nature, as independent from freedom, is on its own accord serendipitously amenable to freedom; the suggestion of unity goes much further than this. It confuses scholars writing on the third *Critique* because Kant can seem, on the one hand, to maintain the "as if" character of what we come to judge about nature, and then, on the other hand, to assert a further unity of freedom and nature. At times, he can appear to wish to have it both ways. But this is simply the fate of a judgment that is reflective. I have been using the language of reference, suggestion, remind, gesture, point to, and so forth to describe how judgments of reflection function. This group of terms captures what it is like *for us to have* judgments that we make in reflection. Judgments of reflection are not knowledge claims; they offer, however, a kind of legitimate testimony about how things are.

What will emerge in this study, however, is that the as-if character of reflective judgments of nature only has purchase insofar as it is referentially related to a *further unity* of freedom and nature. This referentiality will function at once to leave reason dissatisfied in realizing its own aims, and at the same time to point to a robust *possibility* of reason getting what it most fully demands. Put another way, it gives us reason to *hope*; in hope, we do not get what we want, but maintain that it is possible to do so. Reason remains dissatisfied because it only gets the *suggestion* that nature will accommodate reason's ends. Yet this very suggestion is given with reference to the further possibility of reason's absolute determination of nature. That is, the unity of freedom and nature *appears as possible* in the third *Critique*; it is the pattern of unity that makes an appearance. This motive tension drives the third *Critique* and is, in part, what makes it so compelling and dynamic as a work. However, while many of the Idealists and Romantics who furthered Kant's transcendental project after him find a way to justify an inner unity of freedom and nature, the third *Critique* is distinctive in maintaining not only the seriousness of this demand but also, at the same time, the impossibility of fulfilling it.

One of the principal upshots of my reading of the third *Critique* will be to demonstrate how the text offers Kant's readers a markedly different and surprising account of the place of the human being in a larger, even cosmic whole. While the transcendental turn effected in the first and second *Critiques* places the human being at the center of and as source of any ordered whole – of knowing, and as author of the good – the third *Critique* initiates a new context for self-understanding. In the first two *Critiques*, we understand everything in virtue of our own faculties, and measure the good with respect to the good will of the human being; the third *Critique*, by contrast, introduces a kind of exteriority or externality. Hope, after all, refers us to what is outside of us and exceeds us. As Rachel Zuckert defines hope, it is "an attitude of tentative positive expectation ... that [something] could happen, might happen, if all things go well ... in ways we cannot ourselves control."[2] That which we cannot control is, broadly speaking, nature. This book will argue that Kant portrays nature in the third *Critique* as both something genuinely exterior to us and at the same time as a new context in which we must come to understand ourselves. While the new context is not the ancient cosmos of the Greeks and the Judeo-Christian heritage, the third *Critique* does take us back outside of the humanistic center of reason. The natural order as it is rethought in the *Critique of Judgment* is a natural order that is much more hospitable to the ends of human freedom than that of the first *Critique*. Accordingly, insofar as it can be said to inquire into the supersensible substratum of nature (KU 5:176), the *Critique of Judgment* may be understood as developing a new answer to the demand reason makes for metaphysics – one that remains bound by the constraints of the critical system. At the very least, we can see how the text addresses the deepest and most perennial questions of metaphysics as Kant himself articulates them.

In what follows, I will argue that the third *Critique* offers an account of our experience of a more expansive and encompassing system to which both freedom and nature belong. It is in virtue of their places in this larger system, of which both are a part, that freedom finds the possibility of efficacy in the natural order. In establishing a third, independent sphere of judgments of reflection, Kant articulates a system to which the human

---

[2] Rachel Zuckert, "Is Kantian Hope a Feeling?" in *Kant and the Faculty of Feeling*, Kelly Sorenson and Diane Williamson, eds. (Cambridge: Cambridge University Press, 2018), 242–259, 247.

being belongs and which is suited for its ends. Thus, the third *Critique* is not a text made up of discrete topics; its topic is not aesthetics or philosophy of science. Rather, its topic, in answer to the problem of hope, is the system of nature – *reconceived* – to which the human being and mechanical nature both belong. Aesthetic and teleological judgments are those judgments in which this expansive system of nature to which we belong appears to us. This *cosmic sense* of nature is what buttresses the hope we must have in reason's efficacy in the world.

With this interpretative key, then, I will offer a comprehensive account of the third *Critique* as an answer to the following question: What may I hope? Unlike the first two *Critiques*, however, the third *Critique* is not strictly progressive. Paul Guyer, in one of the first full-length manuscripts in English on the third *Critique* (or, on the Critique of Aesthetic Judgment), writes, "we can compare the structure of the *Critique of Judgment* to that of another machine ... an electric motor, in which increasing layers of wire are wrapped around a single central core, every new layer of wire making the motor more powerful."[3] This is an apt description of the argumentative structure of the text. That is, it does not exclusively develop one sustained and unfolding argument, but deepens and complicates its main ideas. In part, this fact about the text is what has allowed it to be treated in such a partitioned manner in the secondary literature and evade definitive interpretation. Yet it does consistently address one question. Each matter treated in the text – beauty, the sublime, art, the sensus communis, organisms, God – is comprehended by Kant according to the schema suggested here. Each matter treated answers to the question of hope and refers ultimately to a unity that at once exceeds the possibilities of the critical system and makes the critical system itself possible. This further means that any book on the third *Critique* that treats it in its entirety inevitably runs into this problem: The initial arguments are proved and supported only by way of the whole.

I develop this reading of the text, first, out of Kant's own discussion of the place of the third *Critique* in his philosophical system. Kant's concept of "territory" will thus form the crux of the interpretation I offer throughout this text. An analysis of his treatment of the territory of reflective judgments emphasizes not only their independence but also especially their role as both a transition between and ground of the other two spheres. How the system is completed offers a picture of how to understand the expansive whole Kant is attempting to articulate. My reading,

---

[3] Paul Guyer, *Kant and the Claims of Taste* (Cambridge: Cambridge University Press, 1997), xiii.

second, is further developed by emphasizing points in Kant's text that have been overlooked as central to its interpretation – the Ideal of Beauty, the sensus communis, genius, organicity, and ethicotheology. These moments of the text, rather than be understood as outliers in the overall movement of the argument that perhaps exceed the critical system, are precisely those moments that suggest the pattern of reflective judgments; these moments all embody a movement of referentiality, where the referent is a more fundamental unity of freedom and nature in the context of a larger system. I will not argue that these moments actually yield said unity, only that their pattern refers to it. To follow an ancient idea related to the arts in particular, these judgments mimic or imitate a unity of freedom and nature; this is to say they reflect it. The Ideal of Beauty provides the template for all judgments of taste. The sensus communis is the ultimate ground of judgments of taste, and, too, of all universality. Genius answers the question of how a human being is able to bring about a product whose production and effect exceed its own capacities. The *life* of living beings refers us ultimately to a system of nature given value in and through the existence of the human being. Ethicotheology develops the inextricable relation of the systems of nature and freedom, leading to faith in God. While much of the history of Kant scholarship has regularly treated these moments as strange aberrations or in the context of concerns alien to the text, we can see, on the contrary, that they gather together and help organize the larger trajectory of the project. Transcendentally speaking, these moments shed light on the conditions for the possibility of things appearing as they do out in the territory. These moments, too, most explicitly answer to the problem of hope as laid out in the Introduction to the book. How this is so can be elucidated by way of how this project fits into the longer history of the reception of the third *Critique*.

The reception of and secondary literature on the *Critique of Judgment* evidence not only the difficulty of the text, as Kant presents it, but also the difficulty of the philosophical task it sets for itself. That the third *Critique* is about the problem of the system of philosophy was clear to Kant's contemporaries and immediate successors. Both Fichte and Schelling published works on the very question of a system of transcendental philosophy oriented by the problem of freedom and nature during Kant's lifetime.[4] Hegel, too, published his own work in 1801 comparing

---

[4] On the importance of the third *Critique* for the development of Fichte's philosophy, see Daniel Breazeale, "'The Summit of Kantian Speculation': Fichte's reception of the Third *Critique*," *Anuario Filosófico* 52:1 (2019), 113–114.

Fichte and Schelling's attempts at establishing a system of transcendental philosophy following Kant, three years before Kant died. Even more than this, however, Schiller and Schelling both take their point of departure from what they find Kant to propose in the third *Critique*, namely that beauty and teleology secure the systematic unity of freedom and nature. For Schiller, beauty is an accomplishment of cultivated individuals and society: It unifies the otherwise opposed aspects of human nature; it is "beauty that can lead him back" to the proper, fully human, path.[5] Schelling, at least in some of his earlier works, argues that art is nothing less than the presentation of the absolute, understood as the primordial unity of freedom and nature, ideal and real. "Art," he writes, "is itself an emanation of the absolute."[6] As such it proves the original, ontological unity of freedom and nature. Hegel follows suit to a point, likewise arguing that beauty in art has a metaphysical significance with respect to the unity of freedom and nature.[7] He also recognizes that the third *Critique* addresses the unity of freedom and nature; he criticizes Kant for subjectivizing this unity, rather than committing himself to it as ontological. That the question of system was a – if not the – central issue for those inheriting Kant's transcendental methodology is evident even in Heine's account of *Religion and Philosophy in Germany*: "This want of a definite system in the philosophy of Kant was the reason why it was sometimes refused the name philosophy. As regards Immanuel Kant himself, there was justice in this; but not as regards the Kantists, who constructed from Kant's propositions quite a sufficient number of definite systems."[8]

If Kant's contemporaries and heirs in the speculative idealist tradition took the third *Critique* principally to address the question of a system of transcendental philosophy and, with this, the metaphysical unity of freedom and nature, we can nevertheless identify a competing strain of Kant interpretation. Frederick Beiser, in his *The Genesis of Neo-Kantianism*, argues that there were two traditions battling over Kant's legacy from the

---

[5] Friedrich Schiller, *On the Aesthetic Education of Man* (New York: Penguin Books, 2016), 33. See especially the Fourteenth Letter, where Schiller describes the "playful impulse" as that which unites "becoming with absolute being" (51).
[6] F. W. J. Schelling, *The Philosophy of Art* (Minneapolis: University of Minnesota Press, 1989), 19. He also argues for the systematic significance of teleology and beauty at the end of his *System of Transcendental Idealism* (1800).
[7] This claim is qualified for two reasons. First, Hegel preserves religion and philosophy as superior to art. Second, Schelling's views on this hierarchy of the presentation of the absolute do not seem to be settled over the course of his scholarship.
[8] Henrich Heine, *Religion and Philosophy in Germany* (Albany: State University of New York Press, 1986), 122.

very beginning. In addition to the rationalistic, speculative idealist tradition, he points to an "empiricist-psychological tradition," represented by Fries, Herbart, and Beneke. When, in the 1840s, the speculative idealist tradition had diminished in influence, it left an "enormous vacuum in the German intellectual scene."[9] This vacuum was filled by the heirs to the empiricist-psychologists and became what we now call the neo-Kantians. In this way, the anti-metaphysical orientation to Kant won out. "The battle to represent Kant's legacy was won – whether rightly or wrongly – by the thinkers of the empiricist-psychological tradition. They won the battle simply because their arguments were later adopted by a slew of thinkers whom we now happen to call ... neo-Kantians."[10]

The neo-Kantian tradition of Kant interpretation played a formative role in orienting the Anglophone reception of and scholarship on Kant. As John E. Smith observes in his Foreword to a 1956 translation of Richard Kroner's *Kants Weltanschauung* (from 1914):

> Kantian scholarship of the past century has been so vast and varied that it would be a matter of great surprise if different schools of interpretation had not developed. The so-called Marburg school is the one best known to English readers, and even those unfamiliar with the details have heard of the "back to Kant" movement associated with such commentators as Natorp, Cohen, and Cassirer.[11]

While the neo-Kantian movement was broad and diverse, we can nevertheless discern in it some key features. As Beiser points out, there was a general aversion toward and mistrust of metaphysical speculation.[12] The rise of the empirical sciences further contoured philosophical sentiment; philosophy could "find a definite place within the division of sciences, only as epistemology. The neo-Kantians had in mind a very specific conception of epistemology: the examination of the methods, standards and presuppositions of the empirical sciences."[13] This influence thus gave shape to how scholars approached Kant's texts. Smith argues that the neo-Kantians and their heirs "were inclined to regard post-Kantian speculation as misguided and thoroughly un-Kantian, a view which in turn led them to

---

[9] Frederick C. Beiser, *The Genesis of Neo-Kantianism, 1796–1880* (New York: Oxford University Press, 2014), 5.
[10] Beiser, *Genesis*, 16.
[11] John E. Smith, "Foreword," to Richard Kroner, *Kant's Weltanschauung: The Ethical and Religious Derivation of Kant's Worldview* (Chicago: University of Chicago Press, 1956), vii.
[12] See also the Introduction to Rudolf A. Makkreel and Sebastian Luft, eds., *Neo-Kantianism in Contemporary Philosophy* (Bloomington: Indiana University Press, 2010).
[13] Beiser, *Genesis*, 6.

strip Kant of all vestiges of metaphysical thought and thereby reduce him to a thinker concerned only with epistemology."[14] While the speculative idealists were concerned with questions of system, of the unity of freedom and nature, and did not shy away from transcendental metaphysics, the neo-Kantians initiated philosophical questioning that was more narrow in its scope and concerns, at least with respect to their interest in Kant.[15]

The secondary literature on the third *Critique* in the Anglophone context embodies this historical movement. First, the lack of engagement with the third *Critique* in favor of Kant's theoretical works is evident enough. One of the few books written on the third *Critique* in English in the twentieth century laments the neglect. Donald Crawford opens his *Kant's Aesthetic Theory* thus: "Many books could be written about Immanuel Kant's *Critique of Judgment*. The fact that so few have been written is one of the surprises in the history of philosophy."[16] When, in 1979, Paul Guyer published *Kant and the Claims of Taste*, he noted that Eva Schaper's study was being published that same year, but otherwise only cited a handful of book-length studies on the text, Crawford's being first among them. In addition to the neglect of the third *Critique*, we also find that the weight on the empirical sciences and emphasis on method shows up in our understanding of Kant's moral theory. Even with the proliferation of interest in Kant's practical philosophy following John Rawls' prominence, much of the scholarship on Kant's moral theory was (and still is) concerned with a kind of scientizing of maxim making – finding a rigorous, almost mathematically logical rule by which we may test our maxims for moral worth.

Second, and more importantly for our purposes, engagement with the third *Critique* has likewise been oriented by epistemological concerns. Guyer's work, along with Hannah Ginsborg's, is exemplary in this regard – one of the main lines of his argument is about the structure of reflective judgments. In this, his concern is with the workings of the mind when we

---

[14] Ibid., vi; vii.
[15] Smith goes much further, asserting that the upshot of the predominance of the Neo-Kantian approach to Kant "lost sight of the main purpose of Kant's thought because we have taken too myopic a view of his philosophy."
[16] Donald Crawford, *Kant's Aesthetic Theory* (Madison: University of Wisconsin Press, 1974), vii. The other early text taking up the third *Critique* that merits mention is J. D. McFarland, *Kant's Concept of Teleology* (Edinburgh: Edinburgh University Press, 1970). A review of the book notes that it is for "The student who wants to acquaint himself with the 'other' Kant, the Kant not of the 'categories of the understanding' and not of 'practical reason' ... but that lesser known Kant of the 'ideas of pure reason and of 'teleological judgment.'" L. Funderbunk, "Book Review of *Kant's Concept of Teleology*," *Kant-Studien* 62:1 (1971), 137.

make judgments of taste. This is not, as it were, a criticism of that text or others that pursue a similar line of inquiry. These examinations of Kant provide helpful reconstructions and insights into the text and into the epistemological dimensions of his thought. But it does narrow the scope of what may be significant about these insights when delineated by questions of knowledge or mind.

Even for those inquiries that have not been principally epistemological in orientation, there has largely been neglect of *system* being the context through which the text is explained. In addition to epistemological concerns, scholars have also asked how the third *Critique* speaks to or adjudicates concerns in Kant's practical philosophy. Henry Allison's *Kant's Theory of Taste* was one of the first to take this up. And, when Guyer came to take up the question of system in Kant in a number of important essays beginning in the 1990s, he, too, emphasized the practical import: "[S]uch a conception," Guyer wrote, "of the single system of nature and freedom is held to be valid only from a practical point of view."[17] Again, these are worthwhile inquiries, and add immensely to our comprehension of how Kant understands the relationship between ethics and aesthetics or teleology. They require supplementation, however, with a broader, more contextual account of the book as a whole.

There has only very recently been a proliferation of Anglophone scholarship interested in the question of system. Guyer, as mentioned earlier, initially wrote a series of essays – collected into a book – on the topic, beginning in 1990s. And, even a cursory overview of the most current secondary literature shows that more and more scholars recognize its import for understanding Kant and especially the third *Critique*. This is further evident in the expansion of inquiries into Kant's thinking about transitions, namely how to find an intermediary or transitional sphere between the theoretical and the practical, the ideal and the empirical.[18] The work with respect to this question is still nascent, especially when

---

[17] Paul Guyer, "The Unity of Nature and Freedom: Kant's Conception of the System of Philosophy," in *The System of Nature and Freedom: Selected Essays* (Oxford: Oxford University Press, 2005), 280. See also Guyer, "From Nature to Morality: Kant's New Argument in the 'Critique of Teleological Judgment,'" in the same volume. See too, Henry Allison, *Kant's Theory of Taste: A Reading of the Critique of Aesthetic Judgment* (Cambridge: Cambridge University Press, 2001). To the extent he is concerned not only to provide a close reading of Kant's arguments but also their systematic significance, he turns already to either the completion of the epistemic or moral projects.

[18] While the "transition" literature focuses heavily on the *Opus Postumum*, there is literature that treats the problem in the third *Critique* as well. On the *Opus Postumum*, see Oliver Thorndike, *Kant's Transition Project and Late Philosophy: Connecting the* Opus Postumum *and the* Metaphysics of Morals (London: Bloomsbury, 2018). Thorndike argues that it is judgment that can effect the transition Kant is seeking. It is worth noting that Klaus Düsing's essay "Beauty as the Transition

considered in relation to those concerns scholars have been addressing for many decades.

These lacunas dovetail with the dearth of writing that seeks a unified interpretation of the text. This may be the most striking feature of the secondary literature to readers. As Fred Rauscher opens his book review of Zuckert's *Kant on Beauty and Biology*: "The slogan for commentators on Kant's *Critique of Judgment* has often been 'divide and conquer.'"[19] The internal problem of the text is captured in John Zammito's articulation of it at the outset of his own reconstruction of the book: "The hermeneutical problem posed by the third *Critique* is why Kant should have brought his treatments of aesthetics and teleology together with systematic intent."[20] Indeed, Zuckert and Zammito have offered two of the main – if not only – attempts to take on this hermeneutical challenge directly and in its entirety.[21] Even here, though, they each privilege reading the text through either an epistemological or practical lens. Zuckert is concerned principally with Kant's claim that judgments of reflection and their principle of purposiveness speak to the "possibility of empirical knowledge."[22] She finds great success in discerning how the third *Critique* contributes to this end. Zammito, on the other hand, takes the culminating moment of the text to be in Kant's claim that "beauty is the symbol of morality."[23] Much of his account of the third *Critique* speaks directly to how our ethical vocation is furthered.

The difficulty of thinking the coherence of the two parts of the text is evident to any reader. They differ in ways that are not so minor: the subject matter, the employment of the a priori principle constitutive of the faculty. The first part of the text, the Critique of Aesthetic Judgment, takes up the topic of the beautiful. Moreover, it treats a *feeling*, namely a feeling of pleasure we have that grounds our judgment of taste. The second part of the text, the Critique of Teleological Judgment, by contrast, takes up the topic of the proper methodology in science, and then turns to topics suited

---

from Nature to Freedom in Kant's *Critique of Judgment*" also appears, along with Guyer's work, in 1990. There will be a further discussion of this literature in Chapter 1.

[19] Fred Rauscher, book review of *Kant on Beauty and Biology: An Interpretation of the Critique of Judgment*. Notre Dame Philosophical Reviews, May 7, 2009.

[20] John Zammito, *The Genesis of Kant's Critique of Judgment* (Chicago: Chicago University Press, 1992), 2. Little has changed, too, in the almost thirty years since Zammito also observed that "a good deal of Anglo-American interpretation chooses neglect the unity of the work for the sake of a few currently interesting arguments about beauty."

[21] This claim excludes those excellent commentaries on the entirety of the text, such as Nuzzo's.

[22] Rachel Zuckert, *Kant on Beauty and Biology: An Interpretation of the Critique of Judgment* (Cambridge: Cambridge University Press, 2007), 5.

[23] Zammito, *The Genesis of Kant's Critique of Judgment*, 3.

to theology. In neither case is there a feeling involved. On the face of it, at least, the two parts of the text seem to have little to nothing to do with each other. Of this difficulty, Allison notes that his initial intent for his *Kant's Theory of Taste* was to "deal explicitly with the thorny question of the unity of the *Critique of Judgment*,"[24] before realizing the book would be inordinately long. Allison is correct about the problem of length – one could not offer a close commentary of the kind his book affords as well as address the issue of the unity of the text in its entirety.

We have thus identified two interrelated themes in the reception of the *Critique of Judgment*. The Anglophone literature, first, has emphasized epistemological over systematic concerns. Second, few have taken on the task of offering an interpretation of the text that treats the whole as a unity. In what follows, I take my point of departure for understanding the text from what I argue is Kant's own: the question of system. In this, I think that the speculative idealist tradition saw something true about Kant, even if they themselves took systematicity in directions he himself patently denied. Systematicity always remained a *problem* for Kant, which marks him off profoundly from his speculative heirs. I take the question of system, then, to orient what I believe constitutes the unity of the text. The problem of systematicity thus forms the horizon for understanding the individual parts of the text on this interpretation. It therefore makes sense that this book treats moments in Kant's text that have been neglected in much of the Anglophone literature. The moments in the text that speak to systematicity are those very same moments that suggest metaphysical leanings the neo-Kantians and the Anglophone tradition would reject.

This book further treats judgments of reflection – and their characteristic principle of purposiveness – principally in their *independence*. That is, judgments of reflection are not examined principally for their epistemological relevance nor under the auspices of practical reason. Reason, as we shall see, is defined by its interests. Reflection, however, is disinterested; this separates the sphere of reflection from both the theoretical and practical domains. Only in its independence and separation, too, will it be able to establish a meditating sphere between those two domains. In this, these judgments also establish a larger, more expansive system of nature to which both the theoretical and practical belong. While the systematicity of freedom and nature speaks to a practical question, this questioning is not, for that, what legitimates or constitutes the system as a system.

---

[24] Allison, *Kant's Theory of Taste*, 6.

The accomplishment of a system is found in Kant's discovery a new faculty and a new a priori principle. It is by now well known that Kant initially set out to write a *Critique of Taste* upon completion of the *Critique of Practical Reason*. This task was the fruition of his early and long-standing interest in aesthetics, revised now under the auspices of the critical system; he had once rejected the possibility of a critique involving aesthetics, but had come to see its possibility after the second *Critique* also established a transcendental ground for a feeling. Angelica Nuzzo describes Kant's turn this way: "For it is the second *Critique* that brought Kant to the radical distinction between the feeling of pleasure and the faculty of desire."[25] Despite his intentions to write only a critique of taste, the trajectory of Kant's research culminates with his correspondence with Karl Leonhard Reinhold, where we find the first use of the title *Kritik der Urteilskraft* on May 12, 1789 (Br 11:39; "judgment" had been the declared object of critique in May 1789, to Herz (Br 11:49)). The shift from *taste* to the *faculty or power of judgment* announces with it a new object of inquiry for the text: It is not merely taste and the feeling of pleasure on which taste is grounded. Already by December of 1787 Kant had recognized that the principal topic of the book was teleology. His now famous letter to Reinhold announces the discovery of a new faculty of the human mind, and, with that, a new transcendental principle belonging to it. "I am now at work on the critique of taste, and I have discovered a new sort of a priori principles, different from those heretofore observed. For there are three faculties of the mind: the faculty of cognition, the faculty of feeling pleasure and displeasure, and the faculty of desire" (Br 10:514). The faculty of feeling and the power of judgment have their own principle: teleology.

The *Critique of Judgment*, then, explicates the judgments that enact the principle of purposiveness. This principle is only ever applied in reflection. Both judgments of taste and judgments of teleology are merely "reflective"; they are not, by contrast, determinative. In some sense, this alone should suffice for us to understand the unity of the text. These are the two cases in which our judgment lacks the determinacy offered under the understanding or of the moral law; we come to invoke the principle of purposiveness in order to make sense of our representations and the objects we find ourselves confronted with. However, that both judgments of taste and judgments of teleology are judgments of reflection that invoke the

---

[25] Angelica Nuzzo, *Kant and the Unity of Reason* (West Lafayette, IN: Purdue University Press, 2005), 72.

principle of purposiveness is, frankly, dissatisfying as an account of the unity of the text. While it is true that both the arts and the sciences as described by Kant fall outside of the domains of cognition and morality, we may still discern a more concrete and determinate relation between them beyond a shared reflective structure and a priori principle.

Perhaps the most sustained effort to forward a thesis that comprehends the third *Critique* as a unity is Zuckert's *Kant on Beauty and Biology*. Zuckert takes the Critique of Teleological Judgment to lead in importance. Her thesis is that the principle of purposiveness "is a necessary, transcendental principle of judging ... because it makes our comprehension of order among natural diversity possible, for it is the form of the 'unity of the diverse' as such, or 'the lawfulness of the contingent.'" She goes on to argue that the subjective character of the judging discloses something key, too, insofar as "the subject must be understood as ... engaged in a future-directed anticipation of an indeterminate, non-conceptually ordered whole."[26] Zuckert is of course correct that the third *Critique* is occupied principally with the possibility of an ordered whole. Teleology, for Kant (as for all thinkers of teleology), is explicitly about an ordered, unified whole. As a causality in accord with ends, teleology names the coming into being of something in just such an ordered, unified way. It is in virtue of its end or purpose that a thing is organized into a coherent whole. While Zuckert's argument and analysis are compelling, it ultimately remains partial in its understanding of the text. As I attempt to show, the whole of a system of laws is only one aspect of what the third *Critique* concerns itself with.

I argue then that we can grasp the difference between the two sections of the book by way of their role in establishing a larger system of freedom and nature, by way of offering accounts of a reconceived nature to which we belong. In this, the difference between the two sections of the book lies in the *scope* of nature being judged. The Critique of Aesthetic Judgment reflectively judges there to be a larger whole to which the human being belongs; this part of the text offers something more akin to ancient cosmologies in seeking to comprehend an order of which human beings are a part. Here, we come to situate ourselves as part of a larger, unified whole that encompasses the domains of freedom, nature, and the human being itself. Thinking of this ordered whole cosmically fits not only with Kant's concerns, but should not surprise us, given the legacy of thinking these issues in the history of Western philosophy. The association of a universe that is beautiful in virtue of its ordering can be traced back even to

---

[26] Zuckert, *Kant on Beauty and Biology*, 5.

the Pre-Socratics. Indeed, the word *kósmos* itself means not only universe but also *ornament* and is the root of our own category of words having to do with things that are aesthetically pleasing (i.e., the cosmetic). In the Critique of Aesthetic Judgment's cosmic sense of nature, we find that we belong already to a meaningful order of things; as a "territory," this meaningful order often remains hidden or covered over when taken up into the spheres of freedom and nature. By contrast, the Critique of Teleological Judgment reflectively judges that the order of nature – as a system of laws and interrelation – can be comprehended as a unified whole by human beings. In the former, the ordered whole is suggested to be an order of rational nature that *exceeds and includes* the human being and in which we are able to find a home. In the latter, by contrast, we find that there is a natural order that is subject fully to the ends of human life. There, we give context and order to nature. Yet it still forms only one part of the human experience – it is the sphere of nature already included within the larger order suggested in the first part of the text. The possibility of nature in this sense – namely, as a determinate sphere, being fully subject to our faculties of cognition – is conditioned by the larger, harmonious system to which we both belong. Both, in being ordered in the ways they are, answer to the question of hope by suggesting that freedom and nature are not in opposition but, rather, are intimately related in ways we cannot comprehend, but we can feel or judge. Even more, in the first part of the text, we find that it is nature itself as it appears to us – in beautiful natural objects and in art through the genius – that suggests we belong to it. In teleology, however, the life of living beings gives us faith in a God who created an order of nature whose highest purpose is moral.

The scope of nature being judged is bound up with the relation this nature has to human beings. Beauty bears an inner relation to human beings; it exemplifies an intimacy of belonging. We are only externally related to nature conceived as a teleological whole – that is, what is essentially human stands outside of nature conceived systematically. While Kant does not explicitly couch the difference between and, ultimately, the relation of the two parts of this way, we find elements of this distinction in the Introduction. Kant writes,

> On this is grounded the division of the critique of the power of judgment into that of the aesthetic and teleological power of judgment; by the former is meant the faculty for judging formal purposiveness (also called subjective) through the feeling of pleasure or displeasure, by the latter the faculty for judging the real purposiveness (objective) of nature through understanding and reason. (KU 5:193)

He repeatedly marks the distinction between the two sections with what it is that grounds the purposiveness of the object – the human subject or the object of our judgment. It is the subjective correspondence of subject and object in judgments of taste, moreover, that Kant names as "essential" to a critique of the power of judgment, as it "alone contains a principle that the power of judgment lays at the basis of its reflection on nature entirely a priori" (KU 5:193). As aesthetic judgments of reflection engage the principle of purposiveness without any purpose, they represent the pure form of the judgment, which is then made more determinate or particular by way of a concept of nature in teleological judgments. That aesthetic judgments of reflection ground purposiveness in the *subject*, too, suggests that these judgments are about an *inner relation* of the human being to something exterior. Teleological judgments, by contrast, are *strictly about what is exterior*. We are thus related only externally to nature in teleology. As a consequence, aesthetic judgments of reflection constitute the "propaedeutic of all philosophy," whereas teleological judgments belong properly only the theoretical part of philosophy, that is, the domain of nature (KU 5:194).

The two parts thus suggest two different possibilities for a transition between the domains of freedom and nature, two occasions for having hope. In pointing us toward a larger, unified whole to which freedom, nature, and human beings belong, aesthetic judgments of reflection suggest a territory that somehow includes freedom and nature already. In this, nature is conceived of much more expansively; it is suggested that it already is contained within a free, rational whole that reveals itself at key junctures in the natural order and our experience of it. Teleological judgments, insofar as they yield the possibility of a completed system of nature, provide the ground that Kant has in mind for the domain of nature and our understanding of it. And, too, nature as a system of laws and of purposes allows us to think of the ends of human reason as the highest purpose of said nature, thus providing something like a more determinate picture of the possibility of freedom making its ends real in the natural order. This is not a nature we belong to, however, as in the Critique of Aesthetic Judgment, but, rather, is a nature that, in the end, belongs to us.

While this schema may not be a complete account of the relation between the two parts of the text, I do think it provides helpful markers for thinking about the expansion of the concept of nature we find in the text as an answer to the problem of hope. Nevertheless, the following chapters will seek to provide an interpretation of the text that supports this basic division and relation.

Chapter Summaries

In Chapter 1, I lay out the basic interpretative key of the text through an examination of hope and of territory. I develop reason's demand for the unconditioned along with the requirement for its self-consistency as the driving force behind the need for hope. I then briefly consider what hope itself is. I move next to how hope is met in Kant's philosophy by way of judgments that we make out in the territory. The territory, I argue, completes Kant's system insofar as it functions both as a transitional and mediating sphere between freedom and nature, and the ground of these two spheres as well. Lastly, I consider how the system that Kant envisions here, along with our encounters out in the territory, may work to recast Kant's Copernican turn and the subsequent centrality of the human subject.

In Chapter 2 I examine the significance of the two principal features of the faculty of judgment: its characteristic activity of *reflection* and its constitutive principle of *purposiveness*. Chapter 2 directly takes up the metaphysical resonances of Kant's account, and the sense beautiful things give us that we belong to a more expansive, even cosmic, order. This chapter will highlight the emphasis on *possibility* out in the territory, and argue that what appears, appears in its possibility. I further argue that what appears to us is the very ground of appearance itself as an orderedness in appearance. Lastly, I suggest that our relation to this orderedness is interpretative, thus opening a future for metaphysical inquiry that is rooted not in speculation, but reflection.

In Chapter 3, I examine Kant's account of the Ideal of Beauty. Contrary to most interpreters, I take Kant at his word that the Ideal forms the measure of the judgment of taste in providing the original pattern that all other beautiful things follow. I further argue that the content of what Kant describes in the Ideal is nothing other than *life*. Life, for Kant, is the unthinkable causal union between force and matter, freedom and nature. All judgments of taste, then, refer us to such a unity, and thus to an outside of the critical system. Nevertheless, in suggesting the possibility of such a union, the beautiful is able to serve as a transition between and likely ground of the two domains of freedom and nature.

Chapter 4 argues that the sensus communis forms the keystone of Kant's critical system. Kant develops his idea of the sensus communis as a response to the *quid juris* of the judgment of taste – by what right may I claim that this is beautiful? As a judgment made out in the territory, without a law, a judgment of taste is always in question. Kant's development of the sensus communis is shown to rely on two senses of its historical usage, both of which address skepticism. Kant's own use of the term, which refers to a sense that we can communicate with all other human beings, discloses to us that all human beings share a way of having the world, and, too, that we share a world in common. It thus grounds the universal character of both cognition and moral life.

Chapter 5 examines Kant's notion of genius and aesthetic ideas. Here, I argue that his discussion of genius forms a kind of Deduction for the possibility of producing objects that exceed our own capabilities. In this, I focus on Kant's descriptions of spirit as what nature gives both to the genius and thereby also to the work of art as what allows it to enliven our minds. Here, as earlier in the text, we find that human beings belong to a nature that is much more expansive than that of the first *Critique*; nature here is spiritualized. The chapter concludes by highlighting Kant's repeated observations that nature is *expressing* itself through genius, and I link this, then, to the communicability that underlies the judgment of taste more generally.

Chapter 6 turns to the Critique of Teleological Judgment. Here, I trace Kant's remarkable line of argumentation from our encounters with living beings (organisms) to culture. Our encounters with living beings justify the use of teleology as a principle to organize our mechanistic inquiries into science. It further allows for us to judge nature, as a whole, as a system. Nature as a system, as we come to see, is oriented not only by human life but also specifically by the work it can do to discharge human beings from its order. If beautiful things remind us we belong in the world, there is a dialectical reversal here suggesting that we do not belong to the natural order. This comes out in Kant's discussions of *culture* and of the *sublime*, which are ways nature appears to discharge us from its influence. Nature thus supports our moral vocation by releasing us from its influence over us.

Chapter 7 focuses on Kant's introduction of a new conception of the relation of the systems of freedom and nature as *reciprocal*. Here, under the auspices of what he calls an "ethicotheology," he describes these two systems as sharing an identical final end, and therefore also being conjoined by that very end. Such a description of this relation is only possible if we view the relation of the two systems from out in the territory. This reflective position further judges freedom as a fact in nature, and opens up the possibility of us being convinced of the existence of God as the author of a nature that now, ineluctably, appears to us as meaningful. In this, nature comes to belong to us.

I

Reason, Hope, and Territory

The purpose of this chapter is to articulate how Kant conceives of his philosophical system and to situate the *Critique of Judgment* and judgments of reflection within it. In examining Kant's system, we can come to understand the centrality of hope and how the third *Critique* addresses it. We need hope because reason's demands are not met. Hope – and its maintenance – is afforded to us in the development of a systematic relation between freedom and nature. This systematic relation is accomplished in judgments of reflection as described in the third *Critique*.

This chapter, then, will argue that the consanguine issues of system and hope motivate and orient the third *Critique*, as well as provide the overarching context for understanding its parts. First, I will lay out what it is that reason wants. What reason wants, Kant argues, is a unified totality. This desire – reason is, definitionally, the faculty of desire – is the central and organizing desire of human life. As such, it orients the use of all of our faculties and organizes all of our other interests. Second, *hope* emerges because we do not find this unity in our experience of things – theoretically or practically. Yet reason's self-consistency demands its possibility: It is only rational to pursue what is possible. Third, I will turn to Kant's notion of system and his conception of it as articulated in the Introduction to the third *Critique*. In virtue of not realizing reason's demand for a unified totality, freedom and nature are brought into relation via a system. This system is established by way of a third, mediating sphere of judgment. Crucially, he names the sphere of judgment a "territory," a motif I will rely on in forming the subsequent interpretation of the text. It is in virtue of being out in the "territory" that we are able to grasp how beauty and teleology serve as both *transition between* as well as *ground of* freedom and nature, thereby establishing and completing the system of philosophy and of human faculties. Fourth, I turn to the broader significance of the territory and the more expansive system of nature and freedom Kant suggests by it.

1.1 What Reason Wants

The demand for systematicity in Kant's philosophy ultimately arises as a demand of reason. To understand what need systematicity addresses, we must begin with the structures of human reason. Human reason demands an unconditioned totality, which can only take shape when things are brought into a systematic relation. In the Dialectic of the *Critique of Pure Reason*, Kant presents this structure. His aim is to lay out the origin of what he calls "transcendental illusion," the illusion we have that metaphysical objects – God, the soul, the cosmological whole – exist, and to offer a positive vision for the use of reason. His argument is that these transcendental ideas are born of reason itself, generated out of reason's syllogistic and inferential character and subsequent demand for the "unconditioned." While our experience, as governed by the understanding, constitutes a world according to the laws of cause and effect, reason seeks to go out beyond what is given in experience and extend the use of its categories. Reason, Kant writes,

> [s]eeks the universal condition of its judgment (its conclusion), and the syllogism is nothing but a judgment mediated by the subsumption of its condition under a universal rule (the major premise). Now since this rule is once again exposed to this same attempt of reason, and the condition of its condition thereby has to be sought (by means of prosyllogism) as far as we may, we see very well that the proper principle of reason in general (in its logical use) is to find the unconditioned for conditioned cognitions of the understanding, with which its unity will be completed. (KrV A307/B364)

While judgments are reached through the determination of the concepts of the understanding to yield experience, reason seeks to discern the condition for what we experience. Moreover, what is given in experience is already conditioned – governed by the principle of cause and effect through which we determine our representations. Reason thus seeks the condition for our given, conditioned experience. It subsequently continues to seek the condition for any new condition thus observed or discovered, ascending to higher and higher principles of unification that make intelligible why things are the way they are. In seeking the highest unity, reason pursues the unconditioned – the ultimate condition for why things are the way they are, and that which has its condition in and of itself. But this, Kant writes, is properly understood as a "need" of reason; it is not for that, to be taken as a transcendental principle of how things *are* (KrV A309/B365).[1]

In demanding the unconditioned, reason comes ultimately to demand the whole, or totality of things. In ascending higher and higher in principles of universality and unification, reason comes to contain the whole of *what is* under its purview. In a totality, each thing is intelligible in virtue of its conditioned and conditioning relation to everything else and to the whole itself. Kant names this totality and the unconditioned causality that stands as its cause "the absolute." The absolute, he reminds us, is valid in every relation. "Now a transcendental concept of reason always goes to the absolute totality in the synthesis of conditions, and never ends except with the absolutely unconditioned, i.e., what is unconditioned in every relation" (KrV A326/B382). Reason thus demands "the absolute whole of appearances," which is nothing other than the "synthetic unity" of our experience, carried "all the way to the absolutely unconditioned" (KrV A327/B384). Reason seeks an absolute, self-standing totality that is, also, a unity; in a totality, all that there is, is part of one larger thing, unified internally.

Reason thus demands, theoretically, that nature be absolutely intelligible to us. This intelligibility, furthermore, is measured in conformity with reason's own structures. What reason wants is for the world to be thoroughly rational, and thus transparent to our reason in virtue of its own rationality. Not only, then, would the entire natural order be unified under one, highest unconditioned, but this unconditioned would be reason itself – the human being and the whole of the natural order would belong to one ultimate rationality. This ideal of intelligibility with respect to how things are is embodied in what Hegel would later call "absolute knowing."

The scope and limits of our experience and possibilities for knowledge, however, preclude such knowing. We thus come to posit metaphysical objects in lieu of our experience of an unconditioned that establishes a highest unity to the way things are. Kant identifies this positing as "transcendental illusion," and argues that we cannot ever rid ourselves of our tendency toward it; the strength of this demand of speculative reason cannot be extirpated. Kant addresses the possibility that critique will in some way be able to curb our propensity to posit metaphysical objects that allow us to think the whole. "Transcendental illusion," Kant writes, "does not cease even though it is uncovered and its nullity is clearly seen into by transcendental criticism" (KrV A297/B353). It can never be made to

---

[1] This is Kant's criticism of Leibniz – he took the principle of sufficient reason to be objective, and not merely subjective.

disappear; the best we can get, he asserts, is not to be deceived by it. It is for this reason that Kant announces at the very opening of the first *Critique* that, "Human reason has the peculiar fate in one species of its cognitions that it is burdened with questions which it cannot dismiss, since they are given to it as problems by the nature of reason itself, but which it also cannot answer, since they transcend every capacity of human reason" (KrV Avii). Coming to consciousness of the source of our desire for metaphysical objects, as well as of the impossibility of ever satisfying this desire is not, for Kant, a remedy for assuaging the desire. We therefore always remain with the desire – we remain in a condition of perpetual striving and with an unending and unyielding "felt need" (WDO 8:136).

Reason is what guides and orients the use of the understanding in our pursuit of complete intelligibility. This pursuit is nothing other than the natural sciences – the fulfillment of our rational desire to know the way that things are. On one side, we cannot extirpate the desire that drives this. On the other, we are fated to our limited knowing; our faculties simply cannot grasp the unconditioned. In this tension, Kant argues, we must assume that it is nevertheless *possible* for us to discern an entirely ordered nature, structured according to a system of universal and intelligible laws. The pursuit of our speculative ends through scientific inquiry is only rational if we take the fulfillment of our ends to be possible. There is a deep claim about reason's self-consistency in Kant's argumentation here: *It is irrational to pursue ends we know we cannot reach*. However, as we do not *know* we cannot reach them, we may have *hope* nevertheless that it is possible.[2] Hope fills in that space between what reason wants and what reason is fated to.

While speculative reason remains in a permanent state of desiring and subsequent dissatisfaction, Kant suggests initially that practical reason may meet a different fate, though its demands are still for the unconditioned whole. "[P]ractical reason," he argues, "has the causality actually to bring forth what its concept contains; and hence of such wisdom we cannot likewise say disparagingly: **It is only an idea**; rather, just because it is the idea of a necessary unity of all possible ends, it must serve as a rule, the original and at least limiting condition, for everything practical" (KrV A328/B385). Reason, in the will, is a causal force in the world; as

---

[2] While Zuckert's *Kant on Beauty and Biology* does not associate *hope* with this, it is this speculative demand that she argues orients and guides the third *Critique*. Further down I will argue why I believe this is an appropriate use of the term.

such, it may be capable of effecting the very thing it seeks in its speculative capacity.

Reason in its practical use also demands an unconditioned whole. This unconditioned whole takes shape, as "a necessary unity of all possible ends," named in the first *Critique* as a moral world, and then in his practical works as the kingdom of ends or the highest good.[3] In short, what practical reason demands is a world that is *morally intelligible* (KrV A809/B837ff). A morally intelligible world would be organized completely by the universal laws of morality; this world would take shape as one in which human reason prevails over nature, in which all human beings respect and promote the ends of all other human beings. This world is perfectly ordered according to the prescripts of reason, and in it, practical freedom and happiness are both made systematic. A morally intelligible world is a world that makes sense morally, such that all human beings are morally good and are happy as a result of this virtue. This is meant, for Kant, to take shape in republican states with laws that embody the form of universality prescribed in the moral law, ethical communities (religion), a cosmopolitan condition in which states relate to each other according to the dictates of peace. In this perfectly rational world, the ends of all human beings are completely coordinated; each is free to pursue his or her own ends and does so in a way that allows for others to do so, too.

The unconditioned totality, from a practical point of view, is a moral world that is caused by the exercise of human freedom. The morally good will is unconditioned; it is the cause of itself when moved to act from duty; the morally good will causes itself to act through its self-legislation and actualization of its freedom.[4] It is in this way that practical reason, through its own efforts, works to bring about the unconditioned totality demanded by reason. As practical reason is nothing other than human freedom, our will in its goodness is the unconditioned causality that causes the whole of the conditioned (human ends).

Kant's most sustained discussion of the proper end of practical reason is in the second *Critique*, in the "Dialectic of Pure Practical Reason," in his treatment of the highest good. It is also in this section that reason's efficaciousness in the practical sphere comes into doubt, and thus will lead explicitly to the need for *hope*.

---

[3] I argue for this at length in *Kant on Practical Life: From Duty to History* (Cambridge: Cambridge University Press, 2013). See especially chapter 4.
[4] For a longer account of this, please see chapter 1 of my *Kant on Practical Life*.

Kant opens the Dialectic thus: "Pure reason always has its dialectic, whether it is considered in its speculative or in its practical use; for it requires the absolute totality of conditions for a given conditioned, and this can be found only in things in themselves" (KpV 5:107). The dialectic of practical reason is found in its object – the thing that it is meant to effect through its own efforts. This end is what the moral law demands, and what it will effect through its own causal activity as principle of the good will. Kant names this end *the highest good*. By the highest good, he writes, he means to designate the *complete* good for a human being. As the complete good, it includes all possible goods for human life; these comprise the moral or rational good, virtue, and the natural good, happiness. While virtue is the supreme good, and good in itself, happiness is only conditionally good. "Happiness is something that, though always pleasant to the possessor of it, is not of itself absolutely and in all respects good but always presumes morally lawful conduct as its condition" (KpV 5:111). That is, it is only genuinely a good when it is conditioned by virtue; the happiness of an evil person is not, in fact, a good. At the same time, virtue is not itself the complete good, as we would not name a virtuous human life without happiness – the satisfaction of our desires – complete.

This description of the highest good is, to a great degree, commensurate with previous descriptions of the highest good in the history of philosophy. Philosophers have long recognized that the highest and complete good for human life involves both moral goodness and pleasure. As Kant notes, however, philosophers have typically sought a *unity* between these two aspects of a good human life. For Aristotle, for example, virtue produces its own attendant pleasure that completes the action; virtue is in itself pleasurable. In the Epicurean (and, later, utilitarian) tradition, it is the pursuit and production of pleasure that is itself the moral good. In Kant's view, these philosophical positions defend an *analytic* unity of virtue and happiness, that is, that they are already inherently related to each other (KpV 5:111). But he takes this idea to be *uncritical*: These philosophers do not have the benefit of the transcendental turn and are simply dogmatically asserting what it is that reason demands.

What is distinctive about Kant's considered conception of the highest good is the independence maintained between our rational and natural ends. Kant insists that they do not mutually entail one another. Because of this, they can only be thought to stand in a synthetic or causal relation. That is, virtue must be thought to be the *cause* of happiness (KpV 5:113). Our happiness is only good if it is conditioned by our virtue, and the totality of our ends can only be thought, as we have seen, as the unconditioned causing the whole of our conditioned ends. Virtue must be what causes our happiness, but without the virtue itself being collapsed into what it is that makes us happy. Happiness must retain its character as the fulfillment of our *natural* desires. In his earliest account of the highest good, in the first *Critique*, there is a *necessary* causal relation between the universal exercise of virtue and the production of happiness. In describing what he names a moral world, he writes of it as "a system of self-rewarding morality," (KrV A810/B837) wherein the virtue of everyone directly causes the happiness of everyone else. In the second *Critique* account of the highest good, and going forward, Kant abandons the notion of such an immediately productive system of causal mechanism. Rather, the relation between virtue and happiness is mediated by a third thing – a certain kind of world.[5] Kant will retain his commitment to the idea that the causal relation between virtue and happiness is mediated through a *world* throughout his practical opus. Kant's account of how virtue causes happiness is not focused on the individual – one's individual virtue does not cause one's happiness. At the individual level, the best one can expect is moral contentment (KpV 5:119).

The establishment of the moral world requires reason to effect itself in and ultimately transform the natural order at a number of sites: the influence of nature on our wills, the character of human relation in unsocial sociability, the proclivity to war between states. At every turn, the demands of reason find a nature that opposes its aims and resists its efforts to establish a thoroughgoingly morally intelligible world. We are obliged to pursue this world by actively pursuing not only a private moral sphere where we treat individuals as ends in themselves, but also in the public sphere of society and civil life. The highest good is where all are both virtuous and happy, and my individual responsibility is to contribute to this.

The dialectic of practical reason comes to focus, then, on how the practically unconditioned (virtue) can cause the whole of the conditioned (happiness), and with this, ultimately effect a world that mediates the relation. This world is accomplished as a transformation of the natural

---

[5] Whether Kant has a theological or secular vision of how the highest good is met – whether in an afterworld or a world here on earth – is a matter of long debate. For our purposes, it is not particularly relevant. What is key is that there is a gap between the unconditioned and conditioned, virtue and happiness (the exercise of our freedom and the satisfaction of natural desires). For a longer account, though, of his argument for the moral world, see chapter 3 of my *Kant on Practical Life*. See also my forthcoming piece "Mapping the Critical System: Kant and the Highest Good," *Journal of Transcendental Philosophy*.

order to accord with reason's laws. Perhaps even more than the difficulty of transforming a nature that resists becoming a moral world, we also find that our natural end of happiness stands outside of the purview of reason. We already know from the opening of the *Groundwork* that reason is ill suited to the task of fulfilling our natural desires. For Kant, our own happiness is, in fact, not up to us. In keeping with its etymology, happiness is a matter of luck; we depend on nature to give it as a gift. "*Happiness*," he writes, "is the state of a rational being in the world in the whole of whose existence *everything goes according to his wish and will*, and rests, therefore, on the harmony of nature with his whole end as well as with the essential determining ground of the will" (KpV 5:124). And in the third *Critique*, happiness is "the kind of end that can be satisfied by the *beneficence* of nature itself" (KU 5:429-30).

The object of the rational will in the highest good, then, is not something that is up to the will alone. That is, the efforts of reason itself are unable to bring about the highest good. Reason, it seems, depends on something else – nature – for the realization of its ends in the practical sphere.

Yet the demand for the highest good is not diminished for all of this. Indeed, Kant's commitment to the realization of reason's ends in the highest good is absolute. The highest good in the world must, therefore, be possible. He writes,

> Now, since the promotion of the highest good, which contains this connection in its concept is an a priori necessary object of our will and inseparably bound up with the moral law, the impossibility of the first must also prove the falsity of the second. If therefore, the highest good is impossible in accordance with practical rules, then the moral law, which commands us to promote it, must be fantastic and directed to empty imaginary ends and must therefore in itself be false. (KpV 5:114)

Unless the highest good – whose realization does not depend entirely on our own efforts – is able to be realized in the world, Kant believes that the moral law that commands its realization is invalid. This is a strong claim; it is also one Kant holds consistently and which parallels that of theoretical reason. The problem, then, is this: Reason, in its practical idiom, has demands that must be realized. And, it is irrational and contradictory for reason to command something absolutely that is impossible. This would destroy the unconditional, sovereign, authoritative nature of reason itself. At the same time, reason's demands do not seem to be able to be realized, in virtue of the interminable dialectic we find between reason and nature.

The satisfaction of reason's ends, then, must depend on something outside of reason, something that undoes or effaces the dialectic of reason and nature. Reason's self-consistency depends on the possibility of realizing the necessary ends it prescribes for itself; it would be in contradiction with itself were it actively to pursue something that it itself takes to be impossible. For reason to maintain its rationality, it must be possible for its ends to be realized. What reason wants is for things to be thoroughgoingly rational, which takes shape in an unconditioned totality, a unified whole. However, our faculties cannot produce such a totality in experience, nor can reason itself produce the moral world. Reason thus depends on something utterly outside of itself to realize its ends. Hope will be the name for our orientation to reason's dilemma, and its proper object will be an exterior nature that can be transformed into a rational whole. Hope, therefore, is needed to maintain the rationality of reason.

1.2 Hope

We may be tempted to think of hope principally as something belonging to practical reason. Kant argues, however, that hope is "simultaneously" *both* theoretical and practical (KrV A805/B833). Kant rearticulates the third question of "What may I hope?" Thus, "If I do what I should, what may I then hope?" He understands this to be at once (*zugleich*) theoretical and practical "so that the practical leads like a clue (*Leitfaden*) to a reply to the theoretical question and, in its highest form, the speculative question" (A805/B833). The object of speculation is the absolute end of reason that lies beyond what we can find in experience. Reason becomes speculative, and not merely theoretical, when it leaves behind what is given through the understanding in seeking to satisfy its desire for the unconditioned. "A theoretical cognition is speculative," Kant writes, "if it pertains to an object or concepts of an object to which one cannot attain in any experience" (KrV A634/B663). Kant's formulation of hope as *zugleich* theoretical and practical will point us in the direction, then, of answering to reason's speculative questions (the highest speculative question being about God as the unconditioned). What are we to make of this practical clue? The practical – as the *ought* – gives us guidance for the theoretical and speculative – as *what is*. The ought, Kant argues, lends a kind of legitimacy to claims we might make about how things *are* beyond what we actually know about them. In this, the practical orients us in how we may take nature to be. It looks as if our practical concerns lead our theoretical ones; we are directed to answers to our theoretical and even speculative (i.e., metaphysical) questions by our practical interests. There can be little doubt that this is the case for Kant. If I am virtuous, I may hope to be happy. Hope, from this perspective, is about the possibility of the harmonization of the practical and theoretical, where the beneficence of nature meets up with our moral vocation. What we hope for, principally, is that there is a moral basis to nature that will allow it to conform to moral claims. As given to us through the laws of the understanding, nature has nothing to do with moral life. Nature is at best indifferent to us, and perhaps even obdurate or hostile. The object of hope is thus a nature amenable to the demands of morality.

The theoretical and practical simultaneity of hope is reiterated again by Kant a bit later:

> I say, accordingly, that just as the moral principles are necessary in accordance with reason in its practical use, it is equally necessary to assume in accordance with reason in its theoretical use that everyone has cause to hope for happiness in the same measure as he has made himself worthy of it in his conduct. (KrV A809/B837)

Hope is practical, first, because it originates in the practical interests of reason. It is theoretical, second, because our practical interest is in how nature is; nature is the object of theoretical inquiry and knowledge. This is why Kant insists that hope is both, *at the same*, practical and theoretical. Hope embodies the unity of reason's dual interests: Practical reason has its own interest in the object of theoretical reason. These interests thus converge in the speculative interests reason has – we hope that the cause of nature is a moral one.

Kant also seems to suggest, however, that hope has a theoretical register in its own right, and not solely one that originates in our practical interests. That is, there is a hope that belongs properly to reason in its theoretical use. He structures an analogy between practical and theoretical satisfaction:

> For all **hope** concerns happiness, and with respect to the practical and the moral law it is the very same as what knowledge and the natural law is with regard to theoretical cognition of things. (KrV A805/B833)

Practically, the demands of the moral law mean that we must hope for happiness. This, in turn, means that we must have a commitment to something theoretical, namely that nature is structured a certain way – amenable to moral life. In the strictly theoretical register, however, the demands of knowledge mean that we must hope that natural laws are cognizable by us. What we hope for is that nature is knowable, and that reason's desire to know will be satisfied. That Kant also takes hope to be aimed at the satisfaction of theoretical reason is confirmed elsewhere in his writings. While he does not address hope as directly in other works as he does at the end of the first *Critique*, we nevertheless find that he regularly invokes hope with respect to the satisfaction of theoretical reason. There are two key examples of this. First, in the *Critique of Pure Reason*, there are numerous instances where he refers to hope in this way. Most notably, he uses the word hope in his famed "island of truth" metaphor at the beginning of the section on phenomena and noumena. After naming "the land of pure understanding" "an island ... of truth" surrounded by a vast sea of illusion, he asks "whether there will be anything to hope for" in this ocean of reason's illusion (A236/B295). Hope here is clearly aligned with reason's interests in discovering the unconditioned out beyond the bounds of experience.[6]

We also find Kant using the word "hope" with respect to reason's theoretical prospects in the *Opus postumum*. The *Opus postumum* is dedicated to the problem of unity and systematicity in the natural order. In any case, the subject matter of this text is nothing other than the completion of a system of nature satisfying the needs of reason in its theoretical use. Hope is the name Kant gives here to how we comport ourselves to the prospects of such completion:

> As far as philosophy is concerned, it is my plan – and lies, so to speak, in my natural vocation – to remain within the boundaries of what is knowable *a priori*: to survey, where possible, its field, and to present it as a circle (*orbis*), simple and unitary, that is as a system prescribed by pure reason, not one conceived arbitrarily. This could not be achieved by the collection of the empirical elements of knowledge, fragmentarily assembled; for this does not allow one to hope for the conviction of completeness. (OP 21:524)

What we hope for is the completeness of a system of natural laws, which is effected, in the *Opus postumum*, by a transition between the metaphysical foundations of science and physics. Theoretical reason thus has its own hope for "the idea of a system combining" the elements of natural science (OP 21:208).

There is no disputing, though, that Kant takes up hope most directly in his practical philosophy. Given Kant's express commitments to the primacy of the practical, this should come as no surprise. Kant thus develops

---

[6] Hope is used in similar contexts, particularly with respect to system, at A12/B26; A616/B644; A743/B771; A756/B784; A764/B792; A796/B824. This last case suggests that theoretical reason finds its satisfaction in the practical use.

numerous sites of hopefulness in his practical writings; these are each about how we come to rethink nature so that the demands of the highest good are seen as possible. The postulates of practical reason are the first sustained engagement with sites of the possible efficaciousness of reason, thought through nature's amenability. Immortality speaks to the possibility of attaining genuine virtue, or holiness, "the complete conformity of dispositions with the moral law" (KpV 5:122), which Kant also names as worthiness to be happy. Kant asserts that "no rational being of the sensible world is capable at any moment of his existence" of attaining such perfection. We must therefore, he goes on, postulate a process of endless progress toward such purification. Immortality is thus the way we think it possible to transform our will to be perfectly in accord with the holiness reason demands of us. It may take an infinite amount of time, but it is possible for reason ultimately to triumph over the influence of nature in our wills.

The postulate of God, however, is Kant's first suggestion of how we think the possibility of *nature itself* as already in conformity with moral life. In this section of the text, Kant does not argue, as one may expect, for a God who sees into the human heart and rewards virtuous individuals with happiness. Rather, God is understood here solely as a "supreme cause of nature" (KpV 5:125). In this way, the existence of God is meant to guarantee that nature as it appears to us under the auspices of the understanding may not be the final word on the order of nature. As the moral author of nature, God allows us to think that nature has an underlying, supersensible causality that is amenable to moral life.

It is perhaps in providence in history, though, that Kant offers the most sustained example of *hope* in his corpus. Kant's development of a cosmopolitan aim in human history, and, in general, his view of a progressive history, allows us to think the possibility of a better future. While human history – which Kant takes to be the work of nature in its wars, competitiveness, and injustices – suggests to us that the moral world as embodied in cosmopolitan peace is impossible, Kant argues repeatedly that we must adopt a progressive view of history in order to take our moral ends as possible. In this, we rethink war as a means to peace, competitiveness as a means to moral discipline, and so on. This "hope for better times" (TP 8:309) is what orients viewing the natural movement of history as having a kind of hidden hand working toward the ends of human freedom.

Hope also plays a role in Kant's writings on religion. Understandably, as both sets of reason's interests lead us to ideas that are traditionally religious matters: the existence of and possible immortality of the soul and God.

Indeed, we might even argue that for Kant, religion is an expression of reason's desires, and a rational religion is one constituted solely by supporting reason's interests. In his religion writings, Kant adds further objects of hope. In a kind of transformation of his argument for immortality as a route to a pure, holy will in the second *Critique*, for example, Kant also notes that one also cannot help but hope for "absolution from his guilt" (R 6:76) from God. He also treats the prospects of miracles, which are indications that nature is not solely ordered mechanistically.

Hope therefore plays a central and decisive role in Kant's philosophy. It is necessary for reason's self-consistency, and the stakes could not be higher. Practically, the validity of the moral law – and thus the whole of moral life – is inextricably bound up with the realization of the ends of reason. Thus, the possibility that nature will conform to the demands of reason is no small matter. Indeed, the needs of reason and the rationality of reason itself all hang on hope, in virtue of reason requiring that nature itself – something outside of its control – be a certain way in order for it to be satisfied. It thus also gives rise to what is one of Kant's most remarkable achievements: the construction of a compelling and all-encompassing philosophical system.

Despite its status as integral to reason's self-activity, however, hope has received relatively little treatment in the scholarship on Kant. Only recently has nascent interest emerged, along with a recognition of the importance of hope. Christopher Insole, for example, does an excellent job arguing for the "irreducible importance" of hope for Kant by way of appeal to medieval theology.[7] He asserts, rightfully, I think, that our understanding of Kant on hope must be keyed to a broader understanding of the universe in which we live; indeed, I attempt to demonstrate this in what follows by drawing out the cosmic sense of nature that Kant develops in the third *Critique*, especially in our experience of the beautiful. Insole, along with Andrew Chignell, both reject earlier interpretations of Kant on hope that collapse hope into the practical or theoretical.[8] On the practical side, hope has been closely associated with moral motivation. This

---

[7] Christopher Insole, "The Irreducible Importance of Religious Hope in Kant's Conception of the Highest Good," *Philosophy* 83 (2008), 333–351. See also Adam Cureton, "Reasonable Hope in Kant's Ethics," *Kantian Review* 23:2 (2018), 181–203, for a recent entrée into the literature emphasizing the centrality of hope for Kant.

[8] Andrew Chignell, "Rational Hope, Moral Order, and the Revolution of the Will," in *Divine Order, Human Order, and the Order of Nature*, Eric Watkins, ed. (London: Oxford University Press, 2013), 197–218; "Rational Hope, Possibility, and Divine Action," in *Kant's Religion within the Boundaries of Mere Reason: A Critical Guide* (Cambridge: Cambridge University Press, 2014), 98–117.

association is not unwarranted; Kant himself sometimes situates hope in the context of the dangers of despair for undermining our moral motivation.[9] On the theoretical side, hope has been closely associated with "belief" taken epistemically; like Insole and Chignell, Zuckert also works to make a distinction between belief and hope.[10]

While these current engagements with Kant on hope make a welcome – if belated – contribution to our understanding of its importance to Kant's philosophy, they overwhelmingly treat hope principally as religious. What I have tried to emphasize here, however, is its supervening systematic importance; it may take shape in also religious ways, but it is not exclusively or even principally a religious matter for Kant.

But what, exactly, is hope? As we have seen, it is neither practical nor theoretical alone. It is both, at once, practical and theoretical. In this, *hope is some combination of will and epistemic status*; it is where the will and the mind meet. Chignell names it an "attitude," which approaches the duality and yet also unity of the phenomenon; Zuckert, too, in "Is Hope a Feeling?" calls it "an attitude of expectation."[11] There are a host of words that aim to get at the mingling of the will and indeterminate cognition that are further candidates to name what kind of thing hope is: assent, stance, comportment, posture, disposition, and conviction among them. Each of these words names the kind of will we have toward something that does not belong to the sphere of the known or knowable. It may be that hope, really, is a special kind of *interest* we take in how things are. Interests, for Kant, belong properly to reason, and thus capture a rational way of relating our desire to objects. It denotes, further, the *active* relation we have to our object – "attitude" may name a broader category of comportment, but fails to capture the active and desirous character of hope. Hope is not a position one adopts once and for all. It is an activity to be maintained – we can lose hope if we do not enact its movement continually. In this, it is close to the medieval theological virtues. Zuckert's examination argues for a similar understanding of hope. She captures the depth and radicality of hope by describing it as a "pre-reflective, felt orientation to the world."[12] It is, she summarizes, some thing that is already natural to human beings; it must, however, be *sustained*. Hope is something we can lose or turn away from

---

[9] Kant does not argue, however, that hope itself can ever be a proper moral motivation. This belongs to duty alone.
[10] Belief, here, is taken in its epistemic register. *Glaube* in Kant more complicated than this, but the epistemic register is certainly one Kant appeals to. See also Rachel Zuckert, "Hidden Antinomies of Practical Reason, and Kant's Religion of Hope," *Kant Yearbook* 10 (2018), 199–217.
[11] Zuckert, "Is Hope a Feeling?," 246.   [12] Ibid., 244.

when the evidence mounts against the possibility of achieving what it is we hope for. We maintain this hope, she argues, in "an alternative way of conceiving of the world, such that it may be understood as more, or (potentially) other, than it has been seen to be empirically – so that one may not come to, but *continue* to hope."[13] The third *Critique*, I will argue, provides a way of conceiving such a world; judgments of reflection in beauty and teleology, we will see, offer an expansive, cosmic sense of nature that speaks to the deepest needs of reason as articulated here.

Hope is not only born of reason's needs but is also circumscribed by reason. If reason's rationality – its self-consistency in pursuing its own demands – hangs on it, then it, too, must be subject to reason. Hope is not a mere wish or fantasy. We must have reason or grounds to hope for something. It is not rational to hope that one will someday become a very short tall person – that is impossible. But just what *kind* of possibility – that is, how possible something must be – for us rationally to hope for it is unclear in Kant.[14] Chignell, in "Rational Hope, Possibility, and Divine Action," takes up the "constraints" that circumscribe hope and lays out the three modal possibilities to which hope may belong: formal, logical, and real. He settles, rightly, on "real possibility," meaning simply, "that we Believe that such a connection is *really possible.*"[15] In this, we have "grounds" to hope; we do not have merely a lack of impossibility formally or logically (A809/B837). There is a positive indication supporting or buttressing our hope – the interest we have in nature's amenability to reason's ends is warranted not only from the perspective of reason's needs but also from nature itself. Zuckert concurs, arguing that Kant takes it "as a philosophical task to give an account (more or less extensive in the different cases) of how these outcomes might be really possible."[16] It is the real possibility of realizing reason's ends that sustains or maintains hope.

The *grounds* of hope, the reason we have in maintaining it are found, I submit, in the *Critique of Judgment*. The scope, limits, and demands of hope – of reason's interest in nature – are what orient the investigation of

---

[13] Ibid., 257.
[14] I treat this briefly in Sweet, "The Moral Import of the *Critique of Judgment*," in *Rethinking Kant Volume 2*, Pablo Muchnik, ed. (Newcastle: Cambridge Scholars Publishing, 2010), 222–236. There, I anticipate Chignell's emphasis on real possibility, noting that the third *Critique* exceeds the postulates in providing something akin to experience of a nature that is amenable to reason.
[15] Chignell, "Rational Hope, Possibility, and Divine Action," 106.
[16] Zuckert, "Is Hope a Feeling?," 249.

the human being's place in nature as put forth in the text. Crucially, and often unacknowledged in the literature, is that reason's interest is met only in something that is outside of reason itself. Reason's interests depend on something beyond reason – nature. It must therefore be in a disinterested experience of nature that hope is maintained. Judgments of reflection have just this combination of independence from the purview of reason as well as an empirical basis, as they are reflections on empirical representations. Only such an encounter can speak to reason's interests adequately.

1.3 Systematicity and the Territory of Judgment

Hope must be sustained in order for reason to maintain its rationality. The structure and arrangement of our faculties of mind preclude the satisfaction of reason's demand for an unconditioned totality. Our experience – as constituted through the faculty of the understanding – yields a nature that is at odds with reason's demands. And, our experience of human behavior and human history further belies the possibility that our moral ends can be realized in the natural order. How is hope sustained? The third *Critique* answers this question first, philosophically and transcendentally, in developing a system in which judgment is introduced as a faculty that mediates between reason and the understanding. In this, we are able to conceive of freedom and nature as related through a third, mediating sphere of "experience."[17] Second, the very judgments of reflection that constitute this third sphere are what give hope to human beings in their experience that the world is fit for us and our ends.

This section will argue that it is the faculty of judgment that functions as the third, mediating sphere in Kant's system. Judgment is what allows for a transition between freedom and nature. *That* judgment provides such a transition is not controversial. But how to conceptualize the need for and the functioning of this transition is far from settled in the scholarship. Versions of Lea Ypi's claim show up in nearly all of the literature on the topic: "It is widely recognized how in the third *Critique*, the unity of the system is promoted through the discovery of the principle of purposiveness

---

[17] Readers of Kant are aware that experience is a technical term in Kant, reserved principally for what is governed by the understanding. However, as judgments of reflection are about empirical representations, they are akin to experience, in contrast say, with mere fantasy or other representations produced through the mind alone.

linked to the capacity for reflective judgment."[18] But scholars have located the need for a transition in multiple places. Düsing names three sites of transition: the determination of the will, society, and the progress of culture in history. More recently, Rohlf offers an expanded defense of the idea that the transition resides in the determination of the will.[19] What I will suggest here, however, does not focus on any one site of transition, but the formal and systematic elements that would allow for such a transition at any particular site. Indeed, in the subsequent chapters, I address the different particular sites in more detail.

I argue here that judgment – judgments of reflection in particular – effects a transition insofar as it occupies what Kant calls the "territory." Kant develops his vision of a philosophical system in the Introduction using a set of geopolitical metaphors. In Section III, when he delineates how freedom and nature (reason and the understanding) may be brought into systematic relation, he argues that the power of judgment serves "as a means for combining [*Verbindungsmittel*] the two parts of philosophy into one whole" (KU 5:176). The combination of freedom and nature is not that of making them into one thing; judgment is the means of binding the two separate things together. He describes how it may accomplish this by invoking the geopolitical metaphorics he has just laid out for the reader. Kant writes:

> But in the family of the higher faculties of cognition there is still an intermediary between the understanding and reason. This is the **power of judgment**, about which one has cause to presume, by analogy, that it too should contain in itself *a priori*, if not exactly its own legislation, then still a proper principle of its own for seeking laws, although a merely subjective one; which, even though it can claim no field of objects as its domain, can nevertheless have some territory [*Boden*] and a certain constitution of it, for which precisely this principle only be might valid. (KU 5:177)

Here, the power of judgment is named as the intermediary between the understanding (nature) and reason (freedom). It is also identified as having its own territory, with its own a priori principle; in this territory, its principle of purposiveness is subjectively valid, that is, it does not legislate over the objects given but only over the subject's judgment. Kant's invocation of the technical terminology of field, domain, and territory will

---

[18] Lea Ypi, "The Problem of Systematic Unity in Kant's Two Definitions of Philosophy," *Kant und die Philosophie in weltbürgerlicher Absicht. Akten des XI. Internationalen Kant-Kongresses* (Berlin: De Gruyter, 2013), 783.

[19] Düsing, "Beauty as Transition," and Michael Rohlf, "The Transition from Nature to Freedom in Kant's third Critique," *Kant-Studien* 99 (2008), 339–360.

be where we can discern Kant's argument for how it is that the power of judgment, with its territory, provides a transition between freedom and nature. The subsequent chapters of the book will further illustrate how judgments of reflection serve to complete the system of philosophy by referring to a prior supersensible unity of the two separate spheres of freedom and nature.

Kant first describes his notion of a philosophical system at the end of the first *Critique*, and this discussion provides an initial clue for understanding his later account. "Under the government of reason," he writes, "our cognitions cannot at all constitute a rhapsody but must constitute a system, in which alone they can support and advance its essential ends" (KrV A832/B860). He goes on to note that

> [P]hilosophy is the science of the relation of all cognition to the essential ends of human reason ... Now the legislation of human reason (philosophy) has two objects, nature and freedom, and thus contains the natural law as well as the moral law, initially in two separate systems but ultimately in a single philosophical system. (KrV A840/B868)

The objects of cognition, which for human beings are nature and freedom, must be brought together as a "whole." They must be brought together under "one idea." He writes, "The whole is therefore articulated (*articulatio*) and not heaped together (*coacervatio*)" (KrV A833/B861). We would not, this suggests, call something a whole consisting of things that are simply gathered together. A "heap" suggests disorder, a multiplicity held together only by proximity.

That the whole must be "articulated," however, provides a clue to what the system of philosophy should be, given the irreducible difference between the spheres of nature and freedom. Kant's use of *articulatio* invokes the principal medical use of the term. In this context, to articulate is to join, as one would the bones of skeleton; indeed, the Latin comes to us from the Greek *enarthrosis*, designating a ball and socket joint. We may still today refer to an "articulated skeleton" to designate that the bones comprising it are all put together properly. For something to be articulated is for it to be put together in just this proper way; moreover, this requires literally being "jointed" (*gegliedert*). Freedom and nature can come to be more than a heap of two independent spheres the way that bones can be joined to one another in the whole of the human body. In becoming joined (or jointed together), they also become part of a larger whole. The metaphor of an organism for the whole goes even further, with Kant likening the whole to "an animal body" (KrV A833/B861). Each part of the whole can only be understood, indeed can only function, in virtue of its relation to the other parts of the system as well as to the idea of the whole. In fact, as this book will demonstrate, judgments of reflection explicitly refer to the idea of the whole as the means by which they join the other two parts together.

Kant's discussion of territory and domain in the opening sections of the third *Critique* describe how it is that judgment joins freedom and nature together, forming a larger systematic whole. Few, if any scholars, have treated this section with any real interest, let alone have taken it as the guiding thread of how to think about the larger system of a purposive nature to which freedom and mechanistic nature both belong.[20]

Kant develops his account of the system of philosophy, its constituent parts, and their relation to each other in geographical and geopolitical metaphors. While we might at first dismiss the seriousness of invoking metaphors for such ground-laying work, we would do well to recall that Kant's reliance on metaphors is nothing new. Throughout his writings, Kant draws upon rich and textured metaphors to illustrate, illuminate, or highlight philosophical arguments. Some are even quite memorable, like the "light dove" of Platonic thinking in the opening pages of the first *Critique*, and some show up over and over as threads woven across his works – juridical metaphors and military metaphors perhaps most prominently.[21] We can think here especially of Dieter Henrich's influential essay on the juridical metaphor Kant employs in the transcendental Deduction of the first *Critique*.[22] Henrich turns to eighteenth-century juridical practices of the Deduction as a way to illuminate Kant's argument. It is hard to overstate the contribution an unfolding of this metaphor has made to our understanding of Kant's text; it provided an interpretative key that Kant clearly intended but did not provide. Similarly, I wish to focus on his geographical metaphors to clarify his conception of reflective judgments as the ground of a philosophical system

---

[20] There is one notable exception to this. Rudolf A. Makkreel treats this section of text adeptly in his *Orientation and Judgment in Hermeneutics* (Chicago: University of Chicago Press, 2015), see esp. 63–69. He does not, however, develop his reading with an eye toward explicating the role of the third *Critique* in Kant's critical system, nor with the intent of articulating the grounding character of reflective judgments.

[21] For an insightful read on a number of Kant's metaphors in the first *Critique*, see David. W. Tarbet, "The Fabric of Metaphor in Kant's *Critique of Pure Reason*," *Journal of the History of Philosophy*, 6:3 (July 1968), 257–270.

[22] Dieter Henrich, "Kant's Notion of a Deduction," in *Kant's Transcendental Deductions*, Eckhart Förster, ed. (Stanford, CA: Stanford University Press, 1989).

and as offering a transition between freedom and nature. This will require both careful textual analysis as well as the kind of historical mining of which Henrich availed himself.

Kant turns to geographical metaphors frequently and principally in his efforts to describe the aims of transcendental philosophy, its constituent parts, and their relations to each other. In this, he appeals to geography as a metaphor when he is concerned with the place of things. Geography, Kant writes, considers things "in terms of the places they occupy" (PG 9:160). The critical project, as Kant understands it, locates the places of our representations, and with this, the uses and boundaries of our faculties. As Jeff Malpas and Karsten Thiel note, "the task of the [first] *Critique* is to relocate metaphysics in its proper place – to achieve an appropriate 'placing' of metaphysics."[23] This "philosophical topology" involves for Kant the exploration of boundaries, surfaces, spheres, planes, domains, nomadism, resting-places, horizons, and paths. He even goes so far as to describe David Hume as a "geographer of human reason," a title he most certainly would have used to describe himself. Thus, Kant regularly turns to geographical terminology when he seeks to provide a description of the places our faculties occupy and their relations to each other. It is worth noting here, too, that in the first *Critique*, it is just this job of "placing" that Kant assigns to reflection in its transcendental mode. In the "Remark to the amphiboly of the concepts of reflection," Kant writes, "Allow me to call the position that we assign to a concept either in sensibility or in pure understanding its transcendental place" (KrV A269/B325). And, further on, it is transcendental reflection that discerns the place where representations "belong" [*hingehören*] (KrV A269/B325). The task of placing our faculties is, in fact, the task of transcendental philosophy. From the beginning of the transcendental project, then, we can see that Kant conceived of the relations between faculties spatially.

The first three sections of the Introduction to the *Critique of Judgment* develop the problem of the gap between freedom and nature and its solution in judgment by way of these metaphors. These sections are meant to motivate for the reader the significance of judgment for Kant's critical project. Section I first announces the division of philosophy into theoretical and practical. The object of theoretical philosophy is nature, or, an analysis of the concept of nature. Practical philosophy has the concept of freedom for its object. This difference in objects, moreover, yields different

---

[23] Jeff Malpas and Karsten Thiel, "Kant's Geography and Reason," in *Reading Kant's Geography*, Stuart Elden and Eduardo Mendieta, eds. (Albany: State University of New York Press, 2011), 195.

principles (KU 5:172). This is a repetition of what Kant has described in the first *Critique* cited earlier; there are two sets of "cognitions" that need to be joined into a larger whole.

In Section II, Kant introduces the geopolitical metaphors. The purpose of this section is to motivate for the reader the problem that the third *Critique* is meant to solve: It concludes with the famed "incalculable gulf" between freedom and nature. Kant begins first by naming a "field." This is the broadest possible relation between concepts and objects; he defines a field thus: "Concepts, insofar as they are related to objects, regardless of whether a cognition of the latter is possible or not" (KU 5:174). The field of concepts thus does not require any relation to their reality. In fact, he later defines the field as "inaccessible" for our cognition, equating it with the "supersensible" (KU 5:175).

Kant turns next to territory and domain, whose relation is key to understanding the importance of judgment for the system. Within the larger field of cognition, he names the "territory" the part "within which cognition is possible for us" (KU 5:174). Then, within the territory, Kant says that there are "parts" in which concepts "are legislative" (KU 5:174); these are domains (*Gebiete, ditio*). Thus, we have a kind of regional mapping or layering. The field is the region of all of our concepts; some of these relate to objects, some do not. Part of this field is characterized by possible cognition (the territory) and within what is possible to be cognized we have parts that are actually cognizable, that is, regions where our concepts are legislative over objects, and thus make them actual.

Before turning to a more thorough account of how we can understand Kant's description of territory, domains, and how they relate to each other, it is worth a caveat about our own understanding of these terms. Kant's uses of the terms differ from our own contemporary usage. Specifically, while the term territory has for us implicit within it a notion of jurisdiction – a territory is subject to law – this is a relatively recent equivocation. Historically, the relation of a specified area of land to authority, sovereignty, and law has been a site of contention and evolution, as Stuart Elden's *The Birth of Territory*, makes clear (among other scholarship in geography, political theory, and legal studies).[24] A survey of contemporary usage of the term, though, finds its intimate association with jurisdiction; indeed, "territorial jurisdictions" is a commonly used phrase in legal, political, and geographical discourses. This term can be understood, as Richard Ford defines our contemporary understanding, as "the rigidly

---

[24] Stuart Elden, *The Birth of Territory* (Chicago: University of Chicago Press, 2013).

mapped territories within which formally defined legal powers are exercised by formally organized governmental institutions."²⁵ It would be patently wrong to associate Kant's notion of territory with jurisdiction. Jurisdiction is from two Latin terms: *ius* (law) and *ditio* (power). *Ditio* is associated with domains for Kant. The difference between territory and domain, in fact, will be a difference in the force or power of the law over the region.

We must remember that in Kant's own time, the relationship between sovereignty and jurisdiction was insecure, and both were continuously contested – often violently. During Kant's life, the state of Prussia increased in size dramatically with the wars in Silesia and the partitioning of Poland. But even naming Prussia a "state" may mislead the contemporary reader; it belonged already to the Holy Roman Empire, which only officially dissolved in 1806. As Prussia grew, it took over the cobbled together regions of the crumbling Holy Roman Empire: duchies, Imperial Free Cities, counties, and provinces. Thus, internally, the authority and reach of law within Prussia was complex, often convoluted, and ever changing. Christopher Clark summarizes its organization in his definitive book on the Prussian state: Prussia, he writes, "was an assemblage of disparate territorial fragments lacking natural boundaries or a distinct national culture, dialect, or cuisine."²⁶ Indeed, the complicated bureaucracy that grew up around this configuration is notorious, if not entirely effective. Clark continues that even "[w]ell into the nineteenth century there were many areas of the Prussian lands where the presence of the state was scarcely perceptible."²⁷ When the state was present, it was often in conflict with more local authorities; when it was not immediately present, the local authorities still ostensibly derived their legitimacy and authority in virtue of their relationship with the Crown. In this, it approximated a loosely federal state, though its constituencies were less well defined.

Our understanding of territory may be closer to how Kant defines a domain, namely a region in which an administration (or faculty) has

---

[25] Richard T. Ford, "Law's Territory (A History of Jurisdiction)," *Michigan Law Review*, 97 (1999), 843.
[26] Christopher Clark, *Iron Kingdom: The Rise and Downfall of Prussia, 1600–1947* (Cambridge, MA: Harvard University Press, 2006), xvi. James Sheehan puts the point this way, "Imperial [HRE] institutions were a labyrinth of overlapping jurisdictions and special privileges, they had no well-defined center, just as the Reich [Prussia] itself had neither a capital nor a single source of sovereignty." James Sheehan, *German History 1770–1866* (Oxford: Clarendon Press, 1989), 15.
[27] Clark, *Iron Kingdom*, xvii.

legislative authority. Each of the two domains has a clearly defined set of objects over which their laws have dominion, the faculties in a domain are "legislative," and thus give the law to its inhabitants. *Gebiete* is an area under specific command; the word ultimately derives from observing or paying attention. A domain is thus the region to which one is attending and looking over. In this, the boundaries of a domain are clearly defined and what is included within these borders is subject to a specific rule. Indeed, the first two *Critiques* are specifically about the laws and set of objects for the concepts of nature (in the understanding) and the concept of freedom (in reason).

Kant seems to have adopted Leibniz's terminological distinctions. Leibniz writes that, "A dominion [*ditio*] is an area of inhabited land served by a common administration."[28] Theoretical philosophy is the domain of cognition – the region of objects over which the understanding is legislative (Kant famously uses another geographical metaphor in the first *Critique*, delineating this domain as an "island of truth"). The domain of practical philosophy is the domain of freedom – the region of objects over which the moral law is legislative. In each case, the region is defined by the scope of the administrative and jurisdictional reach of its legislating faculty.

Crucial for understanding how Kant is conceiving of a system of philosophy, however, is how the two domains relate to each other and to the territory. The two clearly delineated domains are both laid out over and contained within a *territory*. Domains, he writes, are "part of the territory," and he writes, "established (*erreichtet*)" on it (KU 5:174). Domains, then, are spheres of legislation – jurisdictions – carved out of and erected on the vaster territory of possible cognition.

A more robust account of what Kant means by territory is necessary to grasp how the domains may be established on it. For this, we can turn again to the likely source of Kant's use of the term, namely Leibniz. The concept of territory was in transition, mirroring the political developments of the age. In the two hundred years prior to Kant's writing, the concept of territory came to be associated, for the first time, with political or sovereign power. For Althusius (1563–1638), Knichen (1560–1621), and Locke (1632–1704), territory is linked inextricably to law – it is the area subject to a particular jurisdiction. Leibniz, however, maintains a subtle but decisive distinction between territory and jurisdiction. He begins his discussion of territory (*territorium*), with its "fundamental meaning":

---

[28] Gottfried Leibniz, *De Jure Suprematu Principum Germaniae (Caeserinus Fürstenerius)*, in *The Political Writings of Leibniz* (New York: Cambridge University Press, 1972), 114.

"a name common to a state or a dominion or a tract of land."²⁹ But he goes on, next, to address the interests that German jurists have in designating territorial right as the aggregate of laws and rights "which can come to obtain in an inhabited portion of the earth." Territory, then, is a "portion of the earth," *which can come to be subject* to a specific legislation – it is not yet under jurisdiction. He highlights this subtle difference between being subject to positive law and the *potential* for lawfulness in general when he distinguishes between the lord of jurisdiction and the lord of territory. The lord of jurisdiction treats individual cases and has the power to coerce "obstinate private persons." Jurisdiction, in effect, concerns the application and execution of the specific laws to which persons in a designated region are subject. The lord of territory, however, has the power to "do other things whereby the entire land might be brought under his command."³⁰ The lord of the territory does not enforce specific laws, but rather "the entirety of rights."³¹ In this, territory is the portion of land that while not under the authority of any particular enforcement may still be subject to lawfulness in general; it is the region of rightfulness as such.

When Kant designates *territorium* as *Boden*, he indicates that he does not have a legislative space in mind for the territory of judgment. It further suggests, too, his appropriation of Leibniz. Kant does not use the German *Landeshoheit* (typically translated as territory), which, for the German jurists, was a term associated with a jurisdictional region. But invoking *Landeshoheit* would have suggested a kind of legislative or sovereign authority that Kant clearly does not want to associate with territory.³² Rather, in considering territory as *Boden* – as soil or ground (literally – bottom) – Kant indicates that he has the broader geographical region subject to lawfulness in general in mind. It is not, for him, a delimited sphere over which one administration or faculty has dominion. And while later Latin came to understand *territorium* as "land belonging to the dominion of a certain ruler," its earlier meaning is closer to Kant's understanding, as "land about a city."³³ This should not, however, lead us to think that domains, in being circumscribed areas subject to particular laws, have supremacy over the broader territory of which they are a part in virtue of their legislative specificity. On the contrary, as Toyoda notes of Leibniz's rendering, "[t]he power of a lord of jurisdiction was but a 'mild

---

²⁹ Ibid. ³⁰ Leibniz, *De Jure Suprematu Principum Germaniae*, 115. ³¹ Ibid., 116.
³² Kant seems to use the phrase *Landeshoheit* only once, in his *Physical Geography* when contrasting who has propriety over mines. (PG 9:256)
³³ Carl Darling Buck, *A Dictionary of Selected Synonyms in the Principal Indo-European Languages* (Chicago: University of Chicago Press, 1949), entry 19.14.

power of coercion' only enforceable upon private persons. The lord of territory was the one who had actual control of the territory and its people and was therefore its sovereign in the strict sense of this word."[34] In the relation of a jurisdiction to a territory, the enforcement in a jurisdiction is predicated on the broader territorial condition of *enforceability*. Enforceability stands behind the actual force within a jurisdiction and is what makes jurisdiction possible. In this way, then, the legislation within a domain – the power a faculty has as dominion over its objects – is predicated on the territory on which it is located. The soil is the literal ground on which a domain must stand.

The structure of what I am calling enforceability, as necessary and prior to actual enforcement, is further confirmed in a crucial moment of Kant's *Doctrine of Right*. Property rights are the central focus of the establishment of a civil condition for Kant. The purpose of a civil condition, as Kant has it, is to ensure the intelligible possession of things, namely that I may take as *mine* things that are not currently in my empirical possession. Human beings must be able to have security in their use of things – they must be subject to our *wills*, and not merely to our physical possession. We must have dominion over them. For a civil condition to establish such rights, however, Kant argues that prior to such rightful appropriation, the things of the earth must not be nothing, they cannot belong first to no one. The things of the earth must already belong to all of us in a condition of "innate possession in common" (MS 6:250).[35] The determination of property as mine or thine, for Kant, relies on the *determinability* of land found already in its belongingness to the species as a whole. The original communal possession of the earth, Kant argues, is not determinate possession, but rather, determinability of the land as such. Something cannot be possessed by an individual unless it is first, originally, *possessable*. Only on the basis of its being already possessed in common is individual, intelligible possession made possible. Crucially, Kant associates this prior, originally communal possession of land that precedes rightfulness with *territory*: "All human beings are originally (i.e., prior to any act of choice that establishes a right) in a possession of land [*Boden*; this could be rendered 'territory'] that is in conformity with right" (MS 6:262). To be in conformity with right is not the same as being in a condition of rightfulness. To be in conformity with

---

[34] Tetsuya Toyoda, *Theory and Politics of the Law of Nations: Political Bias in International Law Discourse of German Court Councilors in the Seventeenth and Eighteenth Centuries* (Leiden: Brill Publishing, 2011), 87.
[35] This idea is not Kant's alone – advocates of a social contract all have some version of this notion.

right, as Kant has it, is to be amenable to right. In the same way, territory is the region of what is possibly determinable in the domains of freedom or nature. It is the set of objects that are amenable to determination and appropriation by our faculties.

Territory is thus the broader region of land that can become a domain. Territory is the area of land that is possessable; it can be annexed into a domain once possessed and thus subject to the force of law. The territory of which the two domains are a part thus functions as a kind of shared *ground* for both. The power of judgment can, he writes, "be annexed to either of [the theoretical or practical domains] in case of need" (KU 5:168). Indeed, all dominion is a kind of annexation – an appropriation of what *can be* brought under law into a sphere of specific legislation. When this happens, judgment becomes determinate; what is possibly cognizable becomes actually cognized, or determined through a law. A law (moral or cognitive) is enforced on the object in question.

In this, Kant outlines the territory as what grounds the otherwise disparate domains of theoretical and practical philosophy. They are both established or erected on this ground. This is how it may be able to provide the path for us to find a way from one domain to the other despite being separate in their own lawgiving regions. The problem, as Kant now comes to articulate it, is that the two legislative domains are irrevocably distinct, they "do not constitute **one** domain" (KU 5:175). In fact, he argues that there is an incalculable gulf between these two domains:

> [T]here is an incalculable gulf fixed between the domain of the concept of nature, as the sensible, and the domain of the concept of freedom, as the supersensible ... the latter **should** have an influence on the former, namely the concept of freedom should make the end that is imposed by its laws real in the sensible world, and nature must consequently also be able to be conceived in such a way that the lawfulness of its form is at least in agreement with the possibility of ends that are to be realized in it in accordance with the laws of freedom. (KU 5:176)

He continues to describe what makes a transition (*Übergang*) across this gulf possible: "Thus there must still be a ground of the unity of the supersensible that grounds nature with that which the concept of freedom contains practically." The two domains of legislative enactment are separated, Kant suggests, by a gulf – a *Kluft*, a ravine or crevasse – that is so great we cannot see across it (*unübersehbare*). Yet we are called to conceive of a "supersensible that grounds nature," which would make it amenable to the ends of freedom. Judgments in the territory arise from encounters there that indicate just such a supersensible.

Kant's description of the relationship between territory and domain provides the answer for how there can be a shared ground joining freedom and nature. We can imagine a large swath of land with two distant cities, separated by an open region. Each city is established on the land, the land that is then covered over in virtue of its annexation or appropriation. Between them is the land itself, the land upon which each is built. The sphere of *possible* cognition underlies both determinate spheres of freedom and nature and is what appears between them as undeveloped territory. In the jurisdictional spheres, the possible has been made actual through law. Thus, the very ground itself is what admits of an *Übergang*. Kant's geographical and geopolitical metaphors used to describe his system ultimately describe such a mapping of the place of reason (freedom), understanding (nature), and judgment (in reflection).

In Section III, Kant indicates that the land between freedom and nature – the exposed territory – belongs to judgment, specifically, judgments of reflection. This is the passage with which we began our investigation into Kant's notion of systematicity and the question of the role that judgment plays. The power of judgment, Kant writes, is the "intermediary between the understanding and reason" (KU 5:177). He then describes what can only be judgment in its reflective activity: "[I]t too should contain in itself *a priori*, if not exactly its own legislation, then still a proper principle of its own for seeking laws" (KU 5:177). He we see, first, that while the power of judgment has its own principle (purposiveness), it does not legislate over objects with it. What it does do, by contrast, is seek laws; this is what Kant means when he defines reflection: "If, however, only the particular is given, for which the universal is to be found, then the power of judgment is merely **reflecting**" (KU 5:179). Judgment in its reflective activity, then, "can claim no field of objects as its domain, [but] can nevertheless have some territory and a certain constitution of it, which for precisely this principle only might be valid" (KU 5:177). Insofar as judgment "can nevertheless have some territory," it constitutes its own sphere of human experience. Judgments of reflection, moreover, are simply the power of judgment in its *independence*. The power of judgment, we know from Kant's other works, is involved in both the determination of the concepts of nature in experience and in the determination of the will through freedom. But in both of these domains, judgment is determining – that is, it has successfully found a universal rule or law to apply to what has appeared to us and therefore is merely a subsuming power. "The power of judgment in general," Kant writes, "is the faculty for thinking of the particular as contained under the universal. If the universal (the rule, the principle, the law) is given, then the power of judgment is determining" (KU 5:179). In this way, judgment, as judgment, disappears into the determination made.

Even more than this, too, Kant argues in his first *Critique* account of reflection that "all judgments ... require a reflection" (KrV A261/B317). Reflection, here, is what finds the proper faculty and law for our empirical representations. Every empirical representation is *possibly* cognizable by us. Many are actually cognizable as experience or moral claims. Those for which no rule or law can be found remain, for Kant, merely reflective and subject to the principle of purposiveness alone.[36] In determinate judgments, reflection has an end station, and is thus hidden in the process of subsumption of a representation under a law.

To say that judgment in its reflective capacity is territorial is to say that judgments of reflection are, as Kant puts it, heautonomous.[37] Kant writes:

> The power of judgment thus also has in itself an *a priori* principle for the possibility of nature, though only in a subjective respect, by means of which it prescribes a law, not to nature (autonomy), but to itself (as heautonomy) for reflection on nature. (KU 5:186)

Judgment does not prescribe a law to nature; only the understanding can do that. Judgment, however, does reflect on nature and judge nature for itself in accord with its own law of purposiveness. And, Kant here returns us to the very definition of the territory as the region of objects that are *possible* for determination; the a priori principle of judgment is just the "principle of the possibility of nature."[38]

Therefore, as land that has been annexed already into a domain, judgment – and its activity of reflection – remains as a hidden ground insofar as we reside in the domains of cognition and morality. Once we have entered into a jurisdictional domain, the territory is in effect covered over and disappeared from view; objects of possible cognition are brought into actuality. Judgment underlies other arenas of experience in a way that it effaces any traces of itself. At the same time, judgments made out in the territory – judgments of reflection – are beyond the limits of the domains, and so, strictly speaking, beyond the boundaries of experience (taken as what is constituted by the understanding, per the first *Critique*). In judgments of reflection what appears *is the territory* – or ground – itself.

---

[36] For an extended analysis of this, see my "Reflection: Its Structure and Meaning in Kant's Judgements of Taste," *Kantian Review* 14:1 (2009), 56ff.
[37] Heautonomy will also be addressed in Chapter 4 on the sensus communis.
[38] How judgments of reflection embody possibility as such is taken up in Chapter 2.

It is only once we leave the jurisdictional domain – when we exit the city walls, so to speak – that we see the shape of the land on which the city rests.

The objects that belong to the territory of the power of judgment – that reside outside the city walls – and the judgments that arise there are explicitly about the ground the territory offers to the theoretical and practical domains. Thus, judgments of reflection are about the appearance of the ground of the two parts of philosophy; this ground is what allows for a transition between them, and between freedom and nature.[39] The various reflective judgments examined in the third *Critique* – natural beauty, artistic beauty, sublimity, organicity, culture – can each be seen as offering a mediating space between freedom and nature, between the practical and theoretical spheres. Each of these is a judgment made out in the territory, in the independent sphere of purely reflective judgment.

This structure of a transition is consistent with Kant's later conception of it; the later conception, too, provides further clarification to what role the third *Critique* may play in the system of philosophy. At the end of his philosophical career, Kant is increasingly concerned with a transition *within* the sphere of theoretical philosophy. In the last decade of his life, Kant worked on what would become his *Opus postumum* under the auspices of writing a "Transition from the Metaphysical Foundations of Natural Science to Physics." This project – and the need for a transition between the transcendental foundations of a science and its empirical instantiation – has principally to do with the relation between particular laws (which may only constitute a mere aggregate when taken together), and a *system* organized by principles. Kant writes, "Metaphysical foundations of natural science yield something that is certain and a complete system; but their purpose [*Gebrauch*] – the only one which can be envisaged for them – is physics, for which they can give us no material" (OP 21:474). Remarkably, Kant uses the same language and geographical metaphorics – of territory and gulf [*Kluft*] – to describe the problem here as he employed it in the third *Critique*. He writes,

> These two territories [*Territorien*] (metaphysics of nature and physics) do not immediately come into contact; and, hence, one cannot cross from one to the other simply by putting one foot in front of the other. Rather, there exists a gulf [*Kluft*] between the two, over which philosophy must build a bridge in order to reach the opposite bank. For, in order for metaphysical foundations to be combined with physical [foundations] (which have

---

[39] I argue for how this is so more fully in Chapter 2.

heterogeneous principles) mediating concepts are required, which participate in both. (OP 21:474)

The transition that needs to be effected, then, is between a systematic science and its empirical aspect. How this problem – and the promise of a solution – comes to the fore for Kant in the wake of the third *Critique* should be evident enough to its readers. As Eckart Förster suggests in his defining book on the *Opus postumum*,

> That Kant should have felt like putting the new discovery [of viewing nature as purposive and systematic] to a concrete use would hardly be surprising. The sudden possibility of progressing beyond where the *Metaphysical Foundations* had to leave off, and of further extending the a priori investigation in the field of corporeal nature, must have stared him in the face.[40]

Again, when Kant names the possibility of making a transition here, he turns to a *third thing – a set of mediating concepts* that allows for a bridge between two otherwise heterogeneous spheres. This set of mediating concepts provides a link between theory and its application in the natural order. Kant does not argue that we need something that *unifies* the particular laws into a system, but rather that their organization into such a system will require an entirely new set of concepts under which they are arranged.

It will be judgments of reflection – beauty, teleology – that comprise what is out in the territory. They are an entirely new set of judgments, between freedom and nature. They are then capable, too, of mediating between them. Kant is explicit about this, writing that "the power of judgment, provides the mediating concept [*vermittelnden Begriff*] between the concepts of nature and the concept of freedom, which makes possible the transition from the purely theoretical to the purely practical" (KU 5:196). The mediating concept, as the rest of the book will lay out in more detail, is the supersensible ground of nature that unifies it with freedom. While Kant names this as the thing required to allow for a transition between freedom and nature, it will be in the judgments described throughout the text that actually refer to such a unity. As reflective, these judgments do not instantiate this unity, but legitimately interpret what is given in some empirical representations as being like this unity.

---

[40] Eckart Förster, *Kant's Final Synthesis: An Essay on the* Opus postumum (Cambridge: Harvard University Press, 2000), 5.

1.4 Significance of the Territory

It is easy to discern that territory has significance in establishing a "joint" by which the spheres of freedom and nature are able to come into relation; this joint is what allows for two otherwise unrelated spheres to be thought together in some way. It is less obvious, however, that the territory is significant because in establishing this joint, it also displaces what may be seen as a hegemony of reason and the centrality of the human in Kant's philosophy. Yet this is evident at the outset by the need for hope in the first place. Hope is necessary because reason cannot fulfill its demands of its own accord – it depends upon or is conditioned by the natural order's amenability to its ends. Reason thus depends on something that is beyond its purview and over which it holds no sway.[41] Thus, reason's interest can only be met in a sphere of experience not subject to reason itself.

The way this takes shape, though, is in the establishment of the territory and thereby a system that puts reason in a broader, more encompassing context. In this, there is not only an exterior or other to reason in nature, which reason takes as its object to transform. With the territory and the establishment of a larger system, reason is recast as being within and also one part of something that exceeds it.

The import of this shift can be seen by way of contrast, first, to the Copernican turn that Kant makes in his transcendental philosophy. Rather than assume, as most philosophy before him had done, that "our cognition must conform to the objects," Kant argues that "objects must conform to our cognition ... [w]e can cognize of things *a priori* only what we ourselves have put into them" (B xvi/xviii). The transcendentally a priori forms of human thinking are what constitute our experience. Kant goes further, arguing that they constitute *reality*, that is, the way that things *are*. The human being stands at the center of reality: Our epistemology is transformed into ontology. Nature for us is not only constituted by our own faculty of understanding, but the whole of nature is a kind of projection of reason. Reason's theoretical needs, as we saw earlier, demand that we posit a totality of nature that is subject to the principles and structure of reason itself.

---

[41] That reason, which Kant describes as unconditioned, would be thus conditioned by something exterior to it was, for thinkers like Fichte, Schelling, and Hegel, an abysmal contradiction in Kant's thinking. This is the principal motivation for them in seeking an inner unity to freedom and nature, rather than preserving Kant's insight that nature is exterior to reason.

The import of this shift can be seen perhaps even more dramatically, second, by way of contrast to the projection of reason in its practical idiom. The confluence of the primacy of practical reason with practical reason's potential efficacy in the world means that its demands can come to dominate human life in a totalizing way. I will name this totalization Kant's *cosmopolitanism*. This name suggests, of course, Kant's famed theory of a cosmopolitan world order necessary to establish peaceful relations among states. This peace, in turn, is what allows for stability within individual states, and ultimately then for the flourishing of the individuals who comprise such states. The name further suggests Kant's theory of cosmopolitan right – the right each human being ought to have to travel the world and visit foreign lands. This right is predicated on our collective original possession of the earth and the finite character of the globe.

Kant's cosmopolitanism is rooted in a much deeper ground, however, and it is this ground that is challenged by the third *Critique*.

While in the sphere of knowledge it is the faculties of the human mind that constitute reality, in the sphere of morality it is human reason that constitutes the good. Even more than that, human reason is the good, in the most classical sense, that is, akin to the Good of Plato and the subsequent iterations of that notion in the Western tradition. Human reason itself is good, and the origin of all good there is in the world. The opening salvo of the *Groundwork* captures as much: "It is impossible to think of anything at all in the world, or indeed even beyond it, that could be considered good without limitation [*ohne Einschränkung*] except a **good will**" (G 4:393). The good will is the unconditioned good in the world. That is, the will determined to act in its own freedom, through the law it gives to itself, is both goodness itself and that in virtue of which anything else in the world may become good. "Freedom," Kant writes, "is the inner value of the world" (MC 27:344). The actualization or realization of our freedom is the absolute good, conferring worth through its relation to its effects. With this, human beings are no longer called to conform their wills to a transcendental good standing outside of themselves, to which they are subject. Rather, it is human reason itself, in the freedom of the will, which authors and gives the measure of the good to what is external to us.

The demands of reason are such, as we have seen, not simply that we enact a good will in its unconditioned freedom. Rather, this entails, for Kant, that we transform the natural order in which we find ourselves into a rational whole. This demand takes shape subjectively in the highest good as the proper object of the good will; that is, the entire constellation of ends for human beings is given in a moral world. All of our particular ends take part – or, ought to take part – in this objective. The horizon for all human activity, then, is the *world*; specifically, our horizon is the order of nature we are meant to transform into a rational whole. There are, for reason and therefore human activity, no ends or aims outside of these demands.

Kant is clear about the thoroughgoing character of reason's aims and the extent of its demands. We see it, for example, in his theory of right; politics for Kant is a species of morality. The moral good is what prescribes entering the civil condition as a duty (MS 6:267), and also provides the measure for justice in the state. The moral good is what must orient relations between states, and also what dictates our interpretation and understanding of human history. Even science, for Kant, is subject to, at the very least, a moral constraint insofar as he prescribes doing away with anything theory may yield that contradicts the possibility of moral life.

Under the primacy of practical reason, there appears to be nothing in human life that escapes the authority of the moral law. There is, then, no "outside" of the world in which we find ourselves. This comes to its fullest expression in Kant's actual argument for a cosmopolitan right. This right – for individuals to be granted visitation to foreign countries – is based on what he observes as a fact of our finitude, and ultimately elevates to an orienting ground for the political dimension of moral life. He writes, "Nature has enclosed [human beings] all together within determinate limits (by the spherical shape of the place they live in, a *globus terraqueus*)" (MS 6:352). The natural order we seek to transform has a concrete limit – the globe on which we live. The globe is the natural thing we aim to transform into the moral world through political aims.

The highest vocation of human life is manifest as transforming life on the earth. "The greatest problem for the human species," he writes, "to which nature compels him, is the achievement of a civil society universally administering right" (IaG 8:22). This aim provides the content of the highest good, and thus comes to totalize the possible ends of human life. It appears to us, then, that our consciousness of who and what we are is dominated by our boundedness on a globe. This is Kant's cosmopolitan turn – the human being, now the origin and source of the good, has the sole task of realizing that good on the finite sphere of the earth. In this context, nothing escapes the purview of practical reason; there is no "outside" of moral life; subsequently, we may find that there is no "outside" of political life as well. In the idiom of territory and domain, Kant's account of moral life may be an account that runs the risk of keeping us confined inside the walls of one city alone. *The polis, here, becomes our cosmos*, the all-encompassing context of our existence.

In one regard, the project of the third *Critique* is the completion of the Copernican moral turn in Kant's critical system. The nature of nature – as the object of a hope oriented by reason's interests – is seen throughout the text as amenable to the ends of freedom. We thus come to understand ourselves not only as rational beings standing over and against an indifferent and obdurate nature. Here, we find ourselves also already a participant in a nature that is supersensibly, and thus in way, hiddenly, for us. It is nature with a hidden moral author, a nature that sometimes yields hints of its authorship, so we do not despair. At times, too, Kant suggests that *we* – or, our faculties – are the supersensible substratum of nature. We do not have a place within this cosmic order so much as we give the order to the cosmos ourselves. In this, Kant's Copernican turn and his humanistic commitments find their ultimate completion.[42] Reason, human reason, really does come to reign supreme.

If the first two *Critiques* construct a cosmos with the human being as its center, source, and measure – a cosmos whose horizon and limit are circumscribed by the polis – the third *Critique* returns the human being to a broader context and offers an "outside" of what the faculties of the human soul constitute, project, and demand. The territory, first, is a region of human experience over which human beings do not legislate; it is a region, then, that is not subject to us. As we will see in subsequent chapters, the relation we are able to achieve with objects out in the territory is one of accord or attunement. We can come into a kind of harmonious rapport with them. Objects in the territory are beyond what we can understand – we experience them as *excessive* of our own capacities in multiple ways. Moreover, we experience them in their very exteriority, namely as something that is other or exterior to us and our ways of knowing and doing. Thus, as we shall see, they form a kind of disruption to our otherwise everyday course of experience and prompt us to reflect.

Second, as *ground* of the two domains over which we are able to legislate, we find that something outside of us makes possible the success of our attempts to understand and to have effects in the world. Not only do the objects we find in the territory stand outside of our everyday

---

[42] I am, of course, not the first to discern this movement in Kant's critical philosophy. This is the gesture that Hegel himself notes in Kant and then absolutizes in his own work. Fichte, too, resolved the interminable conflicts of reason and nature in favor of just such a humanistically centered cosmos.

experience and legislative capacities, but also, as ground, it displaces from our unreflective perspective of being the center and origin of what is. Something else appears to us as more originary than our own subjectivity.

The territory stands outside of human interests. It remains, in one regard, indifferent to our interests as we have them. At the same time and in another regard, however, the territory also provides for us a context for our interests that exceeds them. Out in the territory we are not in a foreign land but, it will turn out, are granted a deeper sense of belonging to something larger than ourselves. Out in the territory, we have the sense that our human pursuits are part of a much more expansive system of order and meaning. Whereas in Kant's Copernican – or, cosmopolitan – turn, the human being is the source of all meaning, in the territory we find the suggestion of a meaning that in some way precedes or grants us the possibilities for meaning we find in the human world.

The territory can also give perspective on and context to the other two domains. While Kant insists that the theoretical sphere of knowledge can have no bearing on the moral sphere, and clearly the practical sphere is in question with respect to its influence on the natural, the territory partakes of both without being subject to their laws. In escaping determination, judgments of reflection may be able to offer some critical perspective on the other two domains. The expansive capacities of thought and communication cultivated by judgments of taste may offer new avenues for approaching problems in civic life. Indeed, Hannah Arendt's observations about the sensus communis suggest just as much.[43] The teleology section is quite clear in how a reflectively conceived system of nature gives context to the more determinate empirical laws pursued by the natural sciences in the domain of nature.

The territory offers this possibility precisely because it is both independent from the other two spheres and yet also their ground. While the domains of freedom and nature have nothing to say to each other, the territory offers a glimpse of the city walls from the outside and provides a broader vista into which they can be situated. This move displaces the perspective we have from within the cities – where we are their center and horizon – and offers *a new horizon* in which the two domains now sit.

It is easy to see how Kant exemplifies a strand of modern philosophical thinking wherein the human subject is the ground and the measure of all things. But the third *Critique* places Kant in line, too, with

---

[43] This is not to endorse Arendt's description of the sensus communis in Kant. Rather, I am here picking up on the broader insight about the role.

earlier – Ancient and Medieval – sources of thinking that place the human within a larger context and wherein the measure of things is given in something beyond the inner life of humans. What the rest of the chapters in this book will highlight is how judgments of beauty and teleology both grant a sense of belonging to a larger cosmic order, one that exceeds our own making. This larger order to which we belong thus can give context to both our theoretical and practical endeavors, placing each of them in a larger system of which they are only one part, but only in virtue of which can they be thought together.

Our hope, then, is sustained in our encounters with beautiful things and with living things, insofar as they each suggest to us a meaningful order to which we belong, as the subsequent chapters will demonstrate.

2

Reflection, Purposiveness, Metaphysics

In Chapter 1, we saw that Kant argues that the thing that addresses the problem of hope also answers, "in its highest form, the speculative question" (KrV A805/B833). With this, Kant asserts that hope is sustained in virtue of that which speaks to our deepest metaphysical interests. In the Introduction to the third *Critique*, Kant has also already announced that what needs to be sought is a "ground of the **unity** of the supersensible that grounds nature with that which the concept of freedom contains practically" (KU 5:176); that is, there must be a union of the ground of nature with freedom's needs. Kant then goes on to claim that the principle of purposiveness in reflection is what "provides for [nature's] supersensible substratum" (KU 5:196). Judgments of reflection, then, are how we come to judge a supersensible substratum to nature, a supersensible that is in union with human freedom. How do reflective judgments – the judgments characteristic of the faculty of judgment proper – accomplish this? In this chapter, I will demonstrate how judgments of taste speak to our deepest metaphysical interests, and therefore sustain hope, principally in their purposiveness. I argue that they do this, first, through their distinctive kind of objective purposiveness: purposiveness without a purpose. Purposiveness without a purpose can be understood as disclosing to us a basic, fundamental ordering to what appears to us. This is *order itself*, without any specific or particular order. I further argue, second, that judgments of taste speak to our metaphysical interests by way of their subjective purposiveness. Subjective purposiveness, which is embodied in pleasure, yields a more expansive, cosmic sense of human beings' belonging to or being fit for the world. The things that are out there in the world are, in their very structure, not only ordered but ordered for us.

This chapter will first take up Kant on metaphysics. Much of this is certainly a well-trodden path for readers, as it traces some of the key features of Kant's critical philosophy. However, as hope is sustained in what is properly speculative or metaphysical, it will be worthwhile to outline what is essential to Kant's thinking on this matter. Section 2.2 will examine Kant's notion of reflection, the core activity proper to the faculty of judgment. In this section, I will argue that Kant associates reflection with possibility. And, as reflection is reflection on an empirical representation, it is associated with *real possibility*. I turn, third, to purposiveness without a purpose. Here, I develop the idea that judgments of reflection are about the appearance of the territory itself, that is, the appearance of the ground; I further argue that this ground appears to us as *orderly*. In reflection, then, we judge that there appears to be a supersensible ground to nature insofar as it appears in its barest form as orderly. Fourth, I demonstrate that Kant's notion of subjective purposiveness means that, the pleasure we take in beautiful things is indicative of a prior union between our faculties and the world in which we find ourselves. With this pleasure, we find a deeper accord between the way that things are, in their being ordered, and the human soul. This places the human being in a larger system of nature, not merely the mechanistic nature of the laws of the understanding. Lastly, I offer a sketch of what a speculative philosophy that is likewise bound by the critical system might look like. There, we find an *interpretative* metaphysics born of the expansive character of thought we find in reflective activity. I turn to this as an example of the kind of thing that can sustain our hope.

2.1 Kant and Metaphysics

Given Kant's express purpose to limit our metaphysical "illusions," it surely seems out of line to claim that the third *Critique* may rehabilitate speculation. The claim, however, is not that Kant reverses course and allows for metaphysical insight. Rather, reflective judgments and their principle of purposiveness merely *address* the interest we have in metaphysical objects, the same interest that occupies hope. Judgments of reflection and their principle of purposiveness simply *suggest* – since this is as far as reflection can get us epistemologically – the real possibility of a supersensible unity to nature and freedom. The purpose of this section is to remind the reader of the proper objects of metaphysics for Kant, as well as the nature of its limits. In this, too, we will be able to discern what is distinctive about the third *Critique* in opening up a new path for thinking about the objects of speculation that Kant otherwise forecloses in the first *Critique*. This will further help illustrate how the third *Critique* occupies a kind of middle ground between speculation and mere cognition: judgment.

Kant's critique of traditional metaphysics is certainly well known and is well-worn territory amongst Kant scholars and others alike. Whereas traditional or speculative metaphysics professed insight into the essential nature of the human soul, God, and the cosmos, Kant denies any supposed knowledge we could have into objects of metaphysical speculation. He does this, first, by delimiting the boundaries of human knowledge to what can be experienced in space and time in accord with concepts, and, second, by locating the origin of metaphysical speculation not in any objects of experience but in human reason itself. Hence Kant's verdict that human reason suffers a "peculiar fate," namely "it is burdened by questions which it cannot dismiss . . . but which it also cannot answer" (KrV Avii). In this, it may truly be that Kant kills God, as Heine suggests,[1] as our notion of God arises out of human reason itself. By the end of the first *Critique*, Kant's undoing of speculative metaphysics leaves one wondering what future, if any, there may be for theoretical philosophy. Indeed, if the forms of human thought do not apply to "being qua being," what is left for philosophizing?[2] Indeed, what is left for thinking?

Perhaps Kant's most damning – and enduring – criticism of metaphysical speculation is that the source of metaphysical objects appears to be in reason itself. Reason, as we have already outlined in Chapter 1, seeks the unconditioned. In this, reason is not satisfied with what we find in our experience but rather seeks the ultimate condition for it. Reason thus continually draws us toward ideas of metaphysical objects that underlie and make possible all that there is. This metaphysical speculation takes shape in us as three ideas, each constituting a specific discipline within metaphysics: the immortal soul and rational psychology; freedom and rational cosmology; and God and rational theology (KrV A3/B7). More generally, however, we can say that the speculative impulse in us toward metaphysics is cast as a need to know why things are the way they are. This desire to know "why" ultimately leads us to posit – illegitimately, Kant thinks – a fundamental structure to reality. Metaphysics is, in short, reason's answer to the question, "Why does what appears to us, appear as it does?" Reason seeks to answer this question with reference to what lies beyond appearances. Any pretensions we might have to knowledge about

---

[1] See especially the "Part Third" in Heine, *Religion and Philosophy in Germany*.
[2] I am thinking here of the Ancient – initially Parmenidean – presumption of an identity of thought and being. Aristotle, in *Metaphysics* Gamma, makes it explicit as well: "For these axioms hold of all beings . . . they are try of being qua being" Aristotle, *Metaphysics* (Indianapolis: Hackett Publishing, 2016), 1005b22. The presumption of this identity persists dogmatically until Kant, excepting of course those philosophers we may count as skeptics or empiricists. This issue returns in Section 2.5.

the existence or character of such a hidden reality "behind" appearances – that is, the noumenal – in Kant's view, are nothing but transcendental illusion. As we have no intuition of metaphysical objects, that is, they do not appear to us in space and time, we can have no experience or knowledge of them. Metaphysical speculation about them remains idle, and the theoretical philosophy that engages in such speculation is nothing other than a "battlefield," that "perpetually turns round on the same spot without coming a step further" (KrV, Bxiv; Prol 4:256).

Kant thus suggests that theoretical philosophy turn from metaphysical speculation about what underlies objects and the nature of the cosmos toward critique of our own faculties.[3] Critique, like metaphysical speculation, seeks the ultimate condition for the possibility of what there is; it investigates this, though, with respect to our own faculties and capacities for experience and thought. Kant takes the first *Critique* – his principal work in theoretical philosophy – as an "attempt to transform the accepted procedure of metaphysics ... It is a treatise on the method, not a system of the science itself; but it catalogs the entire outline of the science of metaphysics, both in respect of its boundaries and in respect of its entire internal structure" (KrV A4/B8). Metaphysics in a critical idiom, he writes at the end of "The Architectonic of Pure Reason," does not concern the traditional objects of the soul, freedom, and God, but rather "considers reason according to its elements and highest maxims" (KrV A851/B879). Moreover, critique of our faculties must be ongoing and continuous, Kant believes, as a necessary propaedeutic to all philosophizing to insure we do not overstep our cognitive limits.

What remains for theoretical philosophy for Kant, though, remains unclear. As Burkhard Tuschling has put it, "for most readers of Kant the world of Kantian theoretical philosophy seems perfectly ordered and finished."[4] Even beyond Tuschling's own diagnosis, Kant's "positive account" of the speculative use of reason has long troubled scholars; Kant advocates for a regulative role for reason and its ideas, but what shape this takes is left indeterminate.[5] He says only that while reason cannot have an explanatory role in relation to nature – the object of

---

[3] It is worth noting here that critique – the new science of metaphysics for Kant – is carried out by way of transcendental reflection. Reflection, it seems, has consistently been for Kant associated with the problems of metaphysical inquiry.
[4] Burkhard Tuschling, "The System of Transcendental Idealism: Questions Raised and Left Open in the *Kritik der Urteilskraft*," *The Southern Journal of Philosophy* 30 (1991), 112.
[5] An excellent account of the problems in Kant's discussion on this matter can be found in Michelle Grier, *Kant's Doctrine of Transcendental Illusion* (Cambridge: Cambridge University Press, 2001).

theoretical philosophy – it nevertheless bears some relation to the use of the understanding in scientific inquiry.[6] Namely, reason directs the understanding to bring about the "systematic in cognition" (KrV A644/B672). We accomplish this in part through one further aspect of metaphysics that Kant endorses: establishing completeness in the exposition of concepts. Metaphysics, in this regard, takes shape as an analysis of the concepts of nature and of freedom, treated respectively in the *Metaphysical Foundations of Natural Science* and the *Metaphysics of Morals*. Kant expects this project, however, to be brought to its end within two decades of the first *Critique* (KrV A856/B884).

Kant, of course, does not allow that judgments of reflection are making metaphysical claims. However, he is clear that they speak to metaphysical interests not only in *what* it is that they suggest – a supersensible substratum to nature that is in union with freedom – but in that they are not only about our faculties. That is, judgments of reflection are a kind of interpretative engagement with things in the world, based on empirical representations. Judgments of reflection are in the arena of speculative claims in *what* they judge, and *with reference* to what is given in appearance, not merely out of a need of reason. Further, judgments of reflection are about how things are, that is, about what we consider "nature." Even while Kant argues that judgment has its own sphere of experience and thus its own territory, he nevertheless associates the principle of judgment with the theoretical part of philosophy. This is because its object concerns nature, or, *what is*. He writes in the Introduction, "Everything that we might have to say about the proper principles of the power of judgment must be counted as belonging to the theoretical part, i.e., to rational cognition in accordance with concepts of nature" (KU 5:179). The content of the principle, though, will dovetail with metaphysics because it concerns *what is* in virtue of *why* it is the way it is.

The third *Critique* maintains a third way between a complete disavowal of speculation and the absolute idealism of Kant's successors. Hegel, we recall, famously accuses Kant in *Faith and Knowledge* of remaining in "subjectivism," meaning that all we ever come to know are our own faculties. He notes, though, that in the third *Critique* Kant approaches the absolute idealism Hegel himself recommends, but then backs away: "[T]his idea of an intellect that is also a posteriori or intuitive hovered very

---

[6] Susan Neiman offers an account of how this may be understood in *The Unity of Reason* (Oxford: Oxford University Press, 1994), 43–104.

clearly before Kant ... he expressed it and consciously destroyed it again."[7] This intuitive intellect is that which would allow us to grasp how things are in themselves, a possibility Kant consistently denies, of course. Indeed, the third *Critique* does not argue that we come to something like the substance of things, the noumenal. The identity of thought and being that Hegel seeks to recover will not be something Kant endorses. In the third *Critique* we do find that reflective judgments go beyond mere subjectivism, as our judgment is about something we encounter in the world. No identity of thought and being is posited in Kant; thought and being, though, do come into a kind of rapport or fit with one another nevertheless; they emerge in a kind of suspended harmony with one another, as we shall see in what follows. More than this, too, Kant's insistence that metaphysics is not legitimate if it exceeds the boundaries of experience is maintained in judgments of reflection: Judgments of reflection are about a given, empirical representation.

2.2 Reflection

It is as reflective that judgments are able both to speak to our interests in metaphysical matters and remain within the critical confines. By "speaks to" I mean to indicate that what we judge in reflection is substantially relevant to our metaphysical interests. This substantive aspect is given by way of the exercise of the principle of purposiveness in our judgments. Nevertheless, in only speaking to them, they do not fully answer, as they remain "merely" reflective and thus do not grant knowledge. In this, they *suggest* or *refer to* something without becoming determinate in what they judge.

Reflection, or, rather, the structure of judgments in their reflecting activity, will be one key to understanding what makes judgments out in the territory distinctive. This distinctiveness is not only with respect to cognition and morality, which are determining in structure; they are also distinctive with respect to the history of philosophical thinking on the expanse of human experience insofar as they articulate a new kind of encounter as part of human life. Even more than this, judgments of reflection are the express topic of the text – understanding their structure comprises a crucial and necessary component of the two specific judgments of reflection described in the book. While the text names the power of

---

[7] G. W. F. Hegel, *Faith and Knowledge* (Albany: State University of New York Press, 1977), 80.

judgment as the faculty subject to critique, it is only in its reflective activity that judgment constitutes its own sphere of human life. It is in judgments of reflection that the a priori principle of purposiveness is invoked in relation to our representations.

The *characteristic activity* of the power of judgment is to relate the universal and the particular. "In general," Kant writes, it "is the faculty for thinking of the particular as contained under the universal" (KU 5:179). *Reflection* is the means by which the power of judgment engages in its characteristic activity; it is thus the means by which the power of judgment relates particulars and universals. There are two kinds of judgments that result from relating particulars and universals: determining judgments and reflective judgments. It is not until his discovery of the principle of purposiveness belonging properly to the power of judgment itself, however, that Kant comes to develop the latter kind. It may be that it is not the discovery of the principle of purposiveness, but the judgments of reflection in which this principle is active, that names the more novel discovery of the *Critique of Judgment*.

In the third *Critique*, then, Kant describes a new kind of mental *activity*. It is not only a new principle he has found but also a new way the mind relates to empirical representations. Judgments of reflection are distinctive, perhaps above all, in their structure. In Chapter 1, we saw that Kant distinguishes the territory of judgment from the domains of freedom and nature in virtue of the kind of legislative effectiveness they exhibit. The activity of the power of judgment in reflection yields not an application of a law to a case, but, rather, develops an interpretation of something singular.

Kant delineates what is distinctive about judgments of reflection in contrast with determining judgments, which he identifies with cognition. Determining judgments are judgments in which we come to *understand*. Such cognition arises not only from the determination of a concept of the understanding in an empirical representation, but the integration of this particular determination into the stream of our experience – the transcendental unity of apperception operates through the understanding and our intuitions. Determining judgments result in understanding the way that things are, insofar as they are in a way that conforms to our a priori structures of cognition as laid out in the first *Critique*, namely with respect to our faculties of intuition and of the understanding. In this, we also come to understand things insofar as each is a part of a larger series of conditioned things; Kant refers to this as the "nexus of experience" (KrV A227/B279).

In a determining judgment, the universal is given, "which subsumes the particular under it" (KU 5:179). When we cognize something, a particular representation is subsumed under a category of the understanding, a universal. Reflection has a significant role to play in cognition; it does the work to discern which universal – concept or category – is appropriate for becoming determinate in the given representation. That this is the role of reflection in determining judgments is evident in Kant's description of reflection in the first *Critique*, in the Amphiboly.[8] There, we learn that reflection is what discerns the facultative home of our representations. That is, reflection does the work to find the fitting faculty to which a representation belongs: It discerns if a representation can belong properly to the understanding, or whether it is a product of reason's striving for the unconditioned, for example, in a representation we may find in ourselves of God or immortality. Reflection, Kant writes, is the "consciousness of the relation of given representations to our various sources of cognition, through which alone their relation among themselves can be correctly determined" (KrV A260/B316). Thus, in determining judgments, reflection discerns that the categories of the understanding are fit for determining – that is, making determinate – what is given in a representation. We are able to grasp what is given, and, in this, what is given becomes intelligible to us.

In determining judgments, what is given in an empirical representation is cognized not only through the determination of a concept of the understanding but also is determined temporally. All appearances that are cognized are determined *in time* through the activity of the transcendental unity of apperception. Reality, then, as the totality of what appears, is in this domain *understood* as a series of time determinations that are conditioned by those that came before it. Everything we understand – everything determined through the understanding – is understood temporally. All determinate objects of cognition, Kant writes, are part of a "thoroughgoing connection of appearance" (KrV A258/B314). With this, Kant asserts that in experience and cognition, all things appear to us (1) as something, and (2) as a determinate and distinguishable part of a larger whole. What is crucial about determinate cognition is that the concepts of the understanding are always already doing the work of determination. In

---

[8] Kenneth Westphal and Jean-François Lyotard have both demonstrated how this is so. Please see Westphal, "Epistemic Reflection and Cognitive Reference in Kant's Transcendental Response to Skepticism," *Kant-Studien* 94 (2003), 135–171; Lyotard, *Lessons on the Analytic of the Sublime* (Stanford: Stanford University Press, 1994).

virtue of this unflagging activity – both of the unity of apperception as well as the understanding – everything that appears to us in reality appears *as something in particular*. Moreover, they appear to us as something in particular that is conditioned by what came before; they appear to us a part of mechanistic chain of conditioned causality. Their being – what they are – is bound up with the thoroughgoing connection of appearances, and their causal origin is, in some sense, co-given with their determination. When we cognize something, our cognition is constituted at least in part by the conditions for the existence of the thing cognized, that is, its "why."

Determining judgments of cognition thus have the character of *necessity*, specifically, "material necessity in existence" (KrV A226/B279). Material necessity in existence means that the thing cognized exists necessarily, not in virtue of its concept, but in virtue of being caused to come into existence by what has preceded it. This comes out most clearly in Kant's discussion of the Postulates of Empirical Thinking. The third postulate reads, "That whose connection with the actual is determined in accordance with general conditions of experience is (exists) **necessarily**" (KrV A218/B266). Necessity has specifically to do with the coming into being of whatever is cognized; Kant writes that it "concerns only the relations of appearances in accordance with the dynamical laws of causality, and the possibility grounded upon it of inferring *a priori* from some given existence (a cause) to another existence (the effect)" (KrV A227/B280). Determining judgments, then, not only determine a universal rule through the given empirical representation; they also determine these things as "contained somewhere in the nexus of experience," that is, in the temporally bounded succession of appearances, which is further determined according to the laws of causality. This is to say that it is not only the case that we have our experience temporally and successively. There is an inner, causal relation between the successive moments of experience, and this relation is constituted causally. Allison sums up Kant's argument on this point thus: "To regard perceptions [successively] is just to subsume them under an *a priori* rule, which in this case must be the schema of causality."[9] We understand something, then, not only when we determine it through a category (a universal) of our faculty of understanding. We only really understand something when we have cognized it in relation to those appearances that

---

[9] Henry Allison, *Kant's Transcendental Idealism: An Interpretation and a Defense* (New Haven: Yale University Press, 2004), 252.

have come before.¹⁰ *Our understanding of something for Kant necessarily involves understanding how it came into being as – was caused to be – what it is.*

We reflect, however, when an empirical representation is not determinable. "If, however, only the particular is given," he writes, "for which the universal is to be found, then the power of judgment is merely **reflecting**" (KU 5:179). No concept or category of the understanding is able to be made determinate – that is, concrete in experience – for some of our given representations. In this, what is given does *not* conform to our way of knowing. Yet we must still find some way to make these empirical representations intelligible and integrative into our experience. Reflection is the mode by which we attempt this.

We are, Kant recognizes, given to things we simply do not understand. When we find ourselves, as it were, out in the territory, we nevertheless are charged to make what is given intelligible; for Kant this means not only determination via concepts, but understanding its coming into being as part of our larger totality of experience. While we may not come to a determinate understanding, we may still develop a judgment about what is given. When Kant describes what the activity of reflection is, he invokes some key terminology that gives us insight. He associates reflection with consideration (*überlegen*), and, most notably, contemplation. To "consider" has the sense here of staying with the representation, pondering over it; it is a laying over, a stopover that puts us in one place for a time. This stands in contrast to cognition, whose temporality is successive. In reflection, we "linger" [*weilen*] (KU 5:222); the sense is of time stretching out, in contrast with the consecutive temporal determination of everyday understanding. Kant's further invocation of contemplation in this context is indicative, too. The pleasure we find in a judgment of taste, for example, is named by Kant as a merely contemplative pleasure (KU 5:222). Contemplation, in the tradition of European thinking, has typically been reserved for the kind of thinking that characterizes metaphysical speculation. While Kant clearly has foreclosed such a possibility in his own philosophy, it gets a kind of rehabilitation in reflecting on what is given in an empirical representation to us beyond what we can know. In contemplation, we hold the representation in our mind, focusing on it,

---

¹⁰ While I will not take it up in this project, judgments of reflection do suggest an alternative temporality to the successive one developed in the first *Critique*. Rachel Zuckert's chapter, "Aesthetic Pleasure: The feeling of subjective projective temporality," in *Kant on Beauty and Biology*, does an excellent job drawing this out.

taking it from different perspectives in an effort to find a fitting universal and get at the whole. In reflection, Kant introduces a new kind of thinking beyond what is admitted in the first *Critique*.

A judgment is reflective, then, when we fail in our attempt to make something determinately known. We are given to think about, contemplate, and consider what is given, and out of this arrive at a judgment about it. This judgment is merely reflective, Kant will assert, in virtue of it never arriving at an end station. We remain always in the activity of reflection for what we find out in territory – hence, for Kant, the judgment is *merely* or solely reflective. Thus, the activity of reflection that is involved in all judgments is the characteristic and defining activity of a judgment of reflection.

Objects of reflection appear to us not as necessary, but merely as *possible*. In the Postulates of Empirical Thinking, Kant defines the possible as, "Whatever agrees with the formal conditions of experience (in accordance with intuition and concepts)" (KrV A218/B265). Further on in this same section, he explains that the possible agrees with these conditions "in general" [*überhaupt*], or the "objective form of experience in general" (KrV A220/B267). Kant, recall, associates the territory with *possibility* in his description of it in the Introduction. We have seen already that in the domains of the practical and the theoretical, the concepts have an enforced, legislative relation to their objects. As such, these objects are not only brought under a regime of necessity; in their determinacy, they are made determinately actual. Objects in the territory, though, are merely possible objects for cognition. Kant begins his discussion first by naming a "field." "Concepts, insofar as they are related to objects, regardless of whether a cognition of the latter is possible or not, have their field" (KU 5:174). The "field" of cognition is the broadest and most general. In it, only concepts reside; whether any objects are cognizable under such concepts is not at issue. Here, our concepts may lack all objectivity. The territory, though, is further delineated. "The part of the field within which cognition **is possible for us** is a territory for these concepts and the requisite faculty of cognition" (KU 5:174; bold added). The territory, then, is the sphere in which cognition is possible; indeed, it is the sphere in which cognition *remains possible* and does not yield reality or necessity. It is, as "the set of objects of all possible experience," the sphere of possibility itself. What we find in the territory remains possible in its possibility. This is to say that what appears in the territory appears as possible, as not yet, but possibly, determinate. It will be in the domains of freedom and nature that these objects attain reality and necessity; insofar as they remain in the territory, and belong then to judgments of reflection, they are, strictly speaking, given to us in their mere possibility. Some of these objects become subject to and determined by the laws of the understanding and are annexed into the domain of cognition; some of these objects become subject to and determined by the laws of reason, and are annexed into the domain of moral life. The last set of objects remains out in the territory – beautiful things and living beings. These are objects on which we reflect and which we contemplate.

2.3 Purposiveness without a Purpose and the Ordering of Appearance

If reflective judgments are about the merely or purely possible, this takes shape first in objective purposiveness. Specifically, Kant argues that judgments of taste are purposive without a purposive. As we shall see later, this means that when we judge something to be possibly an object, it has the mere form of an object. In this, it is predeterminate, yet it is still organized in some way. It has an ordering to it, even if this never becomes a determinate order. What appears to us appears precisely and solely as *possible*; that this has a form to it ultimately means that what appears is the form of appearance itself, as possibility.

Even though judgments of reflection do not determine an empirical representation through any concept or principle, the activity of reflecting on an empirical representation is nevertheless not without any principle. Judgments of reflection invoke the principle that belongs properly to the power of judgment, namely *purposiveness*. In this, we find that our reflection on an empirical representation and attempt to understand and integrate what we find out in the territory will be brought in under the auspices of an entirely new way of thinking about the coming into being of what we find. Further, this novel approach to what we find can be seen to be not merely possible, but explicitly about an object's possibility.

In reflection, we are thrown out from or displaced from our otherwise everyday course of experience. In reflective judgments, things do not appear to us as part of a thoroughgoing connection, as part of the nexus of experience as described above. Reflective judgments are occasioned precisely when, as we have already noted, "only the particular is given, for which the universal is to be found" (KU 5:179). We are not, for this, without orientation, however. It is in the activity of reflection, Kant argues, that we employ the principle of purposiveness. In the third moment of the Critique of Aesthetic Judgment, Kant defines something as purposive "merely because its possibility can be explained and conceived by us only insofar as we assume as its ground a causality in accordance with ends, i.e., a will that has arranged it so in accordance with the representation of a certain rule" (KU 5:220). In this, something is given in an empirical representation whose existence cannot be (or is not yet) brought under the regime of a connection of appearances determined through the understanding; it stands outside of the mechanistic laws of cause and effect. Instead, we judge certain objects to stand under a causality in accord with purposes.

Human artifacts are perhaps the primary example of objective purposiveness. We encounter them distinctly as objects whose existence is not, in their coming to be, caused by mechanistic causality. Rather, all human artifacts are created in accord with some end. These, however, do not all become judgments of taste. In reflection, we find a universal under which to subsume the vast majority of human artifacts we encounter. Typically, this will be the empirical concept of whatever they may be and thus whatever their use is.

In merely or purely reflective judgments (i.e., judgments of taste), what appears to us is not simply purposive, but purposive without a purpose. That is, what appears to us appears only *as if* it were brought into being in accordance with an end, *as if* it were a determinate object conceived by a being with a will. Kant names this species of objective purposiveness as "purposiveness concerning form." This is to say that an object that appears to have been brought into being in accord with ends, but for which no end can be found, has what we may call the *mere form of an object*. It does not appear *as something with a particular end*, but rather, it merely appears only as object-like. When judging something as purposive without a purpose, what we are left judging is nothing other than how it appears to us as having come into existence. We judge it solely with respect to its form as appearing to have been created in accord with some end. Even more than this, it is the end or purpose of an object that gives it its order. Without an end through which it was brought into being, however, beautiful things thus only appeared *ordered*, but without any determinate order. We may thus say that they have *orderedness* or are *orderly*.

This leaves us judging, though, *possibility* itself. In objective purposiveness, we judge how the "object itself (its form or its existence) ... [is] possible" (KU 5:220). Nevertheless, unlike human artifacts with some determinate purpose, objects that are purposive without a purpose appear to us solely as having been created. Without a determinate purpose to explain their existence, yet still having the form of being purposeful, they essentially appear to us in their possibility. Günter Figal, in his *Aesthetics as Phenomenology*, carefully elucidates the paradox and impossibility of the notion of purposiveness without a purpose. Figal highlights the meaning of the erasure of the end, and observes of purposiveness: "This having-been-produced is inessential even to artworks ... beauty involves the nonessentiality of intention."[11] This is what Kant means when he suggests that art is beautiful insofar as it appears like nature; in nature the "determinate intention" in its production is erased (KU 5:306). Beautiful things appear not as coming into being in intentionality per se, but rather, since the intentionality is effectively effaced, they present coming-into-being itself.

This is further reinforced by Kant's claim that the ground of objective purposiveness is the purpose or end through which something came into being. The "end," he writes, is "regarded as the cause of the [object] (the real ground of its possibility)" (KU 5:200). The ground of a human artifact is the purpose for which it was created. Nevertheless, as beautiful things are purposive without a purpose, they are *groundless*. Thus, Figal continues, "With respect to its cognizability, it is *groundless*. Yet it remains something possible within this groundlessness; it remains that which can be."[12] For something to be purposive without a purpose means that it appears without a ground of its possibility, and thus purely *as possibility*. That things can appear both as possible and as groundlessly so is what Kant must mean in claiming that "[t]he judgment of taste has nothing but the *form of the purposiveness* of an object ... as its ground" (KU 5:221). The ground of the judgment of taste is that things appear to us in their mere possibility.

Recall, too, that possibility is the ground of actuality and necessity. Our judgments made out in the territory, then, are a kind of groundless or suspended ground. So, in the sphere of possibility – the territory of judgments of reflection – this possibility itself has no other ground. Possibility, embodied in orderedness itself, is *what is*. This means that the territory is a kind of groundless ground; the territory serves as the ground of the other two domains, yet this ground embodies a causality that is itself without a ground. Possibility as such, which is itself groundless in its own possibility, is ultimately what we find out there in the territory.[13]

---

[11] Günter Figal, *Aesthetics as Phenomenology: The Appearance of Things* (Indianapolis: Indiana University Press, 2010), 51.
[12] Figal, *Aesthetics as Phenomenology*, 52.
[13] I will come back to and address Kant's own concern with this groundless ground in Chapter 4, on the sensus communis as providing something like a ground for Kant's system.

The territory, as we saw, is both ground of and transition between the two domains of cognition and morality. In each of those domains, what we encounter is subject to legislation – the universal rule under which it is determined. Through such determination, what we encounter becomes part of the nexus of our experience, of what Kant names *reality*. What is real must, prior to being real, be possible. The ground of each domain, then, is the mere possibility of objects at all. Moreover, if possibility is the ground of reality, then what we find in the territory is the structure of the ground itself. So our encounters out in the territory are of the ground, and, as the merely possible what appears to us *appears precisely as ground*. This ground is orderly, and it can become determinately ordered, however, if annexed into one of the two domains. All of this means that out in the territory we find something like an orderedness to appearance. While a more determinate order (or, logic) is not found, what appears to us is the possibility granted by ordering itself.

Objective purposiveness, which in judgments of taste is purposive without a purposive, reveals the structure of the territory as a ground. The ground is itself mere possibility, which appears to us in its barest form, or orderedness. The structure of the territory as described in the Introduction to the third *Critique* – the territory as the sphere of the possible and as ground of the other two domains – is precisely what appears to us in judgments of taste. The territory, we saw, was a region of lawfulness without a law[14] – orderedness without a particular order. Purposiveness without a purpose is how something appears to us as being possible.

2.4 Subjective Purposiveness and a Prior Belonging

Perhaps even more important for speaking to the metaphysical interests of hope is what Kant calls subjective purposiveness. Not only do judgments of taste present to us an orderedness to appearance; they also suggest to us a deeper accord between, or prior belonging to, a larger whole that includes both human beings and what is. This accord is evident in *subjective purposiveness*. In subjective purposiveness, Kant identifies the purposive character of our own pleasure, that is, in the subject, with the suggestion that *what is* is also *for us*. That is, the pleasure we take in a judgment of taste leads us to judge that what appears out in the territory is fit for our

---

[14] This is how Kant describes the free play of the faculties as well (KU 5:241). It should not be a surprise then that this is also what appears to us out in the territory.

cognitive faculties, or purposive for the human subject. This fit is not the fit of proper legislation, as already noted, but a general [*überhaupt*] suitability. If what appears is the *orderedness* of appearance itself, this orderedness is ultimately appropriate for our faculties.

Pleasure is always the product of an agreement. Sensible pleasure or satisfaction occurs when an interest or desire we have meets the object that agrees with it. One's interest in birds, say, is satisfied when birds are there for watching. The object here agrees with what the desire is for. Thus, we say, "such and such agrees with me" to signify that our desire has met its object and we are taking pleasure in it. The satisfaction we take in the good is analogous: We find pleasure in it when the object is in agreement with the concept of it. In the beautiful, what comes into agreement is less obvious; it is the representation of the object and our mental faculties. Kant will thus find in the beautiful a deeper agreement between how things are in the world and our capacities to access these things, a potential prior accord between the world and our ways of knowing. He finds this, in part, because pleasure is not only agreement in this case but also consciousness of this agreement (KU 5:218).

The pleasure we take in a judgment of taste is, as we have noted, a contemplative pleasure (KU 5:222). The pleasure is not, then, a pleasure of the senses, nor does it attend an interest in the object. Rather, it is a cognitive pleasure – Kant even identifies the pleasure in the beautiful as a feeling we have of our "state of mind" (KU 5:217). More specifically, he identifies our "state of mind" with the "free play of our faculties," which is a peculiar kind of agreement between the imagination and understanding that constitutes the activity of reflection itself. Whereas in a determinate cognition the imagination is subsumed under the understanding, in a judgment of taste the two faculties stand in a relation of indeterminate play, a kind of back and forth, a quickening or enlivening: the "animation of both faculties to an activity that is indeterminate but yet ... in unison" (KU 5:219). It is, he goes on, the "sensation of the effect that consists of the facilitated play of both powers of the mind, enlivened through mutual agreement" (KU 5:219). How exactly Kant understands the character of this "play" is a matter still open to interpretation, and has received serious treatment from numerous quarters.[15] That Kant takes this play to be pleasurable in virtue of some agreement, however, is clear from the text.

---

[15] Hannah Ginsborg takes up the issue directly in "Lawfulness without a Law: Kant on the Free Play of Imagination and Understanding," in *The Normativity of Nature*. Ralf Meerbote takes it up in "Reflection on Beauty," in *Essays in Kant's Aesthetics*, Ted Cohen and Paul Guyer, eds. (Chicago:

The free play of the imagination and the understanding is an expression of the general *accord* of these two faculties. Kant describes the relation between the imagination and understanding not only as playing but also a relation of agreement [*zusammen stimmen*] (KU 5:218) or "subjective unity" (KU 5:219). The pleasure we feel, Kant writes, makes us conscious of a "mutual subjective correspondence of the powers of cognition with each other" (KU 5:218). The particular relation of the imagination and understanding that is enacted in reflection is one, Kant thinks, which presents a more basic accord between the two faculties. Picking up perhaps on the Ancient Greek resonances of *Harmonia*, which derives from something being joined in a certain way, Kant describes the relation between the imagination and understanding as a harmony [*Harmonie*] (KU 5:218, 5:210). Rodolphe Gasché, echoing this Ancient sense as well as the German *stimmen* [to tune], describes the free play as a "relational attunement."[16] The imagination and understanding, in the activity of reflection, are simply *tuned in* to one another. They are joined in the way two voices or instruments may be when they meet in a harmony. They do not become one but find a concordant resonance with each other. They are, too, in play. When one voice or instrument alters its sound, its partner is likewise able to find its way back into tune with the other. This is the meaning of when a voice or instrument joins the other in a complementary way: They come into agreement with each other.

Kant takes the mutual agreement of the imagination and the understanding in the free play of a judgment of taste to disclose the possibility of cognition in general. The mere correspondence or accord between these two faculties – which are those involved in determinate judgments – is for Kant a condition for the possibility of the further, determinate relation. In this, the relation between the imagination and understanding, Kant writes, is an "agree[ment] with each other as is requisite for a **cognition in general** [*Erkenntnisse Überhaupt*]" (KU 5:218). He further names the free play a "well-proportioned disposition that we require for all cognition" (KU 5:219). The more fundamental agreement or possibility of being tuned in to each other underlies the possibility of the subsuming relation that constitutes cognition.

University of Chicago Press, 1982), 55–86. Dieter Henrich (*Aesthetic Judgment and the Moral Image of the World*), Paul Guyer (*Kant and the Claims of Taste*), Rodolphe Gasché (*The Idea of Form*), all treat the matter in their respective works.

[16] Rodolphe Gasché, *The Idea of Form: Rethinking Kant's Aesthetics* (Stanford: Stanford University Press, 2003), 47.

It is on account of the possibility of cognition in general embodied in the accord between the imagination and understanding that we find a further, deeper agreement between human beings and the way things are; Kant names this agreement *subjective purposiveness*. The deeper agree is that the way that things are is suitable for our way knowing. If the free play is at bottom disclosive of the possibility of cognition in general, that which occasions it must be fit for our way of knowing in general. "The pleasure," Kant writes, "can express [*ausdrücken*] nothing but [the representation's] suitability [*Angemessenheit*] to the cognitive faculties that are in play in the reflecting power of judgment" (KU 5:189). The pleasurable agreement between the faculties expresses an underlying agreement or prior attunement between the object and our minds:

> For since the ground of the pleasure is placed merely in the form of the object for reflection in general, hence not in any sensation of the object and also without relation to a concept that contains any intention, it is only the lawfulness in the empirical use of the power of judgment in general (unity of imagination with the understanding) in the subject with which the representation of the object in reflection, whose *a priori* conditions are universally valid, agrees; and, since this agreement of the object with the faculties of the subject is contingent, it produces the representation of a purposiveness of the object with regard to the cognitive faculties of the subject. (KU 5:190)

Kant argues that the "representation of the object" agrees with the "unity of the imagination and understanding," a unity that constitutes a condition for the possibility of cognition in general. Objects of reflection, then, agree with our possibilities for knowing how things are. Kant describes this as a "purposive correspondence of an object (be it a product of nature or of art) with the relationship of the cognitive faculties among themselves" (KU 5:191). Our faculties and the way things are, at bottom, tuned in to one another.

Kant goes so far at times to identify the pleasure in the judgment of taste with just this insight about the deeper accord between world and mind. In reflective judgments, we judge objects as "aimed at correspondence with our power of judgment" and "as if [they are] selected for our own taste." Kant writes, "For the judgment of taste consists precisely in the fact that it calls a thing beautiful only in accordance with that quality in it by means of which it corresponds with our way of receiving it" (KU 5:282). Hence Kant's claim in his notes that beautiful things "indicate that the human being belongs in the world" (NF 16:127). The pure possibility presented in the appearance of things out in the territory, and the pleasure that constitutes our encounters with them, suggest to us that the way things are is fit for our cognition. As merely reflective, of course, this is not something known, or even deduced, but a judgment we come to as a result of reflection.

In all of this, what Kant has argued is that the feeling of pleasure we have in a judgment of taste is the feeling we have for the structure of cognition in general. This is the same "objective form of experience in general" that he names as mere possibility. Determinate cognition – knowledge – requires that a concept or rule be determinable in a representation of a given object. In this, a concept is fit for a representation and is able to grasp it fully. In a reflective judgment, no concept is determined; rather, the feeling announces a more general fittingness of things in the world for our faculties. The feeling of pleasure suggests a more general – but also deeper and more grounding – agreement of the way that things are, and our way of knowing. Subjective purposiveness thus completes the objective purposiveness of purposiveness without a purposive. The orderliness of appearance is just that things appear as possible *for us*.

We can further describe the feeling of pleasure in a judgment of taste as a feeling of the promise of intelligibility. First, we have seen that the feeling is of possibility. But possibility is always oriented by or on its way to actuality, so what we feel is that we can arrive at something determinate. Second, the free play is itself the search for some determinate rule – it is the activity of our attempt to make something intelligible. We thus, at least in part, feel ourselves to be on the way to making sense of something.

Reflective judgments thus speak to the needs of reason in speculative metaphysics in virtue of a fundamental ordering to how things are, and a prior accord between how things are and the faculties of the human mind. We may discern that in reflective judgments, we find that there is an orderedness to what appears, an orderedness that *makes possible and grounds* the appearance of particular or determinate things. More than this, too, the appearance of such an orderedness discloses to us the possibility that our faculties are suited to the task of grasping what there is in its entirety. It is nothing other than such suitability of our faculties for *what is* that grounds the possibility of metaphysics in the first place. In the European philosophical tradition, beginning with the Ancient Greeks, speculative metaphysics has been predicated on the identity of thought and being. The insight into the *logos* of the cosmos – the order to the way things are – has its ground in this very identity. Parmenides famously asserts, "[F]or it is the same, to think and also to be."[17] His argument for how things are begins from this assumption, and he proceeds to lay out how things must be, given the possibilities and limits of human thinking. Aristotle, too, predicates his views on this assumption. Of our rules for thinking, he writes, "For these axioms hold of all beings ... they are true of being qua being."[18] It is this very identity of thought and being that Kant argues against in the Antinomies in the first *Critique*. But here, we see the same question answered in a new and innovative way. To "What is the relationship between thought and being?" the third *Critique* answers: harmony, accord, or agreement. It is beyond the limits of the critical system to assert identity; it is within the confines of the critical system, in judgments of reflection, to judge an attunement, however.

The notion that there is a prior fittingness or accord between the human being and the way things are is what gives us a sense that there is a larger whole to which we belong. There turns out to be a common ordering for what is and for the human mind. While for the Ancients the common *logos* of human thought and the cosmos was already part and parcel of our belonging, for Kant the attunement between the two suggests the belonging to larger context. In the Introduction, I described how Kant's Copernican turn – particularly in the practical sphere – led to a cosmopolitan order in which the human being reigned. Indeed, the effective sovereignty of reason is the principal concern of practical life according to Kant. But here, with the accord enacted between human and things in the territory, we find a possible intervention into that idealist Copernican world order. While the domains of freedom and nature both situate the human being as the center and source of what is, judgments of reflection are made precisely when our efforts in this direction fail. In judgments of reflection, the objects in the world push back against being constituted through our faculties. In this, though, the world is still there *for us*. Yet it is there for us in a kind of absolute exteriority. This exteriority is, in a sense, only latent and not *present* in the other two spheres; it is superseded in determination. In the theoretical sphere, we find exteriority only in what lies beyond what we experience and the laws of nature we have come already to cognize. Our experience and knowledge of natural laws are both, in sense, given through our own inner made exterior, and so do not appear

---

[17] Parmenides, *On Nature, Early Greek Philosophy, Volume V: Western Greek Thinkers, Part 2*. Edited and translated by André Laks, Glenn W. Most. Loeb Classical Library 528 (Cambridge, MA: Harvard University Press, 2016), D6; 39.
[18] Aristotle, *Metaphysics*, 1005b22.

to us as absolutely outer. This is to say, the aspects of the theoretical and practical domains that remain outside of what reason itself can do, but on which it depends in part of what is outside of it in nature – the system of natural laws and the as yet unrealized moral world – are both absent from our experience. By contrast, in reflection, what is outside of reason's doing and its purview is in a way, present. Attunement and accord can only be reached with something that is both other than oneself and also present.

Our coming into accord with what is given in an empirical representation, rather than subsuming it under a law of reason or the understanding, maintains the exteriority of what is given. Our relation to it is as what is exterior. The entire task of reflection may be said, then, precisely to achieve an accord – a "relational attunement" – to what there is outside of us. In this, the human being is displaced from their place at the center of the cosmos and returned as a part of a greater whole. It is not, however, a greater whole to which we are *subject*, but in which we stand in our independence and which stands in its independence from us, and with which we can find ourselves in harmony.

It is this accord and the referral to a larger, systematic whole that speaks to the interests of hope. In the territory, we encounter what is beyond our purview – objects there are there in their exteriority and escape the legislative authority of our faculties. Yet we find that what is there in its independence from us is nevertheless still in some way *for us*, it still appears to us as fit for our faculties. As this fitness is discerned with respect to a given thing, too, we do not merely speculate about nature's amenability to human ends. Rather, we have an encounter in which we find that the way things are is already fit for us; that is, it appears to us as for us, giving us reason to hope that it may conform to our pursuits.

2.5 Interpretative Metaphysics

How might reflective judgments speak to the need we have to maintain hope? We have seen how they present an orderedness in appearance as well as suggest a prior accord between the human mind and how things are. Judgments made in the territory bear a trace of metaphysics, which accords with Kant's own description of them as about the supersensible in nature. Unlike the ideas born of transcendental illusion, however, reflective judgments are about encounters with objects given in empirical representations. They are thus able to sustain the *real* possibility that freedom and nature are more intimately related than otherwise appears to us. If speculation leads to empty ideas, reflection leads to substantive interpretations.[19] Here, I will try to fill out, based on Kant's fuller delineation of the free play of the faculties in his treatment of art, how he thinks about the interpretative capacities of reflection. Interpretation is born of our efforts to make intelligible what we fail to understand and is how we further come into accord with how things are when they exceed just such understanding.

In describing the free play of the faculties in judgments of taste, Kant suggests a model of reflection that goes beyond judgments of purposiveness made exclusively about the *form* of what appears.[20] The play between the imagination and understanding is an attempt to understand, and thus, an attempt to understand some *thing*. It is not an empty pleasure that one would associate with a merely formalist aesthetics. Moreover, as oriented by intelligibility, there is a substance or content to the back and forth of the faculties. Thus, the reflective free play of the imagination and understanding is not only a general accord but also a *productive* accord – it leads to a new kind of thinking about something.

We see this productive accord in Kant's fuller description of the free play of the imagination and understanding. In our contemplation of beautiful art, we are spurred to a kind of creative – though still directed – thought. Kant describes the work of the imagination here as being spread "over a multitude of representations, which let one think more than one can express in a concept determined by words" and the mind is opened up for "an immeasurable field of representations" (KU 5:315). Elsewhere he suggests that art (poetry in particular), "*expands (erweitert)* the mind by setting the imagination free and presenting, within the limits of a given concept and among the unbounded manifold of forms possibly agreeing with it, the one that connects its presentation with a fullness of thought to which no linguistic expression is fully adequate" (KU 5:326, my emphasis). Kant's emphasis in these accounts on the lack of linguistic capacity we have to capture our state of mind – a lack of determinate predication – highlights the inadequacy of mere conceptual determination for what we find in the territory. In our contemplative reflection on art, the

---

[19] For an extended account of how the third *Critique* develops a theory of interpretation, please see Rudolf A. Makkreel, *Imagination and Interpretation in Kant: The Hermeneutical Import of the Critique of Judgment* (Chicago: University of Chicago Press, 1990). Makkreel does not, however, link interpretation to the needs of reason in metaphysics.

[20] Descriptions of Kantian aesthetics as "formalistic" dominate much of the Anglo reception of Kant. I think that this interpretation of Kant does not capture what is crucial about his description of beauty, and also what is important about free play. I return to this in Chapter 5, when discussing aesthetic ideas.

relationship between the imagination and understanding is such that the imagination relates a multiplicity of representations to each other and also to various concepts: a "multitude" of them, an "immeasurable field," and an "unbounded manifold" of them. While no one concept is determinable in the representation, many concepts may be associated with the thing, or, as it may be, part of the thing. As the indeterminate thing may be presented in our imagination in multiple ways, we may find that multiple concepts relate to or can be associated with it, even though they do not determine it. Our concepts are thus expanded through these new associations even though they do not determine what appears.

The expansive capacity for thought Kant describes here, moreover, recalls the measure he sets for cognition proper, or knowledge. For Kant, knowledge requires synthetic a priori judgments, which he names "**judgments of amplification** [*Erweiterungsteile*]" indicating that a predicate *adds* to the concept of the subject (KrV A7/B11). These are judgments of enlargement or expansion. We should point out, too, that Kant uses this same notion – and indeed the very same language – to describe what happens in our response to beautiful art.[21] He writes that art "stimulates so much thinking that it can never be grasped in a determinate concept, hence which aesthetically enlarges [*erweitert*] the concept itself in an unbounded way" (KU 5:315). By aesthetic enlargement Kant seems to mean that a concept – its meaning, scope, application, and thereby also relation to other concepts – is broadened and expanded because the representations to which it may be applied are multiplied and diversified even as it is not made determinate. The free play of the faculties in our response to art – to the presentation of aesthetic ideas in art – associates concepts with new representations, ones that are not determined by these concepts, but nevertheless add something to the concepts themselves. Kant describes this as the imagination "giving life" to concepts (KU 5:321).

The free play between the imagination and understanding that takes place when we reflect on a work of art, Kant thinks, actually works to enlarge our concepts. Our concepts are enlarged or brought to more "fullness of thought" because there is a superabundance or excess of content in art. Art, Kant believes, is beautiful insofar as it presents aesthetic ideas. While it is beyond the scope of this chapter to elucidate Kant's

---

[21] We should recall, too, that in the first *Critique*, *Erweiterungsteile* are associated with truth. While it is beyond the scope of this paper to elucidate the possibilities of this further, we may nevertheless remind ourselves of what may be at stake in this association. Judgments of taste and our interpretation of artworks are not about the truth. But they are, in a real sense, about what is true.

notion of aesthetic ideas with much precision (I take it up in Chapter 5 at length), it will suffice to say here that aesthetic ideas are rational ideas made sensible. Aesthetic ideas seek to "approximate a presentation of concepts of reason," the same concepts of reason Kant denies we have metaphysical insight into in the first *Critique* (KU 5:314–5).

Beautiful art cannot be determined conceptually because more is presented than can be brought under a concept. This further means, Kant suggests, that "no language fully attains or can make intelligible" what appears to us in beautiful art (KU 5:314). It is not that we cannot say *anything* but rather that we cannot say it *all*. In attempting to say what we can, though, we come to add to our concepts; there may not be one determinate predicate, but there may be multiple predicates that indeterminately attach to what appears and to each other. In her "Kant and the Pleasure of Mere Reflection," Melissa Zinkin argues that for Kant, the pleasure in judgments of taste is not merely a side effect, but rather constitutive and necessary.[22] This is because, she argues, the pleasure keeps us in that state, seeking to produce and reproduce itself. The continued attention, she argues, is what the pleasure is meant to ensure. And, we might add, the continued attention to and reflection on the empirical representation is what leads us to further intelligibility and also the further expansion of our own faculties.

Moreover, our consideration of art in reflection is not merely fanciful. We do not simply make up associations in our minds. Rather, as reflection is always keyed to what appears, we make associations and thereby expand our concepts with reference to what appears, that is, we *interpret* it. Kant's insistence on the singularity of judgments of taste and the necessity of an empirical representation means that the free play of the imagination and understanding is always oriented by what is given in appearance. Thus, while reflective judgments are not objective, they nevertheless go beyond the merely ideal claims of a merely speculative metaphysics insofar as they are actually about what appears.

Reflection offers the possibility of interpreting and considering how things are. Insofar as it seeks to interpret what appears purely in its possibility, it takes as its object the coming into being of things. This is, in part, how judgments of taste may speak to the interests we have in metaphysical speculation. Our interpretations are, in a sense, speculative,

---

[22] Melissa Zinkin, "Kant and the Pleasure of Mere Reflection," *Inquiry* 55:5 (October 2012), 433–453.

but are nevertheless at the same time about something in an empirical representation.

Reflection, then, can be seen to provide a means by which our metaphysical needs are addressed. We engage in reflection precisely when what appears is in some sense already outside the bounds of "experience" as Kant defines it, that is, experience understood as what is conceptually determined by us. Moreover, we only reflect on what is actually given in an empirical representation. Even though we may not attain determinative cognition or knowledge in the activity of reflection, we do gain an interpretative foothold into what appears. In fact, it may be an advantage to reflection that it does not attain knowledge proper but remains indeterminate; as it is always keyed to what appears, and what appears is continually and consistently changing, interpretation may perpetually speak to what appears in attempts to make judgments about it. Kant's examination of the expansive character of judgments of reflection, too, means that such interpretation has much to recommend to us for thinking. Rather than merely lacking conceptual determination, our encounters call for and admit of much reflective interpretation that amplifies our view of how things are.

3
"Life" and the Ideal of Beauty

We have already seen how judgments made out in the territory serve as both a ground of as well as a transition between the domains of nature and freedom in virtue of being a third, mediating sphere of experience. We have further seen that such judgments present an orderedness in appearance as well as embody a sense for a larger cosmic context to which we belong. What appears to us out in the territory is the ground itself, and this chapter will argue that this ground further *refers* us to a union of freedom and nature as exemplified in the Ideal of Beauty. This union answers directly to the interests of hope. As judgments of taste will be shown to refer us to a union of freedom and nature, they thus speak to hope's concern that it is really possible for nature to be affected and transformed by the force of freedom.

Judgments of reflection are able to complete the critical system and offer a path between freedom and nature because they refer us to *life*. Life, for Kant, names a distinctive kind of causal *unity* between freedom and nature, force and matter. While Kant endorses the possibility of this unity in his precritical writings, within the constraints of the critical system he maintains that we cannot think such a causal relation. Yet it is precisely this union that reason ultimately requires for its satisfaction and that is needed to complete the system of philosophy. *Life, the causal unity between freedom and nature/force and matter, emerges as the measure and pattern for judgments of reflection.* This is brought out in Kant's woefully undertreated and widely misunderstood section on the Ideal of Beauty. While judgments of reflection do not judge *life* per se (this is not possible), they do judge that things are *like life* – or, better, *life-like* – to some degree or other. Judgments of reflection, in their structure, *refer* to or remind us of life.

In referring us to life, judgments of reflection refer us out beyond the limits of the critical system. Judgments of reflection complete the critical system in their grounding and mediating role. Yet the judgments out in the territory are only able to offer a *transition* between freedom and nature insofar as they reflectively judge there to be a *causal union* of these two otherwise heterogeneous domains. Thus, even while completing the system of philosophy and of human faculties, judgments of reflection still refer us to what is impossible and outside of the completed system. A reflective judgment is enough, however, to grant us the real possibility that there is a supersensible underlying nature that allows it to be in union with freedom.

This chapter will develop this argument across three sections. First, we will revisit the demands of reason, focusing on how reason's demand for systematicity is inextricably bound up with an *inner unity* of things. Reason's demands for such inner unity are most fully developed in Kant's discussion of the All, as well as his turn to ether in the *Opus postumum*. In these discussions, Kant describes a model of life on a cosmic scale. In the second section, we will turn to Kant's lifelong concern with the question of life and the possibility of thinking it. Life is the name for the inner causal unity of freedom and nature, of force and matter, in individual things. We turn then, in section three, to the discussion of the Ideal of Beauty in the third moment of the Analytic of the Beautiful. This section demonstrates how Kant takes the Ideal to be a pattern for all judgments of taste, and how this pattern is that of life.

3.1 Reason's Need for Unity

In the Introduction, we examined the needs of reason – both theoretical and practical – for a system of philosophy. That examination focused on the need for a totality; here, we will further delineate how these needs of reason are for the inner relations of this totality to be a unity, and thus focus on the issue of *life*. In a word, life is the name for the phenomenon of the unconditioned coming into contact with the conditioned – something that reason demands but that the understanding cannot think. Kant argues that the oneness reason demands is the unity of freedom and nature. This demand gives proper context to grasping the full import of the Ideal of the Beauty and its systematic role.

In the Dialectic of the first *Critique*, when Kant focuses his attention on the needs of reason, he draws our attention to the ascension from given appearances to the idea of the world, or, a whole of nature. "But the very same world is called nature* insofar as it is considered as a dynamic whole," he writes, looking "at the unity in the existence of appearances" (KrV A419/B447). Nature, as he has it here, means "the sum total of appearances insofar as these are in thoroughgoing connection through an inner principle of causality" (KrV A418/B446nt). This idea leads, famously, to the four Antinomies. We may say that these Antinomies are about nothing other than the coming into being of things – how they come to be how they are. With this, we are concerned not only with the whole of things but also individual things, and, too, change that brings new things about. This leads us, Kant argues, to reason's Transcendental Ideal. Kant takes up what it means for what is given in appearances to be part of a "thoroughgoing determination." He writes, "in order to cognize a thing completely one has to cognize everything possible and determine the thing through it, whether affirmatively or negatively" (KrV A573/B601). He goes on to develop from this the notion of the *All*. In the All reality, everything that is, *is* in and through everything else. It is not that all the things hang together via some external relation; rather, each thing is always already part of the one thing. Each thing, then, is properly understood only as a limitation or negation of this All (KrV A575/B603 – AA583/B661). Kant ultimately describes this need of reason as a movement from "distributive unity of the use of the understanding in experience, into the collective unity of a whole of experience; and from this whole of appearance we think of an individual thing containing in itself all empirical reality" (KrV A582/B660).

Reason's satisfaction is found not only in a totality, that is, in an unconditioned whole of conditioned things. This totality is properly understood as a *one*, constituted by an inner unity of all that there is. The All is "absolute unity"; it is the "absolute unity of complete reality as the original source of possibility" (KrV A587/B615). While this leads reason to the idea of a necessary being – God – the point is that real intelligibility requires that we understand things only when they are given to us as a part of a larger, utterly unified whole. Conversely, each one thing also contains the whole of relations in itself. For human reason, genuine and ultimate intelligibility takes shape only insofar as all things are *unified* with one another. And, the only way for there to be such a one is for there to be a thoroughgoing unity of all force and matter.

The idea of the unity of the All is, of course, not new. The Ancients conceived of the cosmos as one thing – and in its oneness, as a living being. Only in virtue of its unity and life could all individual things, and all change, be properly conceived. It is this very problem that ultimately leads Kant to the notion of ether as developed in the *Opus postumum*. The problem of causality is ultimately given in the phenomenon of change, namely of things coming to be in a way that is otherwise than how they once were (or, were not). In thinking through the problem of change to its limits, Kant arrives where many before him have. Change is possible only if everything that there is, is already internally related as parts of one whole. Change, as well as individuation, is intelligible to us only as a determination, limitation, or internal differentiation of something that is already one. When Kant turns to his discussion of ether in the *Opus postumum*, it is to solve this very problem of causality and change. He argues here for a "world-matter," an "elementary matter" that, "as a given whole, is the *basis* for the unification of all the forces of matter into the unity of experience" (OP 21:602).[1] This need for a unity of All thus takes shape in Kant attempting to deduce, a priori, what Jeffrey Edwards describes as "a physical aether as a universal force plenum."[2] Or, as Stephen Howard aptly summarizes what Kant is interested in here: "Kant considers the ether to be a self-subsistent cosmic whole that is internally self-moving and serves as the basis of all other moveable matter."[3] What reason ultimately demands, Kant argues, is for there to be one thing, and for this one to be constituted by the unity of force and matter. Only this can function as the basis of any unity of experience we may have.

The purpose of this discussion is to draw our attention to the need that reason has for unity, specifically, the unity of force and matter, which throughout his corpus is called *life*. Kant's development of reason's need with respect to how we think about the cosmos as a unity has clear implications for the interests of hope, which are very much keyed to the problem of causality and the possibility of change in the natural order. Human reason demands that the ends of freedom be realized; such realization is met only in the natural order. How, though, can freedom have causality in the natural order? To put it crudely: any action I take may have an effect in the world. This effect, however, appears natural, mechanistic, conditioned. How can it be that freedom has effects such that these effects are embodiments of the freedom itself? If the end of freedom is for the world to be remade into a rational whole, how might this be possible? For this to be a genuine possibility, it now seems, the cosmos must already be constituted by reason as its substratum, its underlying and embodied, constitutive force. The need for life, for the unity of force and matter,

---

[1] For a detailed discussion of Kant's thinking from the Ideal to the ether proofs in the *Opus postumum*, along with the problems in making such a move for Kant, see Förster, *Kant's Final Synthesis*, 80–101.
[2] Jeffrey Edwards, "One More Time: Kant's Metaphysics of Nature and the Idea of Transition," in *Eredita kantiane*, Cinzia Ferrini, ed. (Rome: Bibliopolis, 2004).
[3] Stephen Howard, "The Transition within the Transition: The *Übergang* from the *Selbstsetzungslehre* to the Ether Proofs in Kant's *Opus postumum*," *Kant-Studien* 110:4 (2019), 601.

becomes ever more urgent given the prospect of despair if we come to take our rational ends as unattainable.

Reason, though, will remain dissatisfied with respect to the All and the thoroughgoing unity of all things. Indeed, even the third *Critique* only promises the *possibility* of *agreement or harmonization*. While nature's purposiveness – judged merely reflectively – gives us a sense that nature itself may have a supersensible substratum that accords with the ends of freedom, this does not suggest that freedom may reach out into nature and transform it into something rational. Kant clearly, decisively, and self-consciously opts for *harmonization* instead of *unity* with respect to freedom and nature. We have already noted how those who followed in his wake in the German Idealist tradition were critical of him for just this. "Nature and freedom are not identical," in Kant, writes Figal on the matter. Rather, "the supersensible is given in the sensible and natural aspect of aesthetic experience in such a way that it does not oppose the sensible; supersensible freedom arrives in intuition with the sensible of aesthetic experience without being able to unify with the latter."[4]

Yet it will be in virtue of gesturing toward, or even patterning itself on, such a unity that judgments of reflection are able to complete the system without violating the constraints of the system itself. The harmonization is predicated on referring to unity. While reason will not get what it wants in the third *Critique*, the work that the third *Critique* does is accomplished with reference to the thing that reason demands above all.

3.2 Life as Unity

If what reason ultimately wants is an inner causal unity – the unity of everything that there is, this takes particular shape as the notion of life in Kant. This section will take up Kant's writings on life, and, with this, highlight the centrality of this concept in his thinking. In Section 3.3, I will demonstrate how Kant's argument for the Ideal of Beauty is about life and establishes life – the union of freedom and nature – as the pattern of all judgments of taste.

What life is, along with the difficulty of thinking life, has been a central topic of examination since philosophy's inception. From a reflective perspective, we may wonder at it: there is a strange curiosity that some beings are alive, are animated to grow, move, reproduce, and then have the life go

---

[4] Figal, *Aesthetics as Phenomenology*, 29.

out of them. This is strange enough on the face of it, even stranger in contrast to those beings that do not share in this animation. Aristotle is the first philosopher to take this question up explicitly and in a sustained way, in *de Anima*.[5] Aristotle's account is difficult and probing, and more than provide a clear resolution, what he succeeds in is getting to the heart of what is so perplexing to us when we attempt to think about life. What is this principle that animates matter (or, for Aristotle, corporeal substance, which he distinguishes from mere matter) to growth and movement for a determinate time? How does this principle imbue the corporeal substance, with which it becomes composite, with this growth and movement? *Zōē*, the principle of life, is clearly distinct from matter. Yet it does not appear to be separable from it. While Aristotle may be seen to land on a kind of hylomorphism to address the difficulty, his solution is neither particularly clear nor does it settle the question. This is not a criticism of Aristotle; philosophers and biologists since have not yet offered a coherent, convincing account of how we may understand the relation between materiality and vitality.

Thus, the question of what life is and how we might be able to think it persists. It is still at play in questions of animal life and ecosystems, in issues of etiological functioning, for example. Thinkers like Giorgio Agamben and Jacques Derrida both focus on life hewing quite closely to Aristotle's own development of the thorny problems involved. This is to say that the question of life – of corporeal substance moving itself to grow and to move – is one of the most difficult things philosophers have attempted to think.

Kant has a longstanding interest in the question of life. While he ultimately acknowledges the difficulty – and ultimately, impossibility – of thinking the relation between a principle of life and material substance, his initial foray into the long trajectory of thinking the question is with respect to the vis viva debate. In fact, Kant begins his philosophical career as a twenty-one-year-old student by asking the question of *life* with an essay, "Thoughts on the true estimation of living forces." In this essay, he makes an intervention into the vis viva debate, which had been waged

---

[5] Aristotle begins the text with a kind of list of the difficulties we face in thinking the phenomenon in the first place. Also, it would be wrong to imply Plato is not interested in life as such. Michael Naas' recent work makes an excellent case for the centrality of the concept in Plato's work. Naas does note, though, that there is "no dialogue that poses the famous *ti esti* or 'what is' question with regard to life." Naas, Michael. *Plato and the Invention of Life* (New York: Fordham University Press, 2018), 4.

already for more than fifty years by the time of his writing.[6] The vis viva debate coalesced around attempts to understand how force related to matter, specifically by way of the task of measuring such forces in moving bodies. The debate began in 1686, when Leibniz published a short piece entitled, "A Brief Demonstration of a Notable Error of Descartes and Others Concerning a Natural Law." In it, Leibniz argued against Descartes with respect to his characterization of force; this essay is typically taken to initiate a distinction between kinematics and dynamics. Kinematics studies the motion of bodies with respect what is externally measurable. Dynamics, by contrast, studies the inner forces that are taken to be the underlying cause or source of the movement. The latter is what comes to be associated with living forces – the forces that animate or enliven a thing to motion. These are what Leibniz identifies as "essential forces," which, as Kant writes, "inhere" in a body (GwS 1:17). In this, a material body possesses, or is possessed by, the force that is the source of its motion. Kant's own discussion focuses in part on the question of whether or not a body is moved by forces external to it, or internal to it (GwS 1:139ff).

Even in his early essay, Kant sees the question of the relation of force and matter as one with broader relevance. Living force is the force that is essential to a body when it becomes activated, that is, vivification. Kant himself notes that the difficulty in conceiving how this force comes to life and affects material being also has import for practical life. He writes,

> A similar difficulty becomes apparent when the question is raised as to whether the soul, too, is capable of setting matter in motion ... For the question whether the soul can cause motions, that is, whether it has moving force, is transformed into the question whether its essential force can be determined toward an externally directed action, that is, whether it is capable of acting outside itself on other entities and producing changes. (GwS 1:20)

The question of a living being and its animation, then, is the question of how a force – something immaterial – can come into causal contact with and ultimately affect something material. In his practical philosophy, Kant does not address this issue in any substantive way. For early modern thinkers before him, however, there was much concern with the relation between the soul and the body – how it could be that my soul or will could

---

[6] For detailed examinations of this debate, please see Carolyn Iltis, "Leibniz and the *Vis Viva* Controversy," *Isis* 62:1 (Spring 1971); David Papineau, "The *Vis Viva* Controversy: Do Meanings Matter?" *Studies in History and Philosophy of Science* 8:2 (1977); Mary Terrall, "*Vis Viva* Revisited," *History of Science* xlii (2004).

come to move my body through its own force. Descartes, of course, is perhaps most famous for his inquiries into these matters, and, with this, his development of a theory of the pineal gland as the site where the soul and body may come into contact.[7]

While Kant's attention to the phenomenon of living beings is consonant with the philosophical tradition beginning with Aristotle in *de Anima*, what is important is not only that he is concerned with it from early in his career. Rather, it is how he comes to define life by way of living forces. Life, for Kant, comes to be defined by a specific kind of union between force and matter. In this, he follows Leibniz closely. In this early essay, Kant rejects the Cartesians' view of matter as something inert, acted upon only by external forces. And while he tries in some ways to split the difference between the two, he aligns himself with the Leibnizian view that natural bodies have an internal principle of force.[8] Or, as Edwards sums up the Leibnizian mature position, "it is force that constitutes the inner nature of bodies."[9] Matter, on this account, "does not denote any self-subsistent physical extant."[10]

Kant's preoccupation with this question comes full circle in the *Opus postumum*. It is, in no small part, as an answer to this problem that Kant develops his notion of ether, a kind of "universally distributed worldmatter."[11] It is clear enough from the context of the ether discussions that Kant has in mind issues relating to "moving forces" and to life. His discussion includes the motion of both organic and inorganic bodies – ether is meant to give some possibility to the motion of inorganic substances. The thesis Kant is interested in is this: "a primordial motion of matter and the existence of its moving forces must inevitably be postulated, simply because there is motion in cosmic space" (OP 21:222). It is striking that at the end of his philosophical career, and indeed, of his own life, Kant is still focused on the question of how things come to move, to change, to grow, to affect each other. Thus, we find that at the bookends of the critical philosophy – in the precritical writings on the life sciences, and in the arguably post-critical *Opus postumum*, Kant maintains his interest in

---

[7] See especially, René Descartes, Passions of the Soul, in *The Philosophical Writings of Descartes Vol. 1* (Cambridge: Cambridge University Press, 1985), 340–348.
[8] For a brief synopsis on Kant's essay, see Manfred Kuehn, "Kant's Teachers in the Exact Sciences," in *Kant and the Sciences*, Eric Watkins, ed. (Oxford: Oxford University Press, 2001), 23–27.
[9] Jeffrey Edwards, *Substance, Force, and the Possibility of Knowledge: On Kant's Philosophy of Material Nature* (Berkeley: University of California Press, 2000), 101.
[10] Ibid.   [11] Förster, *Kant's Final Synthesis*, 83.

one of the most basic philosophical questions, namely the relation of force to matter, or, put practically, freedom to nature.

In the context of the critical project, however, Kant diverges from Leibniz and others in the early modern tradition with respect to whether or not we can investigate, let alone even think, the possibility of life as living forces. Kant, with the transcendental turn, will reject a science of living beings; the movement of matter can only be investigated according to mechanistic causalities. He holds a strict distinction between force and matter, and it is beyond the scope of human thinking to cognize a unity in their relation. In his *Metaphysical Foundations of Natural Science*, in 1786, Kant gives voice to his now established view about the issue. Kant defines matter thus: "Matter is the movable in space" (MAN 4:480). "Motion," he goes on, "is the change of [a thing's] outer relations in a given space" (MAN 4:482). Matter also "fills a space" (MAN 4:496), as movable, it "has moving force" and "can be an object of experience" (MAN 4:554). However, matter, "as such," Kant writes, is "lifeless" (MAN 4:544). By this he means that it is inert; it has "no internal determinations or grounds of determination" (MAN 4:453). Matter, then, qua matter, is always subject to that which is external to it, whether that externality is other matter or some living force. Matter is inert: it does not act, but is acted upon. From the perspective of scientific inquiry, moreover, matter, qua matter, is only amenable to mechanical accounts of its being, that is, the kind of accounts that are made possible as knowledge under the regime of the Analytic in the *Critique of Pure Reason*.

Kant thus rejects the *life* sciences, the sciences that purport to account for movement of an object whose determination to motion originates in itself. "Life" he writes, "is the faculty of a substance to determine itself to act from an internal principle" (MAN 4:544). Such motion includes not only the force to move from one place to another but also the nutritive movements of sustenance, growth, healing, and reproduction. In fact, as Jennifer Mensch highlights in her study of Kant's intellectual development with respect to thinking organic life and the possibility of the life sciences, Kant continually found the challenge of thinking living being to be beyond the scope of our capabilities.[12] Of the problem, Kant writes,

> The various appearances of life in nature and the laws governing them, constitute the whole of that which it is granted us to know. But the principle of this life, in other words, the spirit-nature which we do not

---

[12] Jennifer Mensch, *Kant's Organicism: Epigenesis and the Development of Critical Philosophy* (Chicago: University of Chicago Press, 2013), especially chapter 3.

know but only suppose, can never be positively thought, for, in the entire range of our sensations, there are no data for such positive thought. (TG 2:351)

Perhaps the most telling mature discussion of what life is, what it is not, and what we can know about it can be found in Kant's description of organisms in the third *Critique*.[13] In writing the third *Critique*, Kant still rejects the life sciences as earlier conceived. He revisits the question of the biological sciences, however, and the possibilities for investigating living beings under the auspices of reflective judgment. Here he argues for the concept of an organism; we judge that organisms are constituted by what he names *internal purposiveness*. In virtue of its internal purposiveness, an organism is a natural end – it is both "**cause and effect of itself**"; its parts "reciprocally produce each other"; each part exists "**for the sake of the others** and **on account of** the whole" (KU 5:371, 373). Living being, organic life, is "self-organizing." To be a living being is to cause one's own existence, both as a member of a species as well as of an individual. In this, an organism has a kind of self-determination of its existence – in continuing its existence in living and in determining the form of its existence materially.

This organic arrangement of materiality is produced by what Kant names a "formative power." He rejects, though, that this is the same thing as *life*. He writes, "An organized being is thus not a mere machine, for that has only a motive power, while the organized being possesses in itself a formative power, and indeed one that it communicates [*mittheilt*] to the matter, which does not have it (it organizes the latter)" (KU 5:374). Here, the formative power that organizes a being into a living being is one that arranges the parts of the thing with respect to its whole being and its capacity to persist in being. The causality belonging to the formative power, though, is not therefore life. Kant will first reject that this power is akin to art – art is caused by something outside of itself. He will argue, however, that perhaps this "inscrutable property" is "an analogue of life" (KU 5:374–5). The problem he articulates here is the very same one he is "astonished" by in his precritical writings on the topic: either, he suggests, we endow matter with a "property (hylozoism) that contradicts its essence, or else associate it with an alien principle **standing in communion** [*Gemeinschaft*] with (a soul)" (KU 5:375). In either case, what *life* is comes out in the Scylla and Charybdis Kant outlines here, a dichotomy that may

---

[13] We will return to this discussion in Chapter 6.

remain hidden without close inspection. Life here is a *union* between the property of animation or self-determination and material nature. Hylozoism simply ascribes a soul to matter itself, thereby rendering it not matter proper; or we take the soul to be able to come into a union with the matter. These two models of relation differ from the formative power, which merely "communicates" [*mittheilt*] with the matter. Kant's formulation of the formative power is crucial, as it suggests that there remains a distance between the force and the matter. The force that organizes a living being is transmitted to or gotten across to the matter, but it does not come into a union with it. This is a strange kind of causality, and Kant concludes that "the organization of nature is therefore not analogous with any causality that we know" (KU 5:375).

This yields two interrelated claims: what life is for Kant, and his ongoing and persistent interest in how we might be able to think it. Life names a certain kind of unity of force and matter, wherein force activates the matter; life is a compound or composite of a principle of life and corporeal substance where they are inseparable from one another – indeed, they become one thing, a living being. With respect to organic beings, this takes shape with respect to growth, reproduction, movement, and so forth. This unity, this causal relation, is not one that the human faculties are fit to think, however. Living beings, organisms, cannot even be thought properly under the auspices of life – we must still remain in the dark about the way that the formative power communicates itself to the matter it forms. Despite this, Kant will return to the possibility of life, to the possibility of such a unity, intermittently throughout his opus. From his *Reflections*:

> Everything finally comes down to life; that which animates, or the feeling of the promotion of life, is agreeable. **Life is unity** [*Das Leben ist Einheit*]; hence all taste has as its principio the unity of animating sensation. (R 6862, 19:183, my emphasis in bold)

Insofar as life is unity, life is the thing that reason seeks above all else, the thing that reason cannot help but think. And yet Kant denies reason the possibility of thinking life; it remains interminably excommunicated from the confines of the critical system.

3.3 Ideal of Beauty and Life in the Figures

Now that we have a fuller sense of the demands of reason as they take shape in the notion of life, we can better see how judgments of taste specifically speak to these demands. These demands are for nothing other than the intimate causal union of freedom and nature, force and matter, that Kant names life. It will be in the Ideal of Beauty, which Kant argues gives us the pattern for all judgments of taste, that we find how these judgments are patterned after life. As we shall see, we reflectively judge that beautiful things are lifelike, they appear to us as material things formed by and ultimately embodying the immaterial; this is presented in the Ideal of Beauty as the human being thoroughgoingly determined through a morally good will.

As a frame for the following treatment of the Ideal of Beauty, I would like first to point the reader to a remark Kant makes in his moral philosophy that will be instructive. In the section of the *Critique of Practical Reason* entitled, "On the Wise Adaptation of the Human Being's Cognitive Faculties to His Practical Vocation," Kant argues that from the perspective of our moral goodness, it is beneficial to us that we do not have knowledge of God's existence. If we had such knowledge, he suggests, "most actions conforming to the law would be done from fear, only a few from hope, and none at all from duty" (KpV 5:147). To describe such heteronomy, namely acting on the basis of an external ground that merely conforms to the morally good rather than being moved to act from duty to the good itself, Kant writes that "everything would *gesticulate* well, but there would be no *life* in the figures" (KpV 5:147). The suggestion in this passage is that there is an outward appearance of a person's motivations, that there is a difference in the movements of human bodies depending on what their will is. You can tell, he seems to think, whether someone really means something, whether they genuinely intend the good. Such a remark notably depends on taking the human will to have a causal union with the body, namely to be its principle of life. It is this possibility that is more fully developed in the Ideal of Beauty.

While there are a few moments in the practical philosophy where Kant makes a suggestion similar to the one of there being "life in the figures," in the end, this possibility can only be represented aesthetically.[14] In this section, I will reconstruct Kant's argument for the Ideal of Beauty, drawing out the absolute determination of the natural by the rational that he argues for. What will emerge is that the Ideal is the highest measure, and thus also the pattern, of all judgments of taste. While no judgment actually instantiates this Ideal, Kant nevertheless argues that all judgments of taste follow

---

[14] In this way, the observation of there being life in the figures may be consistent with Kant's claims that we can never have access to one's intentions.

this pattern and thus invoke the notion of life and refer to it as their measure.

Scholarship has long neglected or even derided Kant's section on the Ideal of Beauty. Henry Allison's reading of the third *Critique* does not treat it at all.[15] Paul Guyer argues that this section does not tell us anything about beauty, but rather that it belongs principally to Kant's practical concerns. He writes that Kant "was searching for nothing less than vehicles for the representation of the primacy of practical reason itself."[16] As Zuckert points out, too, "Paragraph 17 is the paragraph of the CJ most infrequently discussed in the scholarly literature, often passed over in silence." Even more than this, she notes that Kant's treatment of "human beauty" in this section is, when taken up, "much maligned."[17] By contrast, my examination of the section will show how, in fact, the Ideal of Beauty is a genuine *ideal*. In its function as an ideal, it exemplifies how in the completion of his system, Kant continually refers out beyond the system to the thoroughgoing unity of freedom and nature in *life*. In this, the Ideal provides the pinnacle and archetype of judgments made out in the territory. So while much of the literature ignores or is critical of the Ideal because it seems to exceed the bounds of Kant's critical inquiry, I show how it refers us to what is beyond these bounds, but in a way that is serviceable for the system itself.

Kant introduces his discussion of the Ideal of Beauty in the third moment of the Analytic of the Beautiful, within the context of his much-celebrated treatment of purposiveness without a purposive. The systematic significance of the Ideal of Beauty has remained elusive for Kant scholars, however. In one respect its dismissal as integral to the text makes sense – Kant suggests that the need for a model of an Ideal of Beauty is produced through reason and its attendant "indeterminate idea of a maximum" (KU 5:232). Yet the Ideal, as Kant articulates it, is – despite what at first glance appears to contradict earlier claims about the beautiful – the highest instantiation of the beautiful for Kant. In addition, it is Kant's notion of purposiveness without a purpose that generates the interpretation of Kant's aesthetics as a kind of formalism – that is, what is beautiful is so due solely to its form – yet the Ideal of Beauty poses a counter argument for the supremacy of content as determinative for a

---

[15] Allison, *Kant's Theory of Taste*.
[16] Paul Guyer, "Feeling and Freedom," *Kant and the Experience of Freedom* (Cambridge: Cambridge University Press, 1996), 42.
[17] Rachel Zuckert, "Boring Beauty and Universal Morality: Kant on the Ideal of Beauty," *Inquiry* 48, no. 2 (April 2005), 108, 125.

standard of beauty. The emphasis on formalism accords with an interpretation of the primacy of nature as beautiful in Kant, too. The Ideal, by contrast, as Gadamer notes, marks a movement where Kant "seems imperceptibly to pass over [from nature] into art."[18] Gadamer observes this precisely because the Ideal belies a formalist interpretation of beauty, as Kant describes it in his discussion of art, genius, and aesthetic ideas. Indeed, how Kant thinks about the Ideal of Beauty is consanguine with his discussion of beautiful art.

As elsewhere, Kant takes pains in the opening paragraph of §17 to remind his readers that there is "no objective rule of taste" (KU 5:231). That is, there is nothing in our concepts, or in the object, to which we could appeal in order to demonstrate that an object has met some criterion that would designate it as beautiful. As judgments of taste are predicated on pleasure and not on concepts, Kant asserts, "To seek a principle of taste that would provide the universal criterion of the beautiful through determinate concepts is a fruitless undertaking, because what is sought is impossible and intrinsically contradictory" (KU 5:231). Despite the impossibility of a rule or proof that could be offered for the beautiful, Kant nevertheless asserts that we *must* each, for ourselves, produce a "highest model" or an "archetype" of taste (KU 5:232). While there is no criterion we can apply in each instance of beauty, there still must be an ultimate measure or height that it can reach. It is reason that generates a need in us to produce an idea of what is maximally beautiful – the most beautiful thing available to our thinking. The archetype of the maximally beautiful is that "which everyone must produce in himself, and in accordance with which he must judge everything that is an object of taste, or that is an example of judging through taste, even the taste of everyone else" (KU 5:232). Not only, then, must we produce such a measure, but we must produce it as an archetype for all of our judgments of taste. In order to serve as a measure, Kant further argues, it cannot remain a mere idea. Rather, it must take shape in an *ideal* – a concrete and individual instantiation of the idea. Kant explains the difference between these in the first *Critique*. While human wisdom "in its entire purity" is an idea, the sage, he writes, is an ideal of this wisdom. Namely, the ideal is an "original image" that serves for the "thoroughgoing determination of the copy" (KrV A569/B597). The Ideal of Beauty, as maximum beauty, thus provides us with an example or prototype of the original pattern of what we

---

[18] Hans-Georg Gadamer, "Intuition and Vividness," in *The Relevance of the Beautiful and Other Essays* (Cambridge: Cambridge University Press, 1986), 166.

find beautiful; this example guides us in judging all objects of beauty. In this, all judgments of taste are a kind or copy of imprint of the original Ideal. They have the same form, though perhaps not to the highest degree.

The idea of a maximum that reason generates is functional. That is, it is not merely an inextricable feature of reason that it makes this demand, such that it is arbitrary and must be extirpated. Rather, the ideas we are led to by the demand for the maximum – and their subsequent embodiment in ideals – have "heuristic" value (KrV A663/B692). That is, they may not constitute any experience we have, but they do provide a regulative function. Kant suggests that the ideas of reason may operate as "an analogue of a schema" (KrV A665/B693). An ideal, as a concrete instantiation of an idea, then, is a more determinate analogue (functioning, perhaps, like a symbol). Ideas and ideals "serve as a rule" of judgment, providing the complete and perfect iteration of the thing. Guyer is thus incorrect to suggest that the Ideal of Beauty is referred only to reason itself. He writes, "it is reason which demands outward representation of its effects in a form of beauty, and indeed something maximally beautiful, in order to represent its own character as something maximal or unconditioned."[19] Nevertheless, ideas and ideals of reason serve a clear function, even in the context of cognition. More than this, in the aesthetic context Kant clearly suggests that an ideal would serve that same role with respect to all judgments of taste. For Kant, then, all judgments of taste refer themselves to the ideal of such a judgment as their schema.

But what is it that is maximally beautiful, and that serves as a standard or original image of the beautiful? Kant begins his analysis by first rejecting the possibility that what he has previously delineated as a "free" beauty, which corresponds with a "pure" judgment of taste could fill such a role. For many readers of Kant, this is a stunning turn. The "pure" judgment of taste, which has been intimated to be the highest kind of beauty, is hereby dismissed as a candidate for that which is maximally beautiful. With this, Kant rejects formal beauty – as a "pure" judgment of taste is made with regard only to the form of the object as appearing to have a purpose, and not being grounded on a concept – as the original pattern of beauty. Rather, he writes that "it should be noted that the beauty for which an idea is to be sought must not be a **vague** beauty, but must be a beauty **fixed** by a concept of objective purposiveness, consequently it must not belong to the object of an entirely pure judgment of taste, but rather to one of a partly intellectualized judgment of taste" (KU 5:232).

---

[19] Guyer, *Kant and the Experience of Freedom*, 43.

Kant advocates for the maximally beautiful to involve a concept because for there to be an ideal of something, there must be some idea (i.e., a concept of reason) on which it is based. It is the idea of the thing that provides the end "on which the internal possibility of the object rests," and therefore the measure of what the object is supposed to be (KU 5:233). This is nothing other than the idea of perfection. As there must be something the object ought to be, for it to be an ideal, he denies the possibility that things like flowers, furnishings, or gardens could attain an ideal.

The one thing whose end is determinate enough to admit of perfection and thus ideality is the human being. The human being, Kant observes, "has the end of its existence in itself" and as such "is capable of an ideal of **beauty**, just as the human being, is alone among all the objects in the world capable of the idea of **perfection**" (KU 5:233). The human being, whose end exists in and of itself, is thus capable of providing for itself its own measure of what it ought to be. We set our ends out of our own freedom. Human beings have an absolute relation to ourselves and to everything else insofar as we are the source of what we are and what our ends are. Only humans, then, can admit of perfectability and perfection. We cannot, for example, find the perfect – and thus ideal – horse, rose, or house. None of these has a determinate enough concept of what it is such that an ideal can be posited.

Those familiar with Kant's theory of beauty will be surprised at the apparent equivocation of perfection with beauty, as Kant clearly denies any kind of conditioning relation between these two things. In explicitly denying that the beautiful pleases in virtue of a concept, Kant forecloses the possibility that a thing could be beautiful on account of its perfection. Indeed, just two sections prior to the Ideal of Beauty, in §15, Kant argues, "The judgment of taste is entirely independent from the concept of perfection." Kant argues this because perfection belies beauty's "merely formal purposiveness" by introducing a determinate end (KU 5:226). At the same time, however, Kant notes that "objective inner purposiveness, i.e., perfection, already comes closer to the predicate of beauty" (KU 5:227). Many philosophers have even made the mistake of equating them. We can think here of Plato and the neo-Platonists, for whom a beautiful thing was defined by the height of its goodness; something was beautiful insofar as it instantiated what it is supposed to be. How is it, then, that Kant believes the perfection of the human being can be beautiful and not merely a kind of knowledge – an occasion for the determination of a concept – or even merely a recognition of moral goodness that would effect respect in us? In part, it is not the fulfillment of the concept that pleases us in the ideal. Indeed, Kant's denial that flowers or furnishings could have an ideal, alongside his claim that the only thing in the world that admits of perfection is the human being, suggests to us that we should attend to his claim that an ideal requires an *idea*. Indeed, there is no ideal flower or chair or horse; this is because while there are concepts of what a flower or chair are, there are not ideas of them. Concepts can be fulfilled (come to their fullness [*vollkommen*]) in that they may appear in a kind of completeness in their determination. That is, we may find a horse to which nothing more can be added to make it a better horse. However, we may find many such horses of varying sizes and colors, none of which is an ideal. So, when Kant argues in §15 that beauty is independent of perfection, he seems here to have in mind a perfection associated with concepts, and not the (more perfect) perfection of an idea, found in an ideal.

The very thing that allows for human beings to be capable of perfection is the very same thing that allows the idea of humanity to admit of being beautiful. It is our capacity for freedom that grants human life the possibility of perfection insofar as it is due to our freedom that our existence has its end in itself. At the same time, freedom is less like a determinable concept such as those of the faculty of the understanding and more like what Kant will later outline as an aesthetic idea in his discussion of art and genius. Mere concepts, on the first *Critique* account, are determinable empirically; this means that in grasping what is represented, the concept is fully determined in reality. There is nothing left over, left out, or remaindered. Freedom, on the other hand, is the absolutely unconditioned quality of the human will; it is an unconditioned causality, a cause in and of itself. As such, freedom does not belong to the domain of appearances and cannot be grasped in a representation in the way a mere concept can. Indeed, freedom, Kant reminds us, is "not capable of being presented empirically" (KpV 5:15). Freedom shows up to us as a demand, an imperative of the will, but, according to Kant, we cannot even conceptualize this demand. It presents itself in moral feeling, and the formulations of the moral law, he writes, are simply ways we bring the unconditioned closer to intuition. Freedom, then, cannot be grasped conceptually, nor be presented empirically; insofar as it can be presented, however, it admits of being presented aesthetically.[20]

What does it mean to understand human freedom, in the context of the Ideal of Beauty, as an aesthetic idea? In his description of fine art, Kant

---

[20] Aesthetic ideas will be discussed at length in Chapter 5, in the context of their association with genius.

does not argue that the formal qualities of an artwork make it beautiful, as one might expect. Rather, he submits to the reader that it is the content or aesthetic idea of an artwork – the idea that is presented aesthetically – that makes it beautiful. Kant elucidates aesthetic ideas with reference to a "rational idea," which he names as their counterpart. Aesthetic ideas, Kant writes, "strive toward something lying beyond the bounds of experience, and thus seek to approximate a presentation of concepts of reason" (KU 5:314). What distinguishes an idea of reason from an aesthetic idea is simply this: aesthetic ideas are attempts to make ideas of reason representable to our senses. Beautiful art is nothing other than the presentation of something that, strictly speaking, cannot be presented in its full determinacy. An idea of reason exceeds our capacity for conceptual determination, and thus its presentation to our senses in the aesthetic domain – if done well – can occasion a feeling of the beautiful in us. Because, as Kant describes it, an idea of reason "cannot be adequately presented," it "gives the imagination cause to spread itself over a multitude of related representations, which let one think more than one can express in a concept determined by words" (KU 5:315). Aesthetic ideas occasion the free play of the faculties that constitute the judgment of taste. Freedom as an aesthetic idea, then, is freedom insofar as it admits of being presented at all.

The presentation of freedom takes shape in the morally good human being. In the Ideal of Beauty, Kant describes the attainment of moral perfection – the thoroughgoing determination of the body by freedom. Kant describes the morally good human being as beautiful insofar as freedom animates his or her figure – one's movements, one's gestures, one's comportment. He writes, "the **idea of reason**, which makes the ends of humanity insofar as they cannot be sensibly represented into the principle for the judging of its figure [*Gestalt*], through which, as their effect in appearance, the former are revealed" (KU 5:233). Kant is clear: the freedom that cannot be presented to our senses determinatively nevertheless can have an effect in the figure of a human being who is morally good. There is something, Kant intimates, in the morally good person's embodiment that renders perceptible the moral ideas that determine its action. Further on he repeats the description of the ideal of beauty in the human figure as "the visible expression of moral ideas" (KU 5:235). In the ideal of beauty, the moral idea of freedom is rendered sensible in the human form.

Kant's discussion of the Ideal of Beauty describes the body of a person determined wholly through freedom as organized not only by its physical or organic ends but also principally by moral ends. In this, the freedom that constitutes the activity of moral goodness arranges the physical parts of the body. Freedom, though, exceeds the mere physical relation of the parts to the whole, and imbues the movements, gestures, indeed the entire physical bearing of the morally good person with a moral aesthetic quality. Through the enactment of freedom in moral goodness, the morally good person may form their body through freedom's union with it. If freedom can be a force that organizes our bodily movements, then we can, as Kant indicates, discern "goodness of soul, or purity, or strength, or repose" in the actions of someone else (KU 5:235). However, Kant does not seem to think that all morally good persons can achieve such a standard, indicating that there is something expressed aesthetically in the Ideal beyond simply performing morally good acts. That is, one may enact one's freedom in what one does, yet not necessarily attain the height of beauty in so doing. He writes that if these ideas "were to make visible in bodily manifestation (as the effect of what is inward) their combination with everything that our understanding connects with the morally good ... this requires pure ideas of reason and great force of imagination united in anyone who would merely judge them, let alone anyone who would present them" (KU 5:235). Like the genius – a rare individual amongst human beings – the morally good person who is capable of such beautiful embodiment must be able to "[create], as it were, another nature, out of the material which the real one gives it" (KU 5:314). The morally good person whose freedom forms his or her embodiment makes a unique aesthetic impression on us. The way they carry themselves in their actions exceeds the judgment that they simply act well – their morally good actions are attractive and pleasing in the humility and grace that they express.

The human body, on this account, is organized in all of its activity – all of its liveliness – by the form of freedom, and not simply the principle of organic life. There is nothing that this body does that is not governed by and willed through freedom. What we see when we are brought into contact with the Ideal is not a human body, but freedom personified. This is to say that something like the supersensible – an idea – thoroughly dominates the material or sensible aspect of the thing.

We may also say that in the Ideal of Beauty, freedom is what *animates* the body. In this regard, Kant associates the liveliness of the human being with *spirit*.[21] Indeed, Kant joins the notion of spirit with life in multiple

---

[21] My analysis here appears to go against Zammito's very fine work to distinguish *Lebensgefühl* from *Geistesgefühl* in *The Genesis of Kant's Critique of Judgment*. There, Zammito takes the *Lebensgefühl* to be about the mere fact of living, and not the human (i.e., moral) life of freedom. I think that for

contexts, but foremost when speaking of human life. When Kant writes of beautiful art, he describes spirit as something substantively presented, a kind of presence in the material of the work. He writes about works that are artistic, but lack spirit: "A story is accurate and well organized, but without spirit. A solemn oration is thorough and at the same time flowery, but without spirit. Many a conversation is not without entertainment, but is still without spirit" (KU 5:313). Within human beings, it is spirit that brings the mind to life: "**Spirit**, in an aesthetic significance, means the animating principle in the mind" (KU 5:313). And perhaps most directly, in his "Treaty of Perpetual Peace in Philosophy," he writes,

> By means of reason, the soul of man is endowed with a *spirit* (*mens, nous*) so that he may lead a life adapted, not merely to the mechanism of *nature* and its technico-practical laws, but also to the spontaneity of *freedom* and its morally-practical laws. This life-principle ... proceeds initially and at once from an Idea of the *supersensible*, namely *freedom*, and from the morally categorical imperative of which the latter first informs us. (zeFP 8:417)

Spirit emerges in certain moments of Kant's philosophy as the animating principle of human life. Spirit is the name Kant gives to the force of freedom that comes into union with and imbues materiality with itself. Spirit, as life force, does not merely communicate with matter; it acts on and through material being. Spirit thus appears to be the supersensible that has taken hold of and is directing materiality. Nuzzo describes the principle of life as that which "discloses the traces of the supersensible within the sensible."[22]

Kant further describes the possibility of human freedom having the force ultimately to transform material nature in his writing on medicine. While Kant does not go so far as to argue that reason can reach down into the cells of our materiality and alter them, he does argue that one's reason has "the sheer power ... to master his sensuous feelings by a self-imposed principle determin[ing] his manner of living" (SF 7:100–1). The force of our will can change the way we feel about things, that is, it can alter our natural inclinations. With this, it transforms our natural constitution. Kant notes that he himself tended toward hypochondria, something for which he writes he had a "natural disposition." Hypochondria is "the exact opposite of the mind's power to master its pathological feelings" (SF 7:103). He suggests that while the mechanical oppression in his chest

---

Kant, human *life* is always given in freedom. See Zammito, *The Genesis of Kant's Critique of Judgment*, 292–305.

[22] Angelica Nuzzo, "Leben and Leib in Kant and Hegel," *Hegel-Jahrbuch* 2 (2007), 98.

about which he had become melancholic remained, he overcame his feelings, thus employing the mind's power to do just this. The effect, he writes, is this:

> The result was that, while I felt the oppression in my chest, a calm and cheerful state prevailed in my mind, which did not fail to communicate itself to society, not by intermittent whims (as is usual with hypochondriacs), but purposely and naturally. And since one's life becomes cheerful more through what we freely do with life than through what we enjoy as a gift from it, mental work can set another kind of heightened vital feeling against the limitations that affect the body alone. (SF 7:104)

This is a remarkable passage. It brings together many of the themes treated in the Ideal of Beauty. Kant notes that the disposition he has rationally chosen is public, and that it appears to others both as purposeful and natural. This would indicate that it appears both chosen and thoroughgoing, as if a second nature (we can recall here the idea of making a new nature out of the nature that is given to us). The choice has worked its way onto and into the physical bearing. With this, too, Kant identifies the work of reason in this context to influence one's feelings with a "heightened vital feeling." That is, the activity of the will in altering one's feelings and inclinations yields nothing other than a feeling of life.[23]

It is notable that life returns over and over in these passages to name the efficacious union of freedom and nature in the human being. Life, recall, is defined as "the faculty of a substance to determine itself to act from an internal principle" (MAN 4:544). The internal principle by which human beings are capable of determining themselves to act is found in the will, namely *freedom*. Thus, for Kant, freedom is nothing other than the principle of life – or, as in the "Treaty," the "life-principle" [*Lebensprincip*] – for human beings. That is, freedom is that which animates us and transforms us into living beings. Kant has already identified the principle that animates human beings as freedom in the *Critique of Practical Reason*. In the preface he writes, "**Life** is the faculty of a being to act in accordance with laws of the faculty of desire. The **faculty of desire** is a being's *faculty to be by means of its representations the cause of the*

---

[23] On Kant's remarkable debate with the medical faculty, and their engagement with him, please see John Zammito, "Kant and the Medical Faculty: One 'Conflict of the Faculties,'" *Epoché: a Journal for the History of Philosophy* 22:2 (Spring 2018). In this piece, Zammito further draws our attention to Kant's claim that human beings walk upright as a result of our rational and social vocations (p. 432).

reality of the objects of these representations" (KpV 5:9n). And, continuing the *Reflection* cited previously where Kant writes that "Life is unity," he asserts: "Freedom is the original life and, in its coherence, the condition of the correspondence of all life" (R 6862, 19:183). Thus, the "life in the figures" of the morally good person is nothing other than freedom – as the principle of human life – in its efficacious in the natural order. More than this, too, freedom's efficaciousness is conceived not as a mechanistic or communicative causality but as one that has an inner causal union with material, in the way that the principle of life does in organic bodies. For a human being fully to determine themselves in their living is for the principle of their living as a human being – freedom – to be operative most forcefully.

Returning to the Ideal of Beauty, we can see how it is at once a possibility that lies outside of the critical philosophy, yet does, in fact, function as the absolute measure of the judgments that complete the system. As an original pattern, the Ideal of Beauty stands as the epitome or culmination of what all judgments of taste are; beautiful things are beautiful insofar as they represent or copy this Ideal. The substance of the Ideal is the unity of force and matter, of freedom and nature. In it, freedom determines and dominates the human body. The appearance of such "spirit" in matter is precisely what we find beautiful in fine art – the extent to which an artist can achieve such a feat of imagination is the extent to which a work will be beautiful, as we shall see in Chapter 5.

We may ask how the Ideal of Beauty as Kant describes it forms the height of a judgment whose structure is purposive without a purposive. As Chapter 2 argued, judgments of reflection are about the appearance of the ground; the ground appears as mere appearance. That is, the ground appears in the bare structure of what may appear to us to begin with – things that have a *logos*, or, exhibit orderliness. The Ideal of Beauty suggests that what appears in the territory, as the possible ground of the system of human experience, is an inner causal union of force and matter. The orderliness is thus taken to be the product of a causal union of force and matter – force is what orders the thing. This is what we see hints of in all judgments of taste – traces of the supersensible as it forms and shapes the sensible.

In a way, this seems obvious enough. Purposiveness is nothing other than the notion that an end is the cause of an object. Purposiveness simply is not the kind of causality that is subject to the mechanism of the natural order of the first *Critique*. There, force is external to the object. The very notion of purposiveness involves a different kind of causality, a different relation between force and matter. The height of purposiveness as a causality itself is inner purposiveness, as the Ideal suggests.[24]

This accords with how Kant defines purposiveness, as he likens it to production through a will. A will is a particular kind of force in the world, one that does not have merely mechanistic effects. In this, we see just how much the Ideal of Beauty is a genuine Ideal of the judgment of taste – it is the full determination of force with respect to the matter it forms. All purposive causality must be thought in accord with some kind of inner union of force and matter, rather than an external force, that is, in accord with a notion of *life*.

The beautiful is just that, then, which appears life-like – it reminds us of and refers us to an inner causal union of force and matter, freedom and nature. Insofar as the beautiful takes shape for us on the model or pattern of such a unity, it speaks directly to the interests of hope. What appears to us in beautiful things out in the territory is the possibility of freedom – or force, or spirit – having a causal, determining relation to the natural or material order. Beautiful things are those things whose materiality appears to us as if dominated by a spiritual or free force.

---

[24] This is why, as we see in Chapters 6 and 7, there is a decisive turn for human judgment once we encounter living beings out in the territory.

4

The Sensus Communis and the Ground of the Critical System

While Chapter 1 laid out the territorial understanding of judgments of reflection in Kant's system, Chapters 2 and 3 attempted to fill out two principal ways these judgments function out in the territory. These chapters first examined the most foundational structure of judgments of reflection as revealing a bare, essential orderedness in appearance, and, second, argued that this orderedness also refers us to something that exceeds the critical system, but is the condition of the possibility for it. Beauty was shown here to give a sense of belonging to a larger whole and to remind us of the possibility of unity between freedom and nature. Here, we will examine the transcendental ground of judgments of reflection in the sensus communis. It will ultimately be the sensus communis that legitimates the use of judgment in its reflective activity.

In the sensus communis, Kant explicitly takes up the question of a transcendental ground for judgments of reflection; the sensus communis answers, after all, to the *quid juris* of judgments of taste. This places the sensus communis at the heart of the third *Critique* as well as of the critical system. As judgments of reflection form the ground and transition between the other two domains, and thus allow for the establishment of a system in the first place, the transcendental ground of these judgments is what grounds the entire system. It is, however, an idiosyncratic kind of ground. Being out in the territory means that we effectively do not fall under any jurisdiction – there is no law by which to determine our thinking and acting. In this regard, there thus seems to be a kind of groundlessness to being out in the territory, as we saw in Kant's articulation of purposiveness without a purpose. There is a kind of strangeness or uncanniness to it; to borrow the geopolitical metaphorics, we may say that in virtue of not being within the jurisdictional walls of a domain, we are thereby in a condition of existential *displacement*. The lack of law, place, or ground, however, does not mean it is an abyss. On the contrary, what is most interesting about being out in the territory is that we find that there is still something there, even if what is there is merely the *suggestion* or *promise* of something determinate being there. As we saw in Chapters 2 and 3, Kant describes the territory as a sphere of possibility or appropriability; what appears, appears as possibly something. But what lies back behind these judgments? Without a rule or law given in these judgments, we find that we have no measure for their validity. We only have a *sense*, given in the pleasure we find in beautiful things. It is the sensus communis that grants the transcendental condition for judgments made out in the territory.

The issue the sensus communis is meant to address can be seen by way of Kant's claim that judgments of reflection are "heautonomous" (KU 5:185–6). By this, Kant means that these judgments do not have jurisdiction over the objects they judge. As Allison describes it, "To claim that a judgment is 'heautonomous' in its reflection is just to say that is both *source* and *referent* of its own normativity."[1] How such a judgment may still be legitimate and even universal is what the sensus communis will answer.

The sensus communis, then, completes Kant's transcendental turn; underlying the objective world both materially and morally is the *being in common* we have with other human beings. This comes out in *communicability*. The sensus communis, as we will see, is a basic sense of commonality, of belonging. Such commonality takes shape in a sense that we are communicable – we can be with others and communicate with them. It is, at bottom, a sense that there is a commonality, that we share the world and the way we experience it with other human beings. This shareability is the original fact that legitimates judgments of reflection, and ultimately objectivity itself. The sensus communis, as Kant describes it, thus underlies the possibility of both knowledge (cognition, the sphere of nature) and moral life (the sphere of freedom). At the end of Chapter 5, I will return to how this commonness of our faculties and shareability of the world may also be the substratum of nature, as Kant claims in his discussion of genius.

The sensus communis speaks to the interests of hope in a distinctive way in the third *Critique*. Objects of beauty and their production through genius, and organisms, all suggest to us that *nature* is amenable to the demands of freedom. The sensus communis, by contrast, does not speak to what nature *is* with respect to freedom. The sensus communis, as I will show, serves as the ultimate backstop against the radical skeptical challenge

[1] Allison, *Kant's Theory of Taste*, 41.

to the possibility of knowing. What the sensus communis, and, with it, the possibility of communication at all, proves is that the way that human beings have the world is not only shared with all human beings, but also is, in fact, objective. This means that there is an accord between how things are and the faculties of the human soul that transcends any question about the particular content of what it is we know. This accord addresses the problem of hope at its deepest level, namely whether human beings belong in the world.

Relative to its place in the text as that which grants the right we have to judgments of taste, scholarship in the literature on the notion is negligible. The sensus communis is analogous in the text to the transcendental unity of apperception in the first *Critique* – they both grant the right to claim either knowledge or beauty. And, as judgments of taste are the pure exercise of judgment itself, the sensus communis will be shown to grant the right to use the faculty of judgment more generally. Thus, the proper exercise of all judgment – in synthesizing concepts and intuitions, for example – can be seen to be at stake in this Deduction. And yet inquiries into the sensus communis do not recognize the weight it is due in virtue of carrying the legitimacy of these judgments. Allison, for example, defends the success of the Deduction, but takes its yield to be "relatively modest," arguing that it applies only to pure judgments of taste.[2] Even those examinations of the third *Critique* that treat the sensus communis more robustly do not do so as a central loadstone of the text. The predominance of epistemological concerns in Anglophone scholarship yields discussions that revolve around universal communicability, and our consciousness of this feature of the judgment.[3] While universal communicability is germane to the sensus communis, a purely epistemological focus fails fully to get at what the sensus communis is and does. Communicability is a much more expansive phenomenon than typically described. The European tradition of inquiry fares slightly better, though even here the notion is surpassed in importance by Kant's accounts of play and purposiveness without a purpose. Let us recall, too, that the most widely known appropriation of the sensus communis, by Hannah Arendt, has little in common with Kant's own vision of the concept. Her account treats it as involving an empirical element of consultation of what others think that Kant would clearly reject. Her insights do, however, set the stage for a strain of contemporary interpretations of the sensus communis that seek to

---

[2] Ibid., 160.
[3] We can point here in particular to the work of Paul Guyer, Henry Allison, and Hannah Ginsborg.

articulate its possible political implications or uses. Jean-François Lyotard takes the most care to unpack what the sensus communis actually is perhaps, and Hans-Georg Gadamer discusses it in a manner that is closest in spirit to Kant's own account.[4]

This chapter will unfold in three parts. First, I will lay out the question of the *quid juris* of the judgment of taste as Kant conceives it. The task of the Deduction is to find the ground for the universal claim of a judgment that is based on something subjective, namely pleasure. How, we must answer, can it be legitimate that a judgment grounded on mere pleasure admits of enlisting others in agreement? In this section, I will draw our attention to the way that the judgment of taste is constituted, in part, by its questionable status – when we make a judgment of taste, we both take it as universal but understand that we may be in error. Second, I will briefly trace the historical meanings of the term sensus communis in order to grasp why Kant uses the term himself. There are two principal employments of the concept: the epistemological and the social or practical. In this section, I will emphasize how both uses of the term are meant to address skepticism. In the third section, I will argue for what I take Kant's understanding of the notion to be. I contend that Kant unifies the neo-Aristotelian epistemic function of the sensus communis with the social register of the term in the humanistic tradition and in the Scottish Enlightenment. The sensus communis will be shown to have a dual directionality. It is directed, one, to the organization of an individual subject's faculties; in so doing, it, two, simultaneously discloses that the judgment in which it is involved can be cast over the whole of human subjects. In its dual directionality, the sensus communis opens up onto a deeper accord of our faculties, an accord that suggests to us the possibility of cognition in general. It also opens up onto a distinctive kind of universality among human beings. This is not the universality of reason or subjection to the moral law; it is not the universality of essential sameness. It is, rather, the universality of communicability as such. The human community is the community with whom we can communicate. This is a claim that is beyond language and understanding, and is about the *possibility* of communication at all. When we encounter another human being or human artifact, our sense is that even if we cannot

---

[4] See Hannah Arendt, *Lectures on Kant's Political Philosophy* (Chicago: University of Chicago Press, 1989); Jean-François Lyotard, "Sensus Communis," *Paragraph* 11 (1988); Hans-Georg Gadamer, *Truth and Method* (New York: Continuum Press, 1995), 19–30.

communicate, say, in the same language, the possibility of communication is there. This is only possible in virtue of a shared way of being in the world and of experiencing it. This original fact, Kant argues, underlies the possibility of a universal pleasure as well as answers all skeptical challenges to knowing, to morality, and to judgment in general.

4.1 The *Quid Juris* of the Judgment of Taste

The sensus communis answers the question: By what right do I assert a judgment of taste? That is, how is it legitimate that I assert that the pleasure I take in a representation *ought* to be experienced by others? This is, after all, what it means to make a judgment of taste, rather than simply claim that something is pleasurable. To call something beautiful is simply to assert that one expects others to agree. In this section, we will first outline what a Deduction is for Kant in order to make clear what is at stake in the sensus communis being what entitles us to such claims. We can see that Kant ultimately argues that the sensus communis is the "original fact" that allows for a subjective pleasure to be universal.

Kant opens his discussion of the Deduction in the *Critique of Pure Reason* by referencing jurists and the adjudication of claims. It is here that he introduces his now famous distinction between the *quid juris* and the *quid facti*, between "what is lawful ... and that which concerns the fact" (KrV A84/B116). A Deduction, he goes on, "is to establish the entitlement of the legal claim," given a need for "proof" of what is lawful in a circumstance. A Deduction is necessary when it must be evidenced not that something is the case (is empirically true), but that something is lawful, that is, is in accord with right(s). The purpose of a Deduction is to establish the authority of a claim – to evidence that a claim has proper standing under the law.

Dieter Henrich has offered an illuminating and decisive account about the structure and ends of Kant's Deductions. Henrich highlights the prevalence of "Deduction writing" as a juridical paradigm in Kant's time, as well as Kant's familiarity with the genre. He submits that the aim of a Deduction

> was to justify controversial legal claims between the numerous rulers of the independent territories, city republics, and other constituents of the Holy Roman Empire ... These deductions ... were distributed by governments, with the intention of convincing other governments of the rightfulness of their own positions in controversies that might eventually lead to military

force and thus to the need of finding support from other rulers ... Most of the legal controversies concerned inheritance of territories.[5]

The purpose of a Deduction is to justify a claim in the face of a dispute about its legitimacy. As we observed in the Introduction in the discussion of Kant's use of the term territory, the overlapping and sometimes contradictory jurisdictional regions of Prussia led to a lack of determinacy with respect to dominion and the execution of law. Deductions were needed to adjudicate competing interests in any specific area. In aiming to "justify an acquired right," a Deduction traces such acquisition back to its origins. Simply because one authority exercises dominion over an area at any given time does not therefore justify or legitimate the doing so. If contested, this authority must prove that its acquired position has prior legitimate and legally recognized origins. A Deduction simply is this tracing of an acquired context back to its legitimate origin.

Henrich further notes two crucial elements to Kant's notion of a Deduction that will shape how we can understand the sensus communis as what entitles us to assert a judgment of taste. First, Henrich presciently details how the contestation to our right to assert knowledge in the *Critique of Pure Reason* comes from the skeptic. Indeed, the very act of needing to justify something arises only in the face of skepticism to the very claim. In the first *Critique*, the skeptic denies the possibility of genuine knowledge; in the second *Critique*, the skeptical challenge is to the legitimacy of reason's claim on us; in the Critique of Aesthetic Judgment, the universality of the claim of beauty is in question. As we shall see, given how the argument for the universality of a judgment of taste takes shape, it will be especially relevant that it is ultimately skepticism itself that is at issue in this Deduction. This matters in two key regards: The judgment of taste always has a recognition of possible error built in, and the ultimate ground of a judgment of taste's legitimacy will turn out to be the final word against *all* skepticism.

Second, the origin that justifies a claim may also be something factual. For example, it may be that the fact of one's birth to a father of noble lineage legitimates a claim to a title. One's claim to a title is deduced by way of producing this original fact. Henrich writes, "Most of the origins from which Kant's Deductions are derived exhibit clearly this additional factual element."[6] What we will come to see, then, is how the sensus communis comes to be an original fact that refutes the position of the

---

[5] Henrich, "Kant's Notion of a Deduction," 32. [6] Ibid., 37.

skeptic against claims of universality. It is this structure of a Deduction, in part, that recommends understanding the sensus communis as a kind of ground, rather than, say, an ideal. Thus, arguments like Brent Kalar's, which seek to assert that the sensus communis is regulative, ideal, and something futural do not take adequate account of the placing of the sensus communis in the Deduction.[7] But if the sensus communis is an ideal, it cannot be a legitimating ground of a judgment's claim to assent. By contrast, as Andrea Kern puts the point, "the aesthetic 'should' is to be understood as the request for agreement with a judgment whose standard of correctness is provided by nothing other than the activity of judging itself."[8]

We can understand what kind of entitlement we need in this Deduction, first, by way of the classical triumvirate of truth, beauty, and goodness. Kant famously makes these separate and independent spheres, which leads to the distinctive problem he sets up: How can subjective pleasure be universal? Philosophers have long understood claims about beauty necessarily to involve *both* pleasure and universality. We would not claim something to be beautiful if it did not please us in some way; we also expect others to find the same pleasure in the thing that we do. The beautiful is not merely agreeable, as Kant argues in the first moment of the judgment of taste. Agreeable pleasures are those we do not expect others to share, as they are based on something particular to the subject. Exemplary of an agreeable pleasure would be a taste for spicy food; one may find great pleasure in such dishes, but does not expect that others will feel the same. This is because the agreeable "pleases the senses in sensation" (KU 5:205). We rightly recognize the absolute subjectivity and partiality of such pleasure.

The assertion of beauty – rather than mere pleasantry – is the ascription of a kind of universality. These two aspects of the judgment present a challenge to bring together. Pleasure is subjective, and of itself does not admit of universality. The predominant rationalist orientation of the European philosophical tradition has found its way through this thorny knot in two principal ways, both making beauty objective. One line of thinking develops the idea that beauty is a form or essence that presents

---

[7] Brent Kalar, "The Ethical Significance of Kant's *Sensus Communis*: From Aesthetic to Ethical Community," *Idealistic Studies* 47:1&2 (2018), 43–58.

[8] Andrea Kern, "Aesthetic Self-Consciousness and *Sensus Communis*: On the Significance of Ordinary Language in Kant's Analytic of the Beautiful," *Graduate Faculty Philosophy Journal* 39:2 (2019), 462. Kern's piece offers an interesting take on the demand for universality inherent in the claim that something is beautiful.

itself objectively in the world, the recognition of which is pleasurable. On this model, beauty may be its own formal quality. We can think here of Plato's presentation of Diotima in the *Symposium*. There, Socrates recounts the priestess's argument for beauty as its own form, in which beautiful things participate. Another line of thinking, perhaps more prevalent (though also in Plato and the neo-Platonic accounts), argues that beauty is met when a thing is perfected, that is, when we are able to experience it in its most complete and true form. The pleasure of beauty here is given through a thing's goodness, that is, in its perfecting what the thing is. Both of these accounts of the beautiful argue that the universality of the pleasure we take is based on something objective.

Kant famously denies the objective character of the beautiful, and thus that it has either truth or goodness as its ground. In both the first and second moments of the Critique of Aesthetic Judgment, Kant argues that the pleasure we take in the beautiful is not founded on a concept. This, he notes, is a pleasure in the good, which he claims is distinct from beauty. Having denied the objective character of the beautiful, Kant finds himself with a complicated problem to solve in virtue of remaining committed to the claim of taste being rightfully universal. For Kant, beauty is not some "thing in itself," its own "form." It is also not the perfection of a thing. In denying that the feeling of pleasure in the beautiful may rest on a concept in the second moment of the Critique of Aesthetic Judgment, Kant rejects the idea that there is something in the object that can legitimate the claim to universality. Since the judgment of taste is determined through pleasure alone, Kant commits himself to developing a new kind of pleasure – one that is universal without appeal to being grounded on something objective. Indeed, it is in the second moment that he first takes on the problem he has set up for himself and offers a preliminary solution. While a judgment of taste is not "**objectively universally valid**," Kant asserts that it has "**subjectively universal validity**" (KU 5:215). In this, "the predicate of beauty is not connected with the concept of the **object** considered in its entire logical sphere, and yet it extends it over the whole sphere of **those who judge**" (KU 5:215). When making a judgment of taste, we relate the judgment not to the claim that there is something distinctive in the object, but to a "universal voice"; we ascribe agreement with our judgment to everyone else (KU 5:216). The universality that validates the claim of beauty, and not simply of agreeableness, refers to the whole of human subjects.

It is this problem of pleasure and universality in the context of the denial of an objective character to the beautiful that sets up the Deduction for the judgment of taste, that is, that helps form the question of its *quid juris*. What is it, exactly, that must be proven, that must be put into evidence? What kind of original fact are we looking for in the first place? Kant sets it up with respect to two "peculiarities." The first peculiarity: "The judgment of taste determines its object with regard to satisfaction (as beauty) with a claim to the assent of **everyone**, as if it were objective." The second peculiarity: "The judgment of taste is not determinable by grounds of proof at all, just as if it were merely subjective" (KU 5:281, 284).

These two peculiarities also give shape to the kind of necessity we find in a judgment of taste. Universal judgments are also necessary judgments. While determinative judgments of cognition, as well as moral judgments, have unconditional necessity, judgments of taste yield a *conditional* necessity. The former two each follow a rule, "a determinate objective principle," to which the subject is bound in judgment (KU 5:238). In taking up the modality of a judgment of taste as necessary, Kant posits the notion of exemplarity to get at the perplexity of universality without an objective rule: "As a necessity that is thought in an aesthetic judgment, it can only be called **exemplary**, i.e., a necessity of the assent of all to a judgment that is regarded as an example of a universal rule that one cannot produce" (KU 5:237). It is taken by us to be an example; as such, it is an instance of a certain kind of thing. In a typical example, we are able to state: This is an example of this rule, universal, or concept. As such an instantiation, we are further given to expect that our judgment has necessity in it – we are bound by the way things are to judge it so. In the case of the beautiful, however, we cannot state or give any rule of which the thing is an example. This renders the judgment of taste purely exemplary – it has the form of exemplarity without the rule to which an example typically refers. It is simply the bare form of being an example. Thus, while there is some principle of the necessity of a judgment of taste, it is not objective.

Kant first addresses the issue of the universality of the pleasure we take in the beautiful in his discussion of the second moment of a judgment of taste. Namely, he identifies the free play of the imagination and understanding with the pleasure we take in the beautiful. In so doing, Kant provides an account of pleasure that is not merely subjective, but based rather on universally shared features of human knowing. This thus provides an explanation of how a judgment might both be based on something subjective as well as universal. The pleasure of the free play is in the subject. But, it is also universal, as faculties of mind are universally shared. Yet the issue of the judgment of taste is about the *satisfaction* we take in it, the feeling we have on which it is grounded. The judgment of taste, Kant writes, does not "postulate" that all will agree; rather, it merely "ascribes this agreement to everyone ... The universal voice is thus only an idea" (KU 5:216). When Kant turns to the Deduction, however, he does not simply reiterate this argument about the faculties of the human soul. Surprisingly, he introduces the notion of the sensus communis as the name of the feeling we have for a universal voice. What emerges here is that the universality of human faculties is not simply asserted in Kant; rather, this is what needs to be proved, and an analysis of the sensus communis will provide such evidence.

The problem that the *quid juris* of the judgment of taste must address is thus different from that in judgments of cognition and of morality. The latter two are judgments of unconditional necessity; when we make them, we do not doubt that the connection between the subject and the predicate is necessary. On account of this, the universality we ascribe to them is postulated – we take it as a given that others will and must agree with our judgments. In a judgment of taste, though, we do not, strictly speaking, predicate the subject – the thing about which we are speaking – with beauty; there is no measure by which we could do so. Rather, when we assert that something is beautiful, the predicate (despite our linguistic formulation that "this is beautiful") is really the subject's *feeling* of satisfaction (KU 5:289). This relocates the question of the *quid juris* for such a judgment. It is no longer about establishing necessity between the thing (or, rather, its empirical representation) and some quality it may possess; we do not need here to "justify any objective reality of a concept" (KU 5:290).

What must be justified is that the pleasure we feel is of the kind we can ascribe to others. The Deduction of the judgment of taste is concerned with "the satisfaction in the object ... with the subjective purposiveness of that form for the power of judgment that we sense as combined with the representation of the object in the mind" (KU 5:289–90). The principle of the judgment of taste is, of course, nothing other than the principle that belongs properly to the power of judgment: purposiveness. Specifically, in a judgment of taste, we judge that the representation of the object is subjectively purposive. This means simply that the form of the object is arranged purposefully to suit our faculties, as evidenced by the pleasure occasioned in us. However, there is no means by which we may judge the necessity of this particular combination; we have no further means of discerning whether this pleasure is an instance of the application of this principle.

Part of the distinctiveness of judgments of taste, that is, of judgments made out in the territory, is that we may be wrong. There is no measure of the truth or falsity of the claim; we are not, we must recall, in the domain of truth at all. In some sense, then, it is not quite correct even to describe these judgments as possibly in error. They are always simply undecidable in some way, as "there can also be no rule in accordance with which someone could be compelled to acknowledge something as beautiful" (KU 5:215). We should note that Kant does not seriously take up the possibility of error for judgments of cognition or morality. Doubt, or, a sense that conditions of surety cannot be met, arises in cognition or morality only insofar as one steps back into a reflective, philosophically skeptical mode. Even here, the doubt is not about individual cases, moreover, but the entire enterprise of knowing or of morality. Yet the possibility of being in error about the exemplarity we assert in a judgment of taste is ever present. Kant writes, "Whether someone who believes himself to be making a judgment of taste is in fact judging in according with this idea [of the universal voice] can be uncertain" (KU 5:216). The presence of this possibility is constitutive of how we have the experience of the beautiful and our claims to its universality – the judgment of taste is always open to revision. Cassirer puts it this way: "Since we have no objective knowledge of the rule to which we refer, we can never be certain that the given case actually is an instance of the indeterminate rule."[9] This is what it means to be out in the territory – we are not afforded the security of a law that would guarantee the truth of our judgment. We at once feel that our satisfaction makes a universal claim and at the same time feel that it is in question. Thus, even the *should* of the judgment of taste is peculiar: "The **should** in aesthetic judgments of taste is thus pronounced only conditionally even given all the data that are required for the judging" (KU 5:237). This stands in stark contrast with the should entailed in moral judgments, for example, whose unconditionality is unmistakable in its claim on us.

The *quid juris* of the judgment of taste is then addressed to the possibility that there could be a subjective pleasure that is universal. There is no rule by which to judge whether or not this or that *particular* judgment of taste is such an instance of some ungiven rule; there is no means by which we could secure the necessity of relation between the form of the object and our pleasure. Thus, we are referred to asking about the nature of the pleasure involved. The question thus becomes: What could legitimate a claim to the universality of the pleasure in such a judgment? The measure or rule of the judgment's legitimacy evolves into the possibility of its *universality as such*.

---

[9] H. W. Cassirer, *A Commentary of Kant's Critique of Judgment* (New York: Routledge, 2016), 211.

The Sensus Communis and the Ground of the Critical System

Kant will argue that since a measure cannot be given objectively, that is, in the object, we must seek a "rule of approval" (KU 5:237). We are keen to find that others "approve of the object in question and similarly declare it to be beautiful." That is, the rule is not about the object being judged, nor even about the connection between the empirical representation and the feeling of pleasure. The rule or measure becomes about the agreement of others, which would confirm the universality of the pleasure we feel. Since the ground of the judgment is subjective – pleasure – we can only find its universality in its instantiation in other subjects. Kant comes to formulate the question of the Deduction of beauty this way:

> How is a judgment possible which, merely from one's own feeling of pleasure in an object, independent of its concept, judges this pleasure, as attached to the representation of the same object in every other subject, a priori, i.e., without having to wait for the assent of others? (KU 5:288)

The *quid juris* must only justify the possible universality of my judgment – we need not even wait for the assent of others! The movement of the Deduction thus appears to be thus: The universality of a subjective pleasure could be found in the assent of all other subjects. Then, the question becomes precisely about this possibility at all: Is there something like agreement in general between all subjects? This is what the sensus communis, the sense of communicability we have in the pleasure of the beautiful, ultimately speaks to. The *quid juris* of the judgment of taste may be formulated thus: By what right, by what original fact, is one's claim to the universality of one's pleasure granted? But because there is no rule to ground the universality, we turn to the question of universality as such.

What we see is how the question of the *quid juris* of the judgment of taste evolves to be much more expansive than simply a question of beautiful things. We are ultimately concerned with the universality of judgments as such, or rather, the legitimacy of the use of judgment in and of itself. The judgment of taste is just the pure exercise of the faculty of judgment. This Deduction, then, is about judgment per se; subjective universality will ultimately come to be what underlies objectivity. As Nuzzo points out, "taste reveals the way in which the faculty of judgment in general works."[10] Thus, the Deduction of taste will be about the "power of judgment in general" (KU 5:286ff).

---

[10] Nuzzo, *Kant and the Unity of Reason*, 297. This is in contrast, as we saw earlier, to Allison's assertion regarding the narrow applicability of the Deduction.

4.2 What Is the Sensus Communis?

What is the sensus communis? The term sensus communis has a long philosophical history. Kant's use of the term can only be understood against this backdrop – his invocation of the Latin is a clear indication that he is appropriating a philosophical term. Thus, excavating the background of the term will help us understand not only what Kant has in mind for what the term designates, but, perhaps more than this, the problem it is meant to address. As we will see, both historical usages of the term are meant to counteract a skeptical position regarding the possibility of objectivity and universality, and thereby secure human knowledge by way of having *something in common*.

We can identify, historically, two basic uses of the term sensus communis, or, common sense. These are (1) epistemological and (2) social or practical. Within each lineage, of course, there are multiple articulations of what the term actually designates. The first, older usage of the term designates something epistemological – it is meant to allow for human knowers adequately to know the independent, existing reality in which we find ourselves. Plato and Aristotle first discerned the need for a common sense; it then came to be a focus in neo-Aristotelian thought. It finds a place, too, in Descartes. The common sense is what is taken to unify the other, disparate senses in such a way that they are able to present a coherent world for the subject. Perhaps the first articulation of the problem the common sense is meant to solve is in the *Theaetetus*. There, Socrates notes, "It would be a very strange thing, I must say, if there were a number of perceptions sitting inside us as if we were Wooden Horses, and there were not some single form, soul or whatever one ought to call it, to which all these converge."[11] The problem that Socrates articulates here is this: We have multiple and disparate senses of sight, hearing, touch, smell, and taste. These must somehow be brought together for us to understand that it is one object that looks a certain way, feels a certain way, sounds a certain way when you knock on it, or, tastes and smells a certain way. Without being led or directed to (συντεί'νω) such a unifying point, our senses would present to us a cacophony[12] of sensory data, and, thus, an utterly incoherent world.

---

[11] Plato, *Theaetetus*, in *Plato: Complete Works*, John M. Cooper, ed. (Indianapolis: Hackett Publishing, 1997), 184d.

[12] When Lyotard describes Kant's sensus communis as yielding a "euphony," I think this – cacophony – must be what he has in mind as its other. Jean-François Lyotard, "Sensus Communis."

Aristotle picks up on the problem of bringing our senses together so that they unify and present a coherent world of objects for us. Aristotle treats the issue at most length in Book III of *de Anima*. While scholars are not settled about Aristotle's views on the matter,[13] the question guiding his discourse is clear enough. He is interested in how what is given in each of the five senses may be taken to be identical with, and not incidental to, what is given in the other senses. Without such identification, he writes, "our perception ... would always be incidental, i.e. as is the perception of Cleon's son, where we perceive him not as Cleon's son but as white, and the white thing happens to be Cleon's son."[14] While Aristotle denies that there is a special sense *organ* (αισθητηριον) for producing the unity of the senses, he does suggest that "there is already in us a common sensibility [or faculty] which enables us to perceive them non-incidentally."[15] Aristotle seems to assert that there is in us already the ability to bring together, into agreement, the disparate senses. He goes on to note,

> The senses perceive each other's proper objects incidentally, not in their own identity, but acting together as one, when sensation occurs simultaneously in the case of the same object, as for instance of bile, that it is bitter and yellow; for it is not the part of any single sense to state that both objects are one.[16]

There are, of course, nuanced and detailed debates about what the sensus communis in this particular idiom actually is and does. For our purposes, however, what is of interest is the problem it seeks to address: How do the varied sources of knowledge get organized into a coherent whole? We have the world *objectively*, as a world of that is objective for us. This means that we experience the world as external to us but at the same time as organized and arranged in a way that we can grasp. The sensus communis seeks first to account for how, given the plurality and disparity of "sense data" we take in, we are able to draw the different impressions together into one thing. Second, however, is a more global concern. If we are interested, first, to give an account of how we have the world as a world of objects, we are interested, second, to know that this accords with how the world actually

---

[13] For a brief survey, please see the commentaries on De Anima in the following: R. D Hicks, *Aristotle De Anima*, Trans. by Hicks, Rodier, and Ross, Amsterdam 1965; David Ross, *Aristotle De Anima*, Oxford 1961; D. W. Hamlyn, *Aristotle's De Anima Books II and III*, Oxford 1968. See also D. W. Hamlyn, "Koinē Aisthēsis," *The Monist* 52 (1968).
[14] Aristotle, *On the Soul*, in *Aristotle: On the Soul, Parva Naturalia, On Breath* (Cambridge, MA: Loeb Classical Library, 1957), 425a32–38. 425a25–27.
[15] Aristotle, *On the Soul*, 425a28–29; Hett renders it "common faculty."
[16] Aristotle, *On the Soul*, 425a32–38.

is. The epistemological trajectory of a sensus communis, then, develops in order to account for the possibility that we have the world not only coherently, but correctly. Knowledge requires that we combine our sense data not only coherently but also proper to the objects we cognize. The neo-Aristotelian and Thomistic traditions attempt to demonstrate how the common sense is able to bring together our disparate senses such that the resultant unity corresponds with reality.

Descartes likewise belongs principally to the neo-Aristotelian epistemological tradition of the use of sensus communis. He even invokes the same wax metaphor introduced by Aristotle to describe how the qualities of the object are imprinted onto the mind. Descartes, though, seems to favor an independent and separate sense that organizes and brings into agreement the multiple senses. He writes, "when an external sense organ is stimulated by an object, the figure which it receives is conveyed at one and the same moment to another part of the body known as the 'common sense' [sensus communis]."[17] It is this correct combination of our senses that yields the knowledge of things.

The second and later use of the term is a social or practical invocation; we still employ it today as "common sense." This is the use that Kant himself disavows in his own discussion of it. Kant writes,

> The **common human understanding**, which, as merely healthy understanding, is regarded as the least that can be expected from anyone who lays claim to the name of a human being, thus has the unfortunate honor of being endowed with the name of common sense (sensus communis), and indeed in such a way that what is understood by the word common (not merely in our language, which here really contains an ambiguity, but in many others as well) comes to the same as the *vulgar*, which is encountered everywhere, to possess which is certainly not an advantage or honor. (KU 5:293)

Kant is clearly pointing to the social or practical understanding of the term. This social or practical use of the term has its roots in Roman Stoicism, and comes down through Vico, and, most likely for Kant, the use of the term in the Scottish Enlightenment. Strictly speaking, it refers to what a community holds in common – values, beliefs, customs, mores, and so on. In this, it is closer perhaps to Aristotle's conception of *ethos* as the shared life of a people, their practices, norms, and ways of living. To be someone with good common sense, in this tradition, is to have a kind of practical

---

[17] René Descartes, Rules for the Direction of the Mind, in *The Philosophical Writings of Descartes*, Volume I (London: Cambridge University Press, 1985), 41.

know-how with respect to how things go, and what then will be efficacious in action.

The emphasis on common sense as a measure for know-how arises, at least in part, as a kind of alternative to the early modern commitment to scientific rationality. The uses of common sense that Kant would have been most familiar with can best be understood as developed in a specific historical context. In the wake of Luther's reformation, the dissolution of the moral authority of the Catholic Church led to a much broader crisis in authority. Once the moral authority of the Church had been called into question, so too with it that which rested upon such authority: Its epistemic, scientific, and political authority came crashing down as a consequence. The long Enlightenment that began with Luther's successful declarations against Church practices can, in some sense, be seen as a struggle to reestablish a new authority in the wake of the central pillar of culture and politics crumbling. A principal focus of this endeavor, too, was the challenge of holding together the pursuits of science with a new moral ground.

One way thinkers responded to this crisis in authority was to seek to establish new ultimate grounds that are epistemic and scientific. Perhaps the most definitive articulation of this possibility for a new ground was in Francis Bacon – his *Novum Organon* and *New Instauration* argue for a rejection of history and tradition as bases for our beliefs. His clearly stated goal is to establish a method by which we can arrive at epistemic certainty. He recommends that "the entire work of the understanding be commenced afresh," and repeats, in various formulations, the danger of relying on received or inherited notions. Tradition, and with it, inherited ways of thinking, comes to us in language and speech. He even goes so far in his decrying the "Idols of the Marketplace" to assert,

> There are also illusions which seem to arise by agreement and from men's association with each other, which we call idols of the marketplace; we take the name of human exchange and community. Men associate through talk; and words are chosen to suit the understanding of the common people. And thus a poor and unskillful code of words incredibly obstructs the understanding. The definitions and explanations with which learned men have been accustomed to protect and in some way liberate themselves, do not restore the situation at all. Plainly words do violence to the understanding, and confuse everything; and betray men into countless empty disputes and fictions.[18]

---

[18] Francis Bacon, *The New Organon* (London: Cambridge University Press, 2000), XLIII.

Descartes, as an heir to Bacon, carries on this project in the *Meditations*. Over the course of six days – the same length of time it initially took God to build the world the first time around – he seeks to establish an entirely new foundation for human knowing. Indeed, the structure of the argument proves first the indubitability of human consciousness before proving the existence of God. In seeking to secure knowledge, Descartes recommends "extensive doubt," which will "[free] us from all our preconceived notions."[19] In this lineage of response to the challenge of recovering a new authoritative ground, there is a clear commitment to epistemology as first philosophy. It is further worth noting that Descartes' methodology here is developed specifically to address the skeptic: Methodological doubt may be seen to involve the skeptical challenge at every step of the argument. This methodology exemplifies the intellectual climate of post-Reformation Europe in many ways; what is taken to be the enemy is the doubt and skepticism that have crept in in the absence of the absoluteness of church authority.

By contrast, the humanistic tradition as exemplified by Schaftesbury and Vico puts forward a social or communal answer to the question of authority. In his *Sensus Communis: An Essay on the Freedom of Wit and Humour*, Schaftesbury inveighs against scholasticism as useless; the lack of applicability in the world proves the worthlessness of the epistemological and scientific groundings, devoid of a basis in the human world. "According to the notion I have of reason," he writes, "neither the written treatises of the learned, nor the set discourses of the eloquent, are able of themselves to teach the use of it."[20] The Ancients, by contrast, he praises: "Their treatises were generally in a free and familiar style ... The scene was usually laid at the table or in the publick walks or meeting-places."[21] It comes out in the course of the essay that Schaftesbury disdains the skepticism of those who are critical of what is held in common. The step back of a theoretical skepticism puts one at a remove from other human beings, and, therefore, at odds with them in our actions. Schaftesbury's positive anti-skeptic account thus puts the sensus communis as the measure of right living. It gives us the ideal or rule for what counts as good conduct – whether we are in accord with those with whom we live.

---

[19] Rene Descartes, Meditations on First Philosophy, in *The Philosophical Writings of Descartes* Vol. II (London: Cambridge University Press, 1984), 9.
[20] Schaftesbury (Anthony Ashley Cooper), *Sensus Communis: An Essay on the Freedom of Wit and Humour* (London: Egbert Sanger, 1709), 15.
[21] Ibid., 21.

Vico shares Schaftesbury's humanistic sensibilities. His vision of the sensus communis likewise emphasizes participation in the community; it is principally for him about the primacy of the practical (moral and political) sphere. Gadamer notes this when he describes Vico as providing a "defense of humanistic rhetoric against modern science."[22] However, in drawing on his commitment to the rhetorical tradition, he nevertheless invokes an epistemological aspect. "It is," as John Schaefer puts it, "what connects the trained orator's mind to the public sphere."[23] Common sense, here, connects the truth with rhetorical persuasion, albeit in the service of being public. We must recall, too, that some Renaissance humanism and some classical theories of rhetoric emphasized the public and shared character of the truth. It is for this reason that Gadamer associates rhetoric and the sensus communis with his own more expansive sense of what truth is.[24] Schaftesbury and Vico's humanism privileges the shared realm of common human life over the remote and removed sphere of science and theory.

Lastly, we can look to the Scottish Enlightenment as likely on Kant's radar in his thinking about the term. In this tradition, we see perhaps most clearly the anti-skeptical motivations at the heart of thinking about common sense. This motivation clearly dovetails with post-Reformation concerns for the lack of authority in moral and epistemological matters. It was no doubt the collapse of the central authority of the Church that opened up the possibility for thinkers like Hobbes and Hume to forward such radically skeptical views about moral goodness and knowledge alike. Indeed, Manfred Kuehn notes that much of common-sense Scottish philosophy is a response to skepticism.[25] Reid, while clearly concerned with epistemological skepticism, appeals at the same time to the fact that the "*regulae philosophandi* are maxims of common sense, and are practiced

---

[22] Gadamer, *Truth and Method*, 23.
[23] John D. Schaefer, *Sensus Communis: Vico, Rhetoric, and the Limits of Relativism* (Durham: Duke University Press, 1990), 78.
[24] For an extended account of Gadamer on rhetoric and truth (and also its link to the sensus communis), as well as a very fine historical account of the relation, please see John Arthos, "The Paradigmatic Interpenetration of Hermeneutics and Rhetoric," in *The Gadamerian Mind* (London: Routledge, 2021), 400–417.
[25] See Manfred Kuehn, *Scottish Common Sense in Germany, 1768–1800: A Contribution to the History of Critical Philosophy* (Kingston: McGill-Queen's University Press, 1987), 13. Kuehn's study details the influence of Scottish common-sense philosophy in the period in which Kant was writing. As he puts it, "Scottish common sense figured largely in Kant's intellectual environment both in Königsberg and in the German republic of letters as a whole, and the Scottish doctrine had – at least at times – the strongest attraction for him." Kuehn, *Scottish Common Sense*, 5.

every day in common life."²⁶ He thus uses the sensus communis as a kind of evidence of the effectuality of knowledge. The method of "observation and experiment" is in keeping with how people live, thus falling into line with the notion that skepticism is produced by a certain kind of detachment we might find in philosophical thinking. Common sense – the sense that the common person has for how things are – proves itself in virtue of being widely held and also in its broad efficacy. Even more than this, too, the measure he provides for common sense is whether or not one is led into "absurdity." We can see here remnants of Schaftesbury's commitment to "raillery," irony, and humor, as social measures for judging our own thinking. Both of the thinkers invoke a notion that if a certain sensibility is held in common by many or the whole of humanity, the commonness itself proves its worth.

What is important about this view of the sensus communis is that there is a kind of public test of what one thinks. While the purpose is not cognitive "objectivity" but rather efficacy of action, it is the fittingness with those in our community that provides the measure of rightness. Whether or not our own thinking is right thinking can be answered in it being held in common with others.

Both lineages of the sensus communis are meant to address the same basic issue: What is the measure of a proper judgment? In the epistemological register, this question is oriented by bringing our senses – or faculties – into alignment with each other in order for us to be able to perceive the world objectively. Here, the sensus communis is a faculty of mind that is directed outward toward the world and adequately knowing the objects in it. In the social or practical register, the sensus communis is a faculty that allows us to judge in accord with others in our community. It is a sense for what and how the community thinks; other people provide the measure of one's own judgments. There is a way in which, too, the common sense about how things are lends credibility to claims of objectivity, thereby giving something like "proof" of the epistemic adequacy of our judgments, and with this, evidence of universality. The publicity and commonness of one's judgments is what, for this latter tradition, defends against skeptical claims of groundlessness in both knowing as well as in human affairs. In both trajectories of the sensus communis, moreover, the work that the common sense does is to pick out features of identity across

---

²⁶ Thomas Reid, *An Inquiry into the Human Mind and the Principles of Common Sense* (Edinburgh: Edinburgh University Press, 1764), 3.

disparate things – senses or individual humans – and therefore secure unity and universality to our experience of things.

4.3 Kant on the Sensus Communis

Kant's understanding of the sensus communis invokes both historical uses of the term. As he describes its role, he finds an inner unity of these two seemingly disparate senses. In this, Kant argues that the sensus communis in its epistemic function refers us to the sensus communis in its social or practical register. The objectivity of our judgments will correspond to its shared – or, sharable – quality of human judgment in general. As we have seen earlier, the sensus communis in each tradition is meant to answer a skeptical concern regarding objectivity; first, in the neo-Aristotelian use of the term, by pointing to a faculty that organizes our senses objectively, and second, in appealing to communal judgments as evidence of objectivity. Kant, too, develops his notion of the sensus communis with these philosophical problems in mind, principally around the criterion of universal communicability. He writes, "Cognitions and judgments must, together with the conviction that accompanies them, be able to be universally communicated, for otherwise they would have no correspondence with the object: they would be a merely subjective play of the powers of representation, just as skepticism insists" (KU 5:238). This is a remarkable claim: They must "be able to be universally communicated, **for otherwise they would have no correspondence with the object**." *Kant clearly asserts that universal communicability is inextricably bound to objectivity; he thus builds the human community into the objectivity of our judgments.* With little fanfare, Kant has already made this claim in the first *Critique*. There, in his analysis of opinion, knowing, and believing, he argues that for judgments that do not fall under the jurisdiction of knowledge, we can still hold them to be true. They have a "touchstone" of truth in communicability: The "possibility of communicating" a judgment is that "through which the truth of a judgment is proved" (KrV A820–1/B848/9). Again, truth of a judgment is *proved* if it can possibly be communicated.

Universal communicability thereby folds together the two trajectories of the sensus communis already laid out. We must be able to communicate a judgment, first, which requires the constitutive parts of our cognition or feeling become organized in some way. If the judgment is not to refer merely to our own inner state, we must be capable of bringing various parts together such they present things outside of us. Second, it must be possible for us to communicate this judgment with others, that is, the judgment must be able to be shared.

As we saw earlier in the discussion of the *quid juris*, the judgment of taste is ultimately a claim about the satisfaction we take in a representation. Kant answers the question of the *quid juris* in part by developing the idea that the pleasure we have in a judgment of taste is specifically a feeling of our state of mind. The state of mind in a judgment of taste is nothing other than the free play of the imagination and understanding. Moreover, in virtue of being constituted not by anything private or merely subjective, but rather, by transcendental faculties of cognition, we are warranted in not taking this pleasure to be partial or merely subjective. It still remains, however, how we come to this. Kant thus asks: "[I]n what way do we become conscious of a mutual subjective correspondence of the powers of cognition with each other in the judgment of taste – aesthetically, though mere inner sense and sensation, or intellectually, through the consciousness of our intentional activity through which we set them in play?" (KU 5:218). He goes on to answer that the "subjective unity of the relation" of the imagination and the understanding "can make itself known only through sensation" (KU 5:219). We cannot obtain objective intellection of our own mind. Rather, we have a felt effect of the free play – the harmonious rapport – of the two faculties, as they are "enlivened" in our reflecting on a representation. When we say that something is beautiful, we are announcing to others the character of our own state of mind.

The sensus communis, in the first case, is the name Kant gives to our capacity to be affected by our state of mind sensibly. In §20 Kant identifies our capacity to feel such a pleasure in our state of mind with the common sense: "Thus only under the presupposition that there is a common sense (by which, however, we do not mean any external sense but rather the effect of the free play of our cognitive powers) ... can the judgment of taste be made" (KU 5:238). He further calls the common sense a "subjective principle" by which we are able to determine our pleasure "with universal validity." He makes this identification elsewhere, too: "[I]f indeed one would use the word 'sense' of an effect of mere reflection on the mind: for there one means by 'sense' the feeling of pleasure" (KU 5:295). And again, "the inner feeling of a purposive state of mind" (KU 5:296). In an important regard, the sensus communis refers us to our own mental state. It is a sense for our own state of mind – we feel ourselves, in our pleasure, to be having a certain kind of cognitive activity. Insofar as it is not itself a productive faculty, but a way to sense the relation of our other faculties, Kant draws upon the older, epistemic use of the term. For Kant, the sensus communis grants us consciousness with respect to our mental state, and with this, what we sense is that the pleasure we feel is of a relation of our faculties.

The sensus communis, in this epistemic register, thus discloses to us to the deeper and more general fact of the coordination of our faculties for judging. The sensus communis is a sense we have for the fundamental possibility of the unity of our faculties. Only in working in unison – the agreement of the imagination and understanding in particular – can we lay claim to the objectivity of our cognitions in general. A mere agreement of the imagination and understanding is already "requisite for a cognition in general" (KU 5:218). The sensus communis, in this regard, addresses the skeptical concern about the relation of our faculties in judging objectively. The sensus communis is the sense we have that our faculties work in common with one another; they are not merely operating according to a subjective play, but rather in such a way as to represent the world objectively. Melissa Zinkin's work on the sensus communis argues for the kind of specificity involved in the way the sensus communis senses the relation of our faculties. Zinkin writes that the "*sensus communis* is what makes it possible for us to be affected by, or to feel the actual force of cognitive powers." She goes on to argue that it allows us to sense the "various proportions of the cognitive powers," and thereby have a more refined consciousness of our mental state.[27]

Kant further identifies the epistemic sense we have for the coordination of our faculties with its communal – social and practical – use. The epistemic character of the sensus communis gives security that my individual judgments hold objectively; it confirms that my faculties coordinate with each other, thus grounding my having the world in an objective way. The social character of the sensus communis is about the world appearing the way it does not only to me but also to others; it is a sense that others have the world the way I do, thus proving that the world really *is* that way. Universal communicability is not, then, only about the articulateness (literally, the "joined together") character of our own experience, but the idea that others articulate themselves similarly.

Kant often makes the move seamlessly from the epistemic register to the communal in his discussions of the sensus communis. His arguments typically take shape as a movement from the observation that the pleasure

---

[27] Melissa Zinkin, "Kant's Supersensible Substratum of Humanity," in *Kant und die Philosophie in weltbürgerlicher Absicht, Akten des XI. Internationalen Kant-Kongresses*, Band 4 (Berlin: De Gruyter, 2013), 341.

in the judgment of taste is a pleasure of our transcendental faculties to the claim that it is universal. Such a claim rests, clearly, on the supposition that all human beings have the same faculties of cognition. The Deduction of judgments of taste is, in fact, "so easy" because of this. He writes, "This pleasure must necessarily rest on the same conditions in everyone, since they are the subjective conditions of the possibility of a cognition in general" (KU 5:292). And again, the Deduction "asserts that we are justified in presupposing universally in every human being the same subjective conditions of the power of judgment that we find in ourselves" (KU 5:290). *But what reason do we have for postulating such a thing?* The purpose of the transcendental Deduction in the third *Critique* appears to be to answer this very question. Unless Kant's claim is a dogmatic assertion, there must be some thing that justifies our presupposing universality of faculties amongst all human beings. It is precisely the sensus communis in its social register that supports the claim that our own subjective conditions for experience are the same as for others. The sensus communis is the sense we have that our judgment is shared, that we belong to a community of those who have the world the way we do. And, it will be the *possibility* of communicating with others that provides the original fact proving that we share subjective conditions of judgment.

This should not be confused with questions of what we now call "intersubjective validity." In *Kant and the Claims of Taste*, Guyer tries to tease out the relation of intersubjectivity and objectivity, including noting that in the first *Critique* Deduction, knowledge is secured without intersubjectivity.[28] Guyer does not claim that Kant argued that intersubjectivity is necessary for validity; however, in his analysis of the text, his emphasis on questions of the place of intersubjectivity misses that it is the *possibility* of intersubjectivity itself that Kant is interested in. Kant's insistence is on the possibility of communication, not actual communicative acts. It is in the possibility of communication that the universality of faculties is "proved," the universality that underlies any intersubjectivity. Validity is only the next step – the fact of communicability proves the universality of our faculties.

Judgments of taste are distinctive in that the measure of universal communicability can only be given in a *sense* we have about it. In determinate judgments of cognition, we find – after the fact, if we even seek it – that our judgments are shared. The sensus communis in a judgment of taste thus emerges both to refer us to a larger community

---

[28] Guyer, *Kant and the Claims of Taste*, 248ff.

of judgers who have the world as we do, and at the same time to submit this shareable character of the judgment as a kind of proof of its objectivity. What we feel in a judgment of taste and its feeling of universality – that others should agree – is a feeling that we can communicate this feeling with others. In judgments of taste, communicability turns out to be constitutive of its universality, and not the other way around. Thus, because of the lack of an objective ground in a judgment of taste, along with the uncertainty built into such judgments, the shared character of our experience and the world becomes foregrounded. Without objective grounding, we seek evidence of our right judgment through it being shared. Absent such a possible "proof," we are led to its universal communicability. This is also inherent in determinate cognition, though it is backgrounded in this context. Kant reminds us that universal communicability is "assumed in every logic and every principle of cognition that is not skeptical" (KU 5:239). In one regard, agreement seems to be a kind of backstop against skepticism. In another, deeper regard, it is not the actual achievement of agreement that buttresses our judgments, but rather the possibility of communicability itself. When we communicate with others and find agreement, it grants a kind of further security to the objectivity of our own judgments. In judgments of taste, this confirmation of the legitimacy of our judgment remains always in deferral. However, communicability – the possibility that we can communicate – confirms that we have our faculties in common.

The sensus communis thus displaces us into a more foundational aspect our existence, namely that we have something in common with others. We refer ourselves not only to the transcendental ground of our own judgments; we also take ourselves to be judging in a more broadly *human* way.

> By "*sensus communis*," however, must be understood the idea of a **communal** sense, i.e., a faculty for judging that in its reflection takes account (*a priori*) of everyone else's way of representing in thought in order as it were to hold its judgment up to human reason as a whole and thereby avoid the illusion which, from subjective private conditions that could easily be held to be objective, would have a detrimental influence on the judgment. (KU 5:294)

The communal sense we have is that we belong to a community of judgers. This community is not a specific, particular, historical, or localized community; rather, it is the whole of humanity. Thus, the measure we take of our feeling is whether or not it is shareable with the whole human community. However, because proof of its shared character – its actual universal communicability – cannot be given in experience, it remains a mere idea, and too, is felt as a *should* (rather than, say, a *will*, as in a determinate cognition).

Thus, universal communicability, without any specific thing being communicated, becomes the ultimate measure and ground of a judgment of taste and the employment of its transcendental principle of purposiveness. What must be universally communicated is a feeling, "without the mediation of a concept" (KU 5:295). Universal communicability, is, first universal; in this, in includes all human beings. It therefore transcends any particular language in which we may speak. It is, second, *possibly* communicable. Without a concept, it is unclear what it is we will be getting across to another. Yet we have the sense that others should share our feeling. Kant thus seems to be relying on a notion of *communicability* as such. What human beings have in common, at bottom, is that we can potentially communicate with one another. The sense that we can possibly communicate with any human being we meet reveals to us that we have something deeply in common with them. As Ameriks argues, "Kant probably holds the traditional theory that communication involves the having of matching subjective states."[29] And, then, we can say that the ability to communicate involves the having of matching conditions for the possibility of communicating. This is the original fact to which the Deduction ultimately traces back. We recognize the ability to communicate with the whole of humanity.[30]

Judgments of taste, as we saw initially, are constituted in part by their being in question. In this sphere of human life, then, we are opened up to possible groundlessness and disunity, that is, that all things are in question. At the same time, however, our lack of determinate certainty also has a feeling of necessity. This feeling of necessity is ultimately a feeling we have that we belong more originally to a community of judgers. We have a sense that we can possibly communicate with other human beings – whether such communication becomes determinate is, in a way, irrelevant for this basic feature of our existence. The sense that we can possibly communicate with one another – a possibility that transcends language and history – means, for Kant, that we share our transcendental faculties of cognition.

---

[29] Karl Ameriks, "How to Save Kant's Deduction of Taste," *Journal of Value Inquiry* 16 (1982), 298.
[30] Stuart Hampshire makes the further case for Kant's account of the cultivation of our "social spirit." Hampshire's piece recognizes the unity of humanity found in Kant that is prior to the moral one we must establish. Hampshire, "The Social Spirit of Mankind," in *Kant's Transcendental Deductions: The Three Critiques and the Opus postumum*, Eckart Forster, ed. (Stanford, CA: Stanford University Press, 1989).

This, then, means that we belong to community of beings that have the world in a shared way.

The sensus communis stands, then, as the ultimate ground of Kant's critical system. Out in the territory, where the questionable universality of our judgments is present to us, we are exposed to the barest form of communality – the being in common with other human beings in virtue of our shared way of having the world. That we share a way of having the world becomes the measure that refutes the skeptic. It gives proof to the transcendental character of our faculties, and thus the entire system of transcendental philosophy and the possibility of synthetic a priori judgments. It further gives proof of a being in common with other human beings that underwrites the universality governing moral life. The sensus communis thus meets the interests of hope by securing the deepest accord not only amongst all human beings but also between human beings and the way the world is – it grants the use of judgment, which is nothing other than the copula, the "is": "That is the aim of the copula **is** in [judgments]: to distinguish the objective unity of given representations from the subjective" (KrV B142). Objectivity in its broadest and deepest sense is thus granted by the sensus communis, yielding the sense that human beings do belong in the world.

The sensus communis is a sense for communicability as such. It is the sense we have when we encounter another human being – a sense, before anything else, that we can possibly communicate with them. It is the sense we have when we find ancient cave paintings, when we discover ancient pieces of stones with runes carved in them; the sense of possible communication does not require a face-to-face encounter with another being sharing the same physical shape as ours. The sense for something being communicable underwrites any actual act of speech and, as such, is prior to any truth or moral claim that may be made in such speaking. We may say that the feeling of a judgment of taste and of the sensus communis is a feeling of the promise of intelligibility, the feeling that something could become intelligible to us. It is the very feeling of this possibility.

The being in common we share with other human beings is thus the ground of Kant's transcendental system insofar as it embodies possibility itself – possibility that becomes actual in the other two spheres of human life. The sensus communis makes possible objective judgments of cognition, and also makes possible a more determinate and concrete human community as demanded by the moral law. The community of human judgers, which is given to us in the sensus communis, is thus what completes the transcendental (and, indeed, Copernican) turn.

The sensus communis, the feeling we have that we can communicate with other human beings, proves a shared, universal set of faculties. We recognize in other beings that we have a common way of experiencing the world, and a common world that we share. This "fact" entitles us to claim that the pleasure we feel in a judgment of taste, which is a pleasure of our faculties, should be shared by all. Beauty thus supports hope with a sense of belonging to a broader human community, across the globe and across history. It further confirms that we have the world objectively, sustaining our hope that we are fit for the world in which we find ourselves.

5
Genius, Aesthetic Ideas, and a Spiritualized Natural Order

In Chapter 3, we focused our attention on Kant's discussion on the Ideal of Beauty as one site of thinking the unity of freedom and nature – an ultimately unthinkable unity whose possibility is required for the completion of the system of philosophy. There, we saw how Kant develops this unity from the perspective of the needs of reason. In the Ideal, we find reason, or force, able fully to determine the natural or material order. We now turn our attention to Kant's discussion of genius and aesthetic ideas, which further describes such a unity from the perspective of nature. Here, however, we do not find the possibility of reason's absolute dominion over the natural order. Rather, Kant's description of genius and of the aesthetic ideas as what make beautiful art possible portrays a distinctive kind of belongingness of human beings to nature, through spirit. In Kant's practical philosophy, our participation in the natural order takes shape in the influence of nature on our wills in the form of inclinations, and in the obdurate exteriority of the effects of our will in the world. Nature, there, is the mechanistic natural order that stands in opposition to our rational wills; it is also the mechanical stream into which our free actions seem to disappear. In genius and aesthetic ideas by contrast, we belong to a nature that is excessive: It is the source of *spirit* and, ultimately, life or liveliness. Human beings thus belong to a spiritualized natural order that grants us the gift of genius and great art, and enlivens our minds to pleasurable contemplation that is more expansive than the cognitive possibilities of the first *Critique*.[1] Here, we find Kant arguing for a much more encompassing conception of a natural order that contains within it, harmoniously, human beings and nature.

---

[1] I use "participation" to describe our practical relation to the natural order, and "belonging" for our aesthetic relation. We merely participate in the practical idiom as we find ourselves at a distance from nature in this sphere. Belonging, I think, better captures the fittingness we find for ourselves in the aesthetic order.

Kant's account of genius speaks to the interests of hope insofar as it "deduces" the possibility of artistic production back through a nature to which we belong and which is concerned, it seems, to communicate with us. Nature in this section is communicative, expressive, excessive, and life- and spirit-giving. It answers the question of hope with the portrayal of nature as superabundant, generous, and gift-bestowing. This account of genius presents nature as fundamentally oriented by and related to human beings *intimately* and *spiritually*. It is not, by contrast, the nature of the first *Critique*, standing apart from us, mechanistic and objectified.

Many of the early German Romantics picked up on Kant's account and developed theories of art, philosophy, and human subjectivity out of the description of the imagination given in it. Jane Kneller argues that the "visionary aesthetics" of this period has roots in the imaginative freedom of Kant's genius. Taking a cue from these successors of Kant, she then argues that our rational hope can be maintained in virtue of these visions – we can imagine a world as it ought to be.[2] Kneller's work stands out for taking the issues presented here in Kant as central to his overall project. Lara Ostaric's work is similarly oriented by the larger questions of Kant's philosophy. Her account of genius in Kant emphasizes "the unity of free human activity with nature ... whereby 'nature' signifies the Idea of nature's supersensible substrate."[3] But, of course, whether or not one takes genius and aesthetic ideas to be of import depends upon what one decides is the central purpose of the text. For example, the dominant epistemological concerns of Anglophone literature have led mostly to neglect of these sections. In part, the formalist interpretation of Kant favored in this tradition privileges nature over art. Zuckert describes the phenomenon well in her own apologia: "My aspirations to provide an overarching interpretation of the central, epistemological import of the *CJ* require, moreover, that I neglect several discussions ... notably those concerning fine art and genius."[4] Such a point of departure leads to much consternation about the topic. As Charles Debord puts it in his explication of aesthetic ideas, "Characterizations of Kant's doctrine of aesthetic ideas range from 'peculiar' (Sassen 2003:174) to 'complex, if not abstruse' (Crawford

---

[2] Jane Kneller, *Kant and the Power of Imagination* (Cambridge: Cambridge University Press, 2007), cf. chapters 2–4.
[3] Lara Ostaric, "Kant on the Normativity of Creative Production," *Kantian Review* 17:1 (2012): 76.
[4] Zuckert, *Kant on Beauty and Biology*, 18.

2003:158), or indeed even 'unenlightening' (Crawford 2003:164)."[5] My task here will be to show how genius, art, and aesthetic ideas are crucial to Kant's project of establishing a system of philosophy that relies on a new, expansive possibility of what nature is and how we might belong to it.

This chapter will unfold in four sections. First, I will situate Kant's discussion of art, genius, and aesthetic ideas in the larger movement of the text. Here, I will highlight how the production of beautiful art presents a problem that needs its own solution in Kant's explanation of the beautiful. Second, I will lay out how genius as the gift of nature is a condition for the possibility of the creation of beautiful art. Genius accounts for how the human being is able to bring into being something that exceeds its own facultative capacities. Third, I will develop Kant's notions of spirit and aesthetic ideas, which give further contour to the excessiveness of nature and its contributions to the production of beautiful art. In the final section, I emphasize the communicative elements of Kant's explanation of how beautiful art comes into being. Here, I argue not only that art is fundamentally a communicative endeavor on Kant's account but also that nature is taken to be communicating with us. I link this discussion back to the sensus communis and suggest that this also attunes us to our belonging to this more expansive nature Kant has outlined in the following sections.

5.1 The Turn to Art in the *Critique* of Judgment

First, we must begin with an account of where the turn to art sits in the broader movement of the text. Its placement in the Deduction of judgments of taste seems, on the face of it, puzzling. But, as we will see, Kant's analysis of art is meant to give the conditions for its possibility. And, too, Kant seems to have in mind that there is a fundamental communicative quality to genius and great art.

In the Critique of Aesthetic Judgment, Kant begins with the Analytic of the Beautiful, constituted by his analysis of its "Four Moments." This is followed by the Analytic of the Sublime and then the Deduction. The principal question the Deduction must answer, as we saw in Chapter 4, is how we might be justified in taking subjective pleasure to be universal. After his discussions of the sensus communis as the answer to the *quid juris*

---

[5] "*Geist* and Communication in Kant's Theory of Aesthetic Ideas," *Kantian Review* 17:2 (2012): 177–178. Sassen and Crawford references are to their respective essays in Paul Guyer (ed.), *Kant's Critique of the Power of Judgment: Critical Essays* (Lanham, MD: Rowman & Littlefield, 2003).

of the judgment of taste, Kant turns to the kinds of interests we have that follow from the judgment. While he has already ruled out the possibility of any interest at the ground of the judgment (the first moment), he recognizes he must now account for the interests we find attendant on the judgment; these interests have, historically, confused authors who take them to be constitutive of the judgment of taste itself. The empirical and intellectual interests we have in the beautiful, Kant argues, "attach to [it] indirectly" (KU 5:297) and after the fact of the judgment. These interests follow from the judgment, dovetailing with other aspects of human nature, as Kant explains.

The turn to "On Art in General" in the context of the Deduction and, following the discussion, the two attendant interests, however, is not explicitly developed. Indeed, in a footnote in the Cambridge translation of the text, Guyer and Matthews note that the section "follows the preceding ones without any indication of a major break in the text," and they even go on to question whether these sections should even be counted as a part of the Deduction.[6] Allison and Zammito both also note that this part of the text does not seem to fit with the overarching movement of the argument; Allison describes it as "episodic."[7]

However, in his analysis of the intellectual interest in the beautiful, Kant has claimed that the beauty in nature has "preeminence ... over the beauty in art in awakening an immediate interest" in the soul of morally good person (KU 5:299). The morally good person takes an intellectual interest in nature because nature seems to be communicating with us, expressing itself to us. This is of interest to us for reasons that are already clear – the morally good person is interested in or hopeful that nature is purposive for us. In natural beauty, this interest is awakened immediately. Artistic beauty, by contrast, may only awaken a mediated interest in it from the morally good person. This is because artistic beauty is an *indirect* expression of nature's communication with us. Kant's account of art and genius is meant to describe just how this is so. What emerges, however, is that here Kant describes a nature and a relation to nature that far exceeds any other he has offered.

Investigating the being of art presents an entirely new regime of inquiry. First, in turning to art, Kant turns to the *objects* of our experience out in the territory. Rather than simply focusing his attention on the condition

---

[6] See footnote 22, at 5:303.
[7] Allison, *Kant's Theory of Taste*, p. 271; Zammito, *The Genesis of Kant's Critique of Judgment*, 129–130.

Genius, Aesthetic Ideas, and a Spiritualized Natural Order 135

for the possibility of our judgments of taste, he must address the *production* of the objects with which we find ourselves in accord and which occasion our feeling of contemplative pleasure. It is not only that we *judge* the coming into being of these objects a certain way. Here, Kant actually takes up the coming into being of the objects themselves.

In making sense of how beautiful things come to be, Kant develops an expansive understanding of nature. It may appear at this moment in the text that Kant exceeds the bounds of the critical method, reaching out beyond transcendental a priori structures of the human mind that provide the conditions for the possibility of our experience. But, this is because his transcendental account of how it is possible for human beings to create beautiful art necessarily involves something outside of us, namely nature. The strangeness of the need to give such an account is this: Human beings stand as one moment in a cycle of production and reception that somehow exceeds both our productive capacities and capacities to judge. What emerges in this argument, however, is that a transcendental condition for the possibility of us bringing beautiful art into the world is that we are related to nature as belonging to it in a new and distinctive way. The faculty of genius situates human beings in a larger natural, indeed spiritual, order.

Some recent scholarship has argued that this section of the text is meant to address how beautiful art can have the effect on us that it does. Both Samuel Stoner and Robert J. M. Neal focus their attention on the spectator or apprehension of beauty in art in their approach to Kant on genius; both deny the centrality of interpreting Kant's discussion of genius as about *production*. Stoner argues that we should understand Kant's introduction of aesthetic ideas as an account of how art can be beautiful from the perspective of the *spectator*.[8] Neal emphasizes that Kant's account of beauty here is fundamentally about the ideality of beauty and our experience of it.[9] In one regard, I think that they are right to draw our attention to how art can be beautiful, and how our experience of that beauty may be somewhat different from beautiful nature. However, I think that the focus on the spectator should serve to highlight the actual problem Kant is trying to solve: How can *human beings* produce an object that has the effect on the spectator that it does?

---

[8] Samuel Stoner, "On the Primacy of the Spectator in Kant's Account of Genius," *Review of Metaphysics* 70 (September 2016): 87–117.
[9] Robert J. M. Neal, "Kant's Ideality of Genius," *Kant-Studien* 103 (2012): 351–360.

Kant's turn to art and its production through the genius is a turn to the objects of our judgments of taste, rather than simply our experience of them. However, as we are responsible for the coming into being of these very objects, Kant must also give an account of the condition for the possibility of their existence through us, given that our experience of them is so different from other things. The basic phenomenon is simple: Art, and beautiful art even more so, stands out as being quite distinctive with respect to other things we encounter in the world. Our experience of them does not get brought into our otherwise everyday stream of experience. The other objects of our creative activity – both technical and moral – are brought into being and then are taken up into this stream. That we produce an artistic object must be a wonder; Kant – remember – argues that even the objective effects of free moral action become part of the empirical stream of experience. This fact leaves us in the first *Critique* with an antimony about the status of our freedom. Not only it is remarkable, then, that we are able to produce objects that displace us from our conditioned stream of experience, but it also highlights the necessity of giving some account of how this is possible. While it may not be part of the Deduction that precedes it, it may nevertheless be helpful to think about art as requiring its own kind of account. How can we produce objects that displace us from our own everyday experience? The Ideal of Beauty gave the measure and pattern of the beautiful as a thoroughly spiritualized matter, in the form of a human body completely under the dominion of the force of reason. Genius and aesthetic ideas are Kant's account of how a mere mortal is capable of producing such an object – a matter that is thoroughly spiritualized – outside of ourselves.

5.2 Art, Nature, and Genius

Kant begins his discussion of art, first, by delineating it with reference to the kind of things produced in nature. "Art," he writes, "is distinguished from **nature** as doing (*facere*) is from acting or producing in general (*agere*), and the product or consequence of the former is distinguished as a **work** (*opus*) from the latter as an effect (*effectus*)" (KU 5:303). He goes on to mark the difference between artworks and natural effects as being grounded on production through freedom. Art, then, is brought into being "through a capacity for choice that grounds its actions in reason." He continues his discussion, second, by distinguishing art from science. Here, the relevant difference comes into focus as a distinction between theory and practice; art requires not merely knowing, but knowing how to

Genius, Aesthetic Ideas, and a Spiritualized Natural Order 137

do something, how to bring something into being. Science requires only knowledge, without application. Lastly, Kant contrasts art with handicraft. While handicraft is remunerative – made for the purpose of making money – art "must be regarded as if it could turn out purposively (be successful) only as play" (KU 5:304). Art, unlike a craft, does not have a purpose that stands outside of the object made.

Works of art, Kant holds, stand apart from other objects or products of human skill and invention. Even more than this, Kant's analysis holds that art objects are unambiguously identifiable as what they are. That is, art objects are recognizable as their own category of objects; we recognize art objects as distinct from merely functional or useful objects, or even handicrafts. This is possible because their mode of production marks them as what they are. We recognize art objects as such – they are constituted by having been brought into being through purposive play. Art objects are created for the purpose of being art, and nothing else.[10] Objects bear the pattern of how they came into being (discussed in Chapter 2); thus, we can clearly distinguish objects in nature from human artifacts and, then, within the latter, objects for use and those that are art.

While all art objects are recognizable as art, not all art is beautiful. We can discern that art, qua art, is created through freedom in play. For it to be beautiful art, however, it must further effect a free play of the faculties. Kant returns here to the measure of beautiful art that he has already laid out in the four moments: "Beautiful art . . . is a kind of representation that is purposive in itself and, though without an end, nevertheless promotes the cultivation of the mental powers for sociable communication" (KU 5:306). That is, beautiful art occasions the pleasurable, free harmonious play of the imagination and the understanding.

How, though, is it possible for art – which is brought into being purposively – to achieve purposiveness without a purpose and occasion free play? What is the pattern of productivity in the human mind or will that allows for such an object to be beautiful? The measure Kant sets for this is that beautiful art "seems at the same time to be nature" (KU 5:306).

---

[10] This is more than merely art for art's sake. It is that, but it also captures something phenomenologically so: Art objects are recognizable as their own kind of thing. It is important to note this claim on Kant's part, I think, as at least two things follow from it. First, this means that while other objects may be designed in an aesthetically pleasing way, this does not make them art. Second, it is this free- and self-standing character of art that allows it to instantiate much of what Kant wishes to claim about the beautiful – that it is not grounded on any concepts, that it admits of an Ideal, that it embodies exemplarity, and so on. It further highlights the absolute independence of what we encounter out in the territory. Friedlander's treatment of art in *Expressions of Judgment* picks up on this fact nicely. See especially 60–77.

"Nature," he writes, "was beautiful, if at the same time it looked like art; and art can only be called beautiful if we are aware that it is art and yet it looks to us like nature" (KU 5:306). Nature, which is mechanistic in its causality, is beautiful when its objects appear to have been brought about purposively, that is, in accord with freedom and reason. Yet no purpose may be discerned. Art, however, which is brought into being purposively, may only attain beauty when its purposiveness somehow effaces itself, thus appearing not as intentional but natural. The tension here is clear: An artist has an end to bring about a certain kind of thing; thus, the object will embody this end in its appearance. Beauty, however, requires that no end be present in the thing's appearance, the intention of the artist must be present for the thing to come into being, but then disappear in the object itself. Gasché asks the question succinctly, "If art, qua art, including beautiful art, inevitably presupposes a design, what must happen to the definite concept behind the design of the beautiful arts if their products are to be judged beautiful?"[11]

The question, then, is how it is possible that art, which is created by human beings in their freedom, can appear as a product of nature. *Genius* is Kant's answer to this apparent contradiction in how there can be art that is also beautiful, that is, how a product of human beings does not fall into the familiar stream of everyday experience. As both Zammito and Bruno detail in their studies, by the time Kant was writing, the notion of genius not only had developed its own history but also had come to the fore of discourse in Kant's age.[12] What we find here is much like what we find with Kant's appropriation of the sensus communis – a philosophical concept that he both accepts and transforms. He finds a key place for the concept of genius in his own schema that both draws from and works over its meaning.

Genius is a kind of faculty – a talent or predisposition – for artistic production that nature grants to human beings. It allows for nature to work through human beings and to present something of itself to us in the work that is created. Kant defines it thus:

> **Genius** is the talent (natural gift) that gives the rule to art. Since the talent, as an inborn productive faculty of the artist, itself belongs to nature, this could also be expressed thus; **Genius** is the inborn predisposition of the mind (*ingenium*) **through which** nature gives the rule to art. (KU 5:307)

---

[11] Gasché, *The Idea of Form*, 185.
[12] Paul Bruno, *Kant's Concept of Genius: Its Origin and Function in the Third* Critique (New York: Continuum, 2010); Zammito, *The Genesis of Kant's Critique of Judgment*.

Genius, Aesthetic Ideas, and a Spiritualized Natural Order 139

Genius, specifically, has to do with a relation to *rules*. Art, as Kant initially defines it, presupposes rules for its creation. Beautiful art, however, cannot be derived from any rule. This presents the aporia in which the genius stands. How is creation by design or rule ultimately presented as without rules? This contradiction is superseded in the work of the genius, who channels a special kind of rule of nature into the work.

Kant delimits the rule of the beautiful work first, as original. "**Originality**," he writes, "must be its primary characteristic" (KU 5:308). In the work of beautiful art, the art itself is ultimately the origin of its own rule. Its rule is not one that is followed or is taken from elsewhere, such as the natural order (conceived mechanistically), the mind of the artist, or any other sphere. In this way, the work of art appears to us as self-standing. It not only appears as a distinctive kind of object; it originates its own rule for the presentation of its content. It is not enough that the work is *unique*. Rather, its production and existence are themselves the very origin of the rule it embodies. Friedlander describes this aspect of the work as "appear[ing] to exist for itself, as though completely self-enclosed and detached from an order of reasons."[13] The genius is the one who mediates this originality in the rule nature gives. In the *Anthropology*, Kant describes genius as a "talent for inventing" (*Anth* 7:224) by contrast with mere discovery. We can see this, too, in Kant's description of how nature works *through* the artist. In this, the artist him- or herself does not, indeed cannot, appear in the presentation of the work. Kant goes so far as to note that "the author of a product that he owes to his genius does not know himself how the ideas for it come to him, and also does not have it in his power to think up such things at will or according to plan" (KU 5:308).[14] The beautiful work of art, and not the artist, is the originating source of the rule of its appearance.

Originality is also constrained in the *kind* of rule by which the genius produces beautiful art. While the work of beautiful art originates its own

---

[13] Friedlander, *Expressions of Judgment*, 63–64.
[14] Here we see clearly Kant's adherence to the ancient notion of artistic genius that persists through the Latin use of the term. Kant reminds the reader that the Latin genius refers to the "spirit given to a person at his birth ... from whose inspiration those original ideas stem." We cannot also help but be reminded of Socrates' criticism of artists for just this reason in both the *Apology* and the *Ion*. In the *Apology*, he chides the poets for not being able to offer an account of the meaning of their own work; in the *Ion*, he accuses artists of mere inspiration, of being out of their minds (not in possession of reason), and attached only to a muse. Kant himself seems to recall this association in the *Anthropology*, notes how, in antiquity, the idea that poets were "inspired" (or possessed) meant that "lively and powerful images and feelings pour into him, while he behaves passively, so to speak" (*Anth* 7:188).

rule of presentation, this rule is not determinate. In Chapter 2, we saw how judgments of reflection made out in the territory are explicitly about what appears. In this, they present an orderedness in appearance itself. The union of mere appearance with the presentation of an ordering – or, here, rule – should shed light on Kant's descriptions in this section of the text. A beautiful work of art thus presents an original rule that is not a determinate one – this is simply another way of saying that it is purposive without a purpose. It has the form of a rule, or of being brought into being through a rule, but no particular rule is determinable. Figal's suggestion of beautiful art as "decentered orders" is instructive. There are orderings in every work, but there is not one, centered order. He suggests that "one should first take up Kant's indication of the fabric-like character of some free formations."[15] The moments of the order, he goes on, are "never static . . . variable . . . every moment can be assigned in a manifold way, and depending on what other moment one views it from, it can enter into a new coherent correspondence."[16] Artworks represent something that appears organized; what it is organized into, however, never becomes determinate. *That* the work is ordered is evident enough. One determinate account of this order, however, is not given in the work and is not possible even through interpretation of it. (How this is so will be treated in Section 5.3.)

Kant goes on, second, to delineate a crucial aspect of the rule that must constitute the beautiful. Conscious that a lack of a pregiven rule to follow may yield a lack of rules or "nonsense," Kant insists that beautiful works of art are able to serve as models, that is, they are "**exemplary**" (KU 5:308). We might imagine such nonsense as the random strokes of a brush by an elephant on a canvas; each piece would certainly be unique, but would in effect have no meaning or order. We may likewise imagine the ramblings of a madman in the same vein. There must be some rule to the work, and the rule must serve as an example. As exemplary, models are not meant to be imitated in style, content, and so forth; rather, they come to "serve . . . as a standard or rule for judging" (KU 5:308). Exemplarity, here, has a homologous structure to the originality of the work of art. While beautiful art presents its origin in itself, it also sets its own example, qua exemplarity as such. Both are singular and self-standing within each work of beautiful art. As we saw in Chapter 4, exemplarity has the mere form of being an example, but without anything that is being exemplified. But, as an

---

[15] Figal, *Aesthetics as Phenomenology*, 56.   [16] Ibid., 57.

example, it embodies a universal rule, and thus demands assent. Beautiful art thus presents itself in such a way that other things may become examples of it. The difficulty of explaining what is entailed in exemplarity without referential content – a particular rule – is not lost on Kant:

> Since the gift of nature [genius] must give the rule to art (as beautiful art), what sort of rule is this? It cannot be couched in a formula to serve as a precept, for then the judgment about the beautiful would be determinable in accordance with concepts; rather, the rule must be abstracted from the deed, i.e., from the product, against which others may test their own talent, letting it serve them as a model not for **copying** but for **imitation**. How this is possible is difficult to explain. (KU 5:309)

The notion of exemplarity here is meant to signify that the beautiful work of art presents a universal but indeterminate rule. That Kant has introduced the notion in the section on modality gives the clue to what it is at stake in the rule-character of the work. It must make a claim on us – we find ourselves bound by its necessity. Beautiful art originates its own rule of presentation; this rule is indeterminate, yet universal and demanding. Beautiful art makes a claim on us – what claim, exactly, is likely never settled. This, I think, is consanguine with Hannah Ginsborg's emphasis on normativity in Kant's aesthetics; the beautiful work of art is, in a way, about its own normativity.[17] Without a determinate rule given, however, what remains is the rule-character of the work and the sense of universality it embodies.

But how is the beautiful work meant to serve as an example? What kind of standard does it set? The Ideal of Beauty, we saw, set a standard for the pattern of judging the beautiful. The standard there was of a thoroughgoing determination of material nature by the force of reason – reason could reach all the way down to become the sole cause of the body. In the beautiful work of art, the standard is similar. Some have noted a seeming "paradox" of Kant's claim that the beautiful work of art is to be imitated; the question is what, exactly, is to be imitated? Martin Gammon observes that the problem of genius and influence has a pre-Kantian history – how can a genius produce works that are at once original, yet meant to serve as a model for others who are also supposed to be original? What is exemplary about a beautiful work of art can be seen in Kant's distinction between

---

[17] See Ginsborg's collected essays on these topics in *The Normativity of Nature: Essays on Kant's Critique of Judgment* (Oxford: Oxford University Press, 2015).

copying and imitation as two ways other artists relate to the work.[18] Kant writes that the rule serves other artists, "as a model not for copying but for imitation" (KU 5:309). The difference here is subtle but telling. When we copy something, we simply take its matter and rehearse it; it remains external to us. If we, say, copy someone else's style, we might wear the same outfit they wear, but in a way that the outfit does not quite become us. Imitation, by contrast, is a kind of active appropriation – we become the thing imitated. The reason that the Ancient Greeks centered their aesthetic theories on imitation is because they took *mimesis* as just such a transformation. This is why, for Plato, the arts were taken to have such a formative role – they literally could work to form the soul a certain way through repeated engagements with works of art. Our souls take on the shape of what we imitate. If we imitate the lamentations for the dead as depicted in Homer, we become someone prone to enact such base things. For Aristotle, too, the catharsis or purging of fear and pity when taken up in watching a tragedy was only possible because we ourselves went through the events of the play. What the beautiful work of art is an example of is not a particular rule to be copied, to be applied externally to the next work of art. It is an example of an *activity* of rule-giving by way of genius and aesthetic ideas, an example of original creation. A genius *invents* something; it thus inspires other artists not to copy the thing invented, but also to invent something themselves. Beautiful artworks are examples of original invention, and are to be "emulated" by other geniuses, who are "thereby awakened to the feeling of [their] own originality" (KU 5:318).

Genius is the name for the naturally given talent a person may have for being open to such a rule coming to be in the work of art, from out of nature itself. Kant takes pains to insist that the capacity for producing beautiful art – being a genius – is something naturally given and cannot be learned. This is intimately related to the kind of rule we find present in beautiful art. Kant's implication with contrasting art and science, genius and copying, is that those things involving determinate rules can be *known*. Kant's logic seems to be thus: Rules govern how things are, in our experience and in the world. Whatever truth is attained through the possession or understanding of rules is both accessible to all, as well as mundane. This is the difference, Kant asserts,

---

[18] Gammon traces Kant's ultimate resolution to the paradox to the work of Winckelmann and Tetens. See Martin Gammon, "'Exemplary Originality': Kant on Genius and Imitation," in *Journal of the History of Philosophy*, 35:4 (1997), 578.

between a Newton and Homer; what Newton learned could be known, and therefore replicated and known by others, what Homer presented cannot. Kant writes,

> Thus everything that Newton expounded in his immortal work on the principles of natural philosophy, no matter how great a mind it took to discover it, can still be learned; but one cannot learn to write inspired poetry, however exhaustive all the rules for the art of poetry and however excellent the models for it may be. The reason is that Newton could make all the steps that he had to take ... entirely intuitive not only to himself but also to everyone else, and thus set them out for posterity quite determinately; but no Homer or Wieland can indicate how his ideas, which are fantastic and yet at the same time rich in thought, arise and come together in his head, because he himself does not know it and thus cannot teach it to anyone else either. (KU 5:308–9)

There is a way in which even the greatest minds of science are merely copying – they are learning what already is. Rules are binding; science merely discovers the rules to how things are. Beautiful art, as Kant has it, makes us feel bound by it, although there is no particular rule by which we are bound. And, in art the rule is singular to the work and created only in and for it.

Kant's account here reflects his doctrine of the faculties. Science does not only discover the rules of nature. It does this in virtue of the extent to which nature conforms to the possibilities we have for thinking rules and relations through the faculty of the understanding. Beautiful art, by contrast, lies beyond the possibility of what we can know, of the rules and relations we can understand. While in science reason can stretch the scope of the use of the understanding significantly, in beautiful art something wholly other is at issue. What is presented does not conform to rules and relations we can understand but challenges and exceeds them.

It is for this reason that Kant argues that the rule for beautiful art cannot come from us and must come from beyond what our faculties themselves can produce. We can master the mechanical aspects of art – techniques, styles, and so forth. This, Kant calls the "**form**" of art, arguing that it "require[s] a talent that has been academically trained" (KU 5:310). It is only genius that can "provide the rich **material** for products of art" (KU 5:310). We cannot, of ourselves, produce something that exceeds our own capacities.

5.3 Spirit and Aesthetic Ideas

What is it, then, that makes art beautiful? How can genius create such material for us? Aesthetic ideas provide the rich material that exceeds what the faculties of the human mind can comprehend. *Spirit* is what allows the human mind to present what exceeds it in these very ideas. Spirit is also what distinguishes art that is beautiful from that which is not. "One says of certain products," Kant writes, "of which it is expected that they ought, at least in part, to reveal themselves as beautiful art, that they are without spirit ... A poem can be pretty and elegant, but without **spirit**" (KU 5:313). We find spirit both in beautiful art, and in the artist, "Spirit, in an aesthetic significance, means the animating principle in the mind." Kant describes how spirit works to animate or enliven the faculties – spirit "purposively sets the mental powers into motion," into *play*. Nature, then, grants to genius the spirit of a live mind, which is then able to take shape in the work produced in the presentation of aesthetic ideas.

Spirit animates the mind by way of aesthetic ideas, which constitute the material we contemplate that sets the play of the faculties into motion. Kant thus identifies spirit as "the faculty for the presentation of aesthetic ideas" (KU 5:314). A certain liveliness of the mind is what allows it to present aesthetic ideas, which are otherwise out of reach for our faculties; they exceed what we could otherwise, of our own accord, present. The relationships between the different faculties that Kant has already described in his critical project do not admit of presenting aesthetic ideas – they remain impossible for us unless a special kind of relationship between the imagination and understanding is achieved. This relationship is what the animating principle of spirit allows. By enlivening the imagination and understanding, by waking them up to a free, playful relation, aesthetic ideas may be either produced (through the genius) or contemplated (by the spectator).

But what is an aesthetic idea such that a new relation of the faculties born of spirit is necessary? Kant defines aesthetic ideas this way:

> [B]y an aesthetic idea, however, I mean that representation of the imagination that occasions much thinking though without it being possible for any determinate thought, i.e., **concept**, to be adequate to it, which, consequently, no language fully attains or can make intelligible. –One readily sees that it is the counterpart (pendant) to an **idea of reason**, which is conversely, a concept to which no **intuition** (representation of the imagination) can be adequate. (KU 5:314)

Aesthetic ideas are a counterpart and pendant (*Gegenstück* and *Pendant*) of an idea of reason. The key feature of an idea of reason is that it is a concept for which we can have no intuition. The ideas of God, freedom, and immortality, as we know from the first *Critique*, exceed the possibilities of time and space that constitute any intuitions we may have. Our faculties are structurally precluded from having a representation of these ideas in the imagination. As a counterpart or pendant, an aesthetic idea is both contrary and complementary to an idea of reason. First, they are counterparts: Where an idea of reason is conceptually unbounded such that no intuition could match it, an aesthetic idea inverts the relation between representation and thought. An aesthetic idea is too rich in imaginative representation for any single concept to determine it. There is too much given to the senses for any particular thought to be adequate to it. Second, aesthetic ideas complement ideas of reason. Aesthetic ideas, Kant writes, "seek to approximate a presentation of concepts of reason (of intellectual ideas), which gives them the appearance of an objective reality ... The poet ventures to make sensible rational ideas of invisible beings, the kingdom of the blessed, the kingdom of hell, eternity, creation, etc." (KU 5:314). On the one hand, aesthetic ideas are the other of ideas of reason, as they invert the site of excessiveness in the relation of the faculties. On the other hand and at the same time, however, this inversion is taken as an attempt to meet the excessiveness of the other. Aesthetic ideas are sensible presentations whose matter attempts to present what is not presentable.

We are not able of our own accord to produce the excess in imaginative content that complements the ideas of reason. This stands in stark contrast with the ideas of reason. The ideas of reason are our fate in virtue of reason's demand for the unconditioned. Aesthetic ideas are only possible insofar as nature bestows the gift of genius, and thereby opens the way for nature itself to give the rule to art in aesthetic ideas. Aesthetic ideas come to us by way of nature, we must rely on its grace to enliven the faculties of the mind such they become capable of expressing what exceeds them. Aesthetic ideas are what nature does for us as a complement to reason's unmet needs. Nature, thus, provides the complement to the ideas of reason from itself; it even, Kant argues, "serves that idea of reason" (KU 5:315).

Ideas of reason and aesthetic ideas share in exceeding the bounds of experience. Their kinship is what will allow for us to have something like an encounter with the supersensible. We find ourselves subject to the ideas of reason. That is, we cannot help but come to them; it is not up to us whether we think about the existence of an unconditioned being, the whole of the cosmos, and our immortal souls. The best we can get is *critique*, that is, conscious recognition that we are unable to discern the reality or truthfulness of the ideas to which we are ineluctably led.

We cannot extirpate the tendency to come to them. In this, coming to the ideas of reason is not really up to us. In the same way, producing aesthetic ideas, which may provide complementarity to the ideas of reason, is also not up to us. Bringing forth beautiful art is not something that we can simply decide to do and then make happen of our own accord. As Brigitte Sassen notes, "Genius is a capacity that is *given*, not one that can be commanded at will or controlled."[19] When taken together, these two forms of finitude point to a human being whose experience of themselves is as part of larger whole. In this larger whole, we are subject to the demands of reason we ourselves do not produce, and the genius is given an unbidden gift to create. The way we are subject to these movements is profoundly intimate. Even more than this, we are led out beyond the bounds of experience by forces to which we are ourselves subject – reason and nature – but of which we are not in control. The larger whole of nature and the cosmos to which we belong show up in our minds and in our wills, insuring that their order is reflected there regardless of our own doing. And, the drive to metaphysics that possesses reason suggests to us that there is more than meets the eye; in aesthetic ideas, there is more that meets than eye than our minds can grasp.

In producing material that exceeds our capacity for conceptualization, the imagination takes center stage. "The imagination (as a productive cognitive faculty)," Kant writes, is "very powerful in creating, as it were, another nature, out of the material which the real one gives it" (KU 5:314). The productive power of the imagination is a feeling of freedom, as it is not bound to subsume its representations under any given law. The "material [of the imagination] may be lent to us by nature, but the latter can be transformed by us into something entirely different, namely into that which steps beyond nature" (KU 5:314). Nature grants genius the power to transform nature into something that goes beyond itself. The material that nature gives to the genius passes through the productive force of the imagination and emerges as something even more than nature can bring about. Kant describes this process of the creative imagination as *enlarging* concepts. Whereas a determinative judgment subsumes the imagination under the understanding, here, the imagination borrows a concept of the understanding and, through multiple associations with other concepts, produces content that breaks out beyond what the concept itself can determine. This is the opposite of reason's drive pulling the

---

[19] Brigitte Sassen, "Artistic Genius and the Question of Creativity," in *Kant's Critique of the Power of Judgment: Critical Essays*, Paul Guyer, ed. (New York: Rowman and Littlefield, 2003), 171.

concepts of the understanding beyond experience to their limit. In that, they are not enlarged, but emptied out. In the creative play of the genius, more content is associated with the concept, thus amplifying its possible referents and relations:

> In a word, the aesthetic idea is a representation of the imagination, associated with a given concept, which is combined with such a manifold of partial representations in the free use of the imagination that no expression designating a determinate concept can be found for it, which therefore allows the addition to a concept of much that is unnameable, the feeling of which animates the cognitive faculties and combines spirit with the mere letter of language. (KU 5:316)

What nature lends to human beings in genius is an ability through spirit's enlivening to free up one's imagination with respect to the understanding. Through this relation of these two faculties, genius is able to give expression to aesthetic ideas, an abundance of material that exceeds and thus also enlarges the concepts of the understanding. An aesthetic idea thus looks like an indeterminate rule – there is an idea that is indeterminate not because it is vague, but is rather because as an idea, its content is too rich to be determined by us in one way. We cannot reduce an aesthetic idea through determination, though we can expand and multiply these determinations.

We are now poised to describe the cyclical movement of the excess of nature that takes shape in spirit, genius, art, and freedom. First, nature exceeds itself insofar as it gives the gift of genius to human beings. In a note from the early 1770s, Kant names this the "original fruitfulness [*Ursprüngliche Fruchtbarkeit*] of nature [that is] the ground of beautiful art" (R 752; 15:329).[20] The name for this excessiveness of nature is spirit, a principle of life that moves the mind of the genius. The genius is then able, through the movement of spirit, to express aesthetic ideas in materiality. This new materiality – beautiful art – is itself a transformation of and exceeding of material nature. Material nature becomes spiritualized through the efforts of the genius. The genius accomplishes this by seemingly imbuing the work of art, in the aesthetic ideas, with spirit itself. The beautiful work of art, finally, enlivens the mind of the spectator. If spirit is what allows the genius' faculties to enliven in such a way as to produce aesthetic ideas, the spectator detects this very spirit when their mind is

---

[20] Jeremy Proulx takes this up in his essay "Art and the Fecundity of Nature," in *Kant und die Philosophie in weltbürgerlicher Absicht: Akten des XI. Internationalen Kant-Kongress* (Berlin: de Gruyter, 2013).

enlivened in contemplating them. In the free play of the spectator, we exceed the otherwise mundane capacities of our faculties and ourselves become spiritualized.

If spirit is the name for the excessiveness of nature, *freedom* is the name for the way the human being exceeds nature. While this is not practical freedom, it is nevertheless a freedom from the constraints of nature. In the movement of spirit from nature, through the genius, and then in art and the spectator, the excessiveness of nature in its gift of genius and spirit ultimately results in the human being coming to exceed nature, thus, be free. Moreover, Kant identifies this excessive freedom with life. We see this, first, in the opening of the text, where Kant names the pleasure we take in the beautiful a *Lebensgefühl*, a feeling of life. But it is not only a feeling of life, but, rather, a feeling of the "promotion of life" (KU 5:244). There is, Kant argues, an increase in our capacities through reflection. The feeling of life is associated for Kant with an expansion of our mind as well as its strengthening (KU 5:326). While Kant's descriptions of the expansion and strengthening of the mind are indexed to poetry as the highest form of art, he is clearly noting the benefits of the free play of the faculties. The expansion of the mind, as we saw in Chapter 2, enlarges concepts and the representations with which they may be associated, as well as opens up and reconfigures the way concepts are brought into relation between themselves. It is a kind of "free association." The imagination is freed up to make new associations between representations and concepts. Our mind is also made stronger; Kant writes that poetry

> strengthens the mind by letting it feel its capacity to consider and judge of nature, as appearance, freely, self-actively, and independently of determination by nature, in accordance with points of view that nature does not present by itself in experience either for sense or for the understanding, and thus to use it for the sake of and as it were as the schema of the supersensible. (KU 5:326)

Insofar as we feel ourselves in our freedom, we are made stronger. In our experience of beautiful poetry, we feel our capacity for reflection on nature; this feeling is, for us, explicitly about independence from and freedom with respect to it. We feel ourselves in our distance from nature, that is, in not being determined by it. We are able to consider it and our own activity, take our own perspective on it. The movement of spirit out of nature, then, culminates in the free activity of the human mind in its contemplation of beautiful art. Friedlander is thus right to argue that this broader movement of spirit can be named "culture," or, as he puts it, "the human form of life that encompasses these terms."²¹ Culture, which Kant argues is a movement of nature itself,²² is thus one way nature shows itself to us as a place we belong, and not as something external to our being. It is an intimate space of human activity.

What Kant has outlined in his account of genius, aesthetic ideas, and spirit is a more expansive nature than we have seen prior in his writings. This nature exceeds itself, and is the source of liveliness and a feeling of our own freedom. The human being is quite at home in this spiritualized nature. Indeed, part of our reflection on art is about this possibility of nature itself. One of the "points of view" we take in our reflective state is "the schema of the supersensible" (KU 5:327). The supersensible, in the first *Critique*, is mere transcendental illusion and thus off limits for any productive inquiry. But here Kant seems to suggest that we can "[play] with the illusion [*Schein*] ... yet without thereby being deceitful, for it itself declares its occupation to be mere play" (KU 5:327). In reflection, Kant describes us as able to "play" with the illusion of the supersensible. Unlike in the first *Critique*, where we are simply subject to reason's demand and thus unwillingly given to illusion such that we must engage in critique to keep it at bay, here we recognize the illusion as such and are able to play with a schema of the supersensible in our own mind. We do so freely, actively, and by our own will. We do so, further, with engagement with an empirical representation via a work of art. In this way, our engagements with art serve to maintain our hope that there is a supersensible substratum to nature that is in union with freedom.

When Kant argues for the condition of the possibility of beautiful art, he portrays an expansive, spiritualized nature. In this account, human beings are a part of this larger expansive of nature – it exceeds us in every way, but in a way that ultimately raises us up into what is most our own, namely our freedom.

5.4 Nature's Supersensible Substratum: Communicability and Life Revisited

Kant further associates this movement of spirit with communication. Nature can thus be seen to contribute to the cultivation of our deepest human feature, which joins us with all other human beings:

---

[21] Friedlander, *Expressions of Judgment*, 70.
[22] See Kristi Sweet, "Kant and the Culture of Discipline: Rethinking the Nature of Nature," *Epoché: A Journal for the History of Philosophy*, 15:1 (2010): 121–138; see also Chapter 6.

communicability. In Chapter 4, we demonstrated how Kant argues that the sensus communis is ultimately about the fact that human beings can communicate with one another. This fact provides the final bulwark against skepticism, and operates as the foundation of the critical enterprise. The sensus communis is about our being in common with other human beings, as expressed in the fact of communicability, which reveals a shared supersensible substratum to all human beings. Nature, then, in promoting communication, also promotes our being in common and the possibility of establishing a rational world order as prescribed by reason.

Nature promotes our communicative capacities through beautiful art. Communication involves the relation between the imagination and understanding. "The aptitude of human beings for communicating their thoughts," Kant writes, "also requires a relation between the imagination and the understanding in order to associate intuitions with concepts and concepts in turn with intuitions" (KU 5:295). As our engagement with beautiful art strengthens our mind and the use of these very faculties, Kant's first definition of beautiful art is about the possibilities for communication it encourages. Beautiful art, he writes, "is a kind of representation that is purposive in itself and, though without an end, nevertheless promotes the cultivation of the mental powers for sociable communication" (KU 5:305). We also see Kant associating and evening defining aesthetic ideas by way of linguistic expression. Because there is no determinate thought adequate to the abundance of content presented in aesthetic ideas, "consequently, no language fully attains or can make intelligible" (KU 5:314); they "let one think more than one can express in a concept determined by words" (KU 5:325); and

> no expression designating a determinate concept can be found for it, which therefore allows the addition to a concept of much that is unnameable, the feeling of which animates the cognitive faculties and combines spirit with the mere letter of language. (KU 5:316)

While these passages highlight the unnameability or un-sayability of aesthetic ideas, Kant's clear meaning is not that we are unable to speak. Rather, it is that there is too much we might say, although it will always remain indeterminate and incomplete. This appears to be the process of strengthening our minds as well as our speech: The attempt to make the unnameable intelligible builds up our ability to put our thoughts into words, that is, to communicate ourselves.

Kant further describes beauty – in both nature and art – as nature's attempt to communicate with us. First, Kant presents the communicative

Genius, Aesthetic Ideas, and a Spiritualized Natural Order   151

element of the beautiful as something directly from nature. Second, the task given to the genius is to communicate. In both cases, Kant emphasizes the expressive character the beautiful, linking such expression to communication. The beautiful is trying to tell something to us; the genius facilitates this telling in beautiful art. All beautiful things are expressions of ideas:

> Beauty (whether it be beauty of nature or of art) can in general be called the **expression** of aesthetic ideas ... in beautiful nature the mere reflection on a given intuition, without a concept of what the object ought to be, is sufficient for arousing and communicating the idea of which the object is considered as the **expression**. (KU 5:320)

This comes out plainly in Kant's discussions of natural beauty. It is the sense we have that nature is trying to tell us something that leads to the intellectual interest in nature. On the side of the subject, it is a moral disposition that takes an interest in natural beauty; on the side of natural objects, however, our interest is *because* they appear to us as trying to get something across to us. He describes our experience of beautiful nature this way: "The song of the bird **proclaims joyfulness and contentment with its existence**. At least this is how we interpret nature, whether anything of the sort is its intention or not" (KU 5:302, boldface mine). Bird song is not beautiful merely in its form. Rather, we find in it a proclamation of something: an idea that the bird's song is expressing. Kant rather explicitly argues that the reason we take such an interest in natural beauty is that nature is communicating something with us. He calls it a "cipher [*Chiffreschrift*; literally 'cipher writing'] by means of which nature figuratively speaks to us," and argues that natural beauties "contain a language that nature brings to us and that seems to have a higher meaning" (KU 5:301–2). Natural beauty, Kant maintains, appears to us a kind of code-writing, symbolic and encrypted. It seems to contain a hidden message for us. Because it is nature speaking to us directly, the interest we may take in it is immediate.

The communicative vocation of the beautiful is further confirmed by the division of the arts, which is given by analogy with "the kind of expression that that people use in speaking in order to communicate to each other" (KU 5:320). The arts are thus organized according to the mode by which they communicate aesthetic ideas. Rhetoric and poetry communicate via speech; sculpture, painting, and architecture (the "pictorial" arts) communicate via "shapes in space," which Kant relates to human gesture (KU 5:322); music communicates via tone and thus sensation.

It also appears that the vocation of the genius is to facilitate nature's expressive intent with respect to human beings; the genius must be able to make aesthetic ideas communicable. Nature supplies the material – the aesthetic ideas – for beautiful art, but the genius must be able to present these ideas in a way that makes sense. While the genius must be original, he or she must not produce mere *nonsense* [*Unsinn*]. In order to get aesthetic ideas across, the genius must also give the idea a "pleasing form which [is] ... the vehicle of communication" (KU 5:313). The genius must therefore also have taste. As we saw in Chapter 4, taste is the faculty by which we discern what may be universally communicable. While the judger of beautiful art has taste when they have a sense for what others will also find beautiful, the creator of beautiful art must present aesthetic ideas such that they can be universally received. Kant goes on to suggest that the genius must hit "upon the **expression** for" aesthetic ideas (KU 5:317).[23] And again, the job of the genius is the "exposition or the expression of aesthetic ideas" (KU 5:317). This is what spirit grants to the genius:

> The latter talent is really that which is called spirit, for to express what is unnameable in the mental state in the case of a certain representation and to make it universally communicable, whether the expression consists in language, or painting, or in plastic art – that requires a faculty for apprehending the rapidly passing play of imagination and unifying it into a concept (which for that very reason is original and at the same time discloses a new rule, which could not have been deduced from any antecedent principles or examples), which can be communicated without the constraint of rules. (KU 5:317)

The communicative endeavor of nature, genius, and art is impossible to ignore in Kant's accounts. Nuzzo sums Kant up by claiming that "[g]enius is the faculty of 'communication' of aesthetic ideas."[24] The difficult thing to think about the ubiquitous communicative endeavor of beauty, however, is that it never becomes evident *what* is being communicated, only *that* something is. Or, rather, we are able to discern a range of *what* is being communicated, but it will never become determinate and final in beauty. Our intellectual interest in the beautiful is mediated, therefore, because nature's speaking to us is mediated by the genius and work of art.

Kant connects the sense we have that nature is communicating with us to the suggestion of a supersensible substratum to nature. At the end of the Dialectic of the Critique of Aesthetic Judgment, Kant writes that "three

---

[23] Kant himself bolds "expression" [*Ausdruck*] no fewer than four times in these sections.
[24] Nuzzo, *Unity of Reason*, 309.

ideas are revealed" by the preceding Deduction. The first of these ideas is "that of the supersensible in general, without further determination, as the substratum of nature" (KU 5:346).[25] It is simply that there is a supersensible substratum to nature that matters – that is, that nature is more than the mechanistic nature we find in the cognition and morality. The second idea revealed elaborates on the import of this initial suggestion, the supersensible substratum relates the natural order specifically to human beings. It is "the principle of the subjective purposiveness of nature for our faculty of cognition" (KU 5:346). Even though the supersensible substratum is not made determinate – that is, it is not, say, claimed to be rational – it nevertheless is what allows us to feel at home in nature. It is what yields the fittingness of things we find out in the territory for our faculties, and ultimately speaks to the interests of hope. We can think of this analogously with the sensus communis. There, we presume a shared supersensible substratum for all human beings – the universality it of our faculties, which is disclosed in the sense we have that we can communicate. This same supersensible kinship is thus found in nature insofar as it appears to be communicating with us. While this was pointed toward in the Ideal of Beauty in the model of *life* as the highest perfection of beauty, what the discussions of genius and aesthetic ideas suggest more forcefully is that *life* is, in fact, what underlies the mechanistic natural order and the entire human sphere together. Kant's opening salvo in naming the pleasure we take in the beautiful a *Lebensgefühl* thus appears as a feeling not only of the liveliness of our own faculties but also the liveliness – indeed, fruitfulness – of nature thus conceived. The *Lebensgefühl* associated with beauty is a feeling for life itself as a larger context to which both humans and nature belong.

Kant's emphasis on the communicative endeavor that is shot through all aspects of the beautiful gives further contour, too, to the sensus communis. While the sensus communis is a sense for the universal communicability of things with other human beings, we may find an expanded notion of it on the heels of the rest of the Deduction. The sensus communis may also be seen as a kind of receptivity to nature's endeavor to get something across to us. While Ostaric argues that "genius' action is the result of her receptiveness to nature's supersensible substratum,"[26] the spectator must have a

---

[25] While it would be too far afield to address the issue here, it may be that this note of Kant suggests that he did indeed take the sections on genius and beautiful art properly to be part of the Deduction.
[26] Ostaric, "Kant on the Normativity of Creative Production," 81.

similar receptive engagement with the work. We experience the beautiful as having the promise of intelligibility in much the same way we might another human being speaking another language to us. While what beauty promises is grounded on an excess presented in imagination and thus yields the pleasure of the free play of the faculties, the sense we have for communicability underlies both promises. If taste is a sense for what others will also judge as pleasurable, we may also say that it is a kind of attunement to the communicative endeavors of nature. We recognize that nature is trying to get something across to us, even if we are unable to decipher what it is that is being said.

In the way that the sensus communis yields a sense of belonging to a larger human community, the communicative endeavors of nature yield a sense that we belong to it, or, at least, that we can commune with it. Here, it is not a foreign entity that stands in the way of our ends, but rather can sustain our hope that nature is possibly for us.

Interlude: Transition to the Critique of Teleological Judgment

The most essential difference between the Critique of Aesthetic Judgment and the Critique of Teleological Judgment is the kind of purposiveness they each treat. Both take up the faculty of judgment and its constitutive principle of purposiveness; however, the purpose that constitutes the purposiveness of each half of the text is different. The purposiveness of the Critique of Aesthetic Judgment is a *subjective* purposiveness, which takes the human subject as its purpose; the purposiveness of the Critique of Teleological Judgment is an *objective* purposiveness, which focuses on the purpose of objects either in themselves, or with respect to other objects. In the former, what we find out in the territory is judged insofar as it is related to us intimately, to our faculties and also our freedom. In the latter, what we find out in the territory remains exterior to us, and we relate to it in its exteriority, that is, scientifically; it remains objective for us. In teleology, we discover the possibilities we have for conceiving of nature in accord with ends, in individual objects as well as at a systematic level.

This essential difference accounts for the distinctive pictures that emerge of the human being's relation to nature in each section. As we saw in

Chapters 1–5, what we find out in the territory discloses to us a sense of belonging to nature; this is precisely because in subjective purposiveness, we judge nature to be for us and our faculties through a feeling that relates us to it. Moreover, it is not just nature to which we belong, but nature conceived expansively, as lively and spirited, and even cosmic, insofar as we have a sense of larger system to which both nature and freedom belong. We are a part of a larger context of nature, integrally and holistically. Beauty suggests a union of freedom and nature that lies beneath or beyond the spheres of human life, and thus gives context to them. In Chapters 6 and 7, nature will remain external to us, as an object of inquiry. Even as such, however, as we shall see, we nevertheless conceive of its organization with respect to the human being. This conception will not be of a union, however, but of a mutually conditioning, reciprocal relation.

The results of the Critique of Aesthetic Judgment may further be seen as the condition for the development of the Critique of Teleological Judgment. The Critique of Aesthetic Judgment allows us – reflectively – to hold that nature is suited to our faculties. Our encounters with things out in the territory disclose a harmonious rapport between those things and our faculties. The Critique of Aesthetic Judgment thus forwards a broader and more encompassing claim about how we are related to nature, given what we find in the sphere between morality and cognition. This suitability underwrites the Critique of Teleological Judgment. That is, the Critique of Aesthetic judgment has confirmed for us that nature is fit for our cognition; the Critique of Teleological Judgment gives more determinate orientation for how, then, we may investigate nature according to the systematicity we seek in its laws.

The system of nature that Kant describes in the Critique of Teleological Judgment sits within the larger, completed system of freedom and nature envisioned in the first half of the text. The system of nature conceived teleologically is how we situate the *domain* of nature within the larger system, while we remain out in the territory. In the Introduction, I suggested that one of the things that the territory affords is a perspective on the domains – one could view the broader expanse of land on which a domain is erected – the contours that underlie the city, that is, the ground on which it is built. One may discern the outline of the borders of the domain, as well as observe both its distance from and proximity to other domains. From this vantage point, the domains can also be viewed with respect to each other. From a facultative point of view, we see that we are able, from the territory, to relate the domain of the understanding (nature) to the ends of reason, both theoretical and practical, by way of the principle of purposiveness. This is what the Critique of Teleological Judgment is doing.

The Critique of Teleological Judgment thus takes the domain of nature as its object, standing outside of it and reflectively interpreting it as a whole and ultimately in a larger context. Within the domain of nature, we find empirical laws of nature as determined through the understanding. We seek, however, to discern a systematic relation of laws within the domain, and also to relate the domain as a whole to the ends of human freedom. The second part of the third *Critique* is about the possibilities and limits of such investigations.

6

The Domain of Nature as System: Ends

If our experience of beautiful things out in the territory reminds us that "human beings belong in the world," our teleological judgments of nature suggest, by contrast, that we do not belong to nature. Nature, nevertheless, is still *for us*. The way in which nature is for us, however, is peculiar, and the proposed conception of a system of nature makes a kind of double movement with respect to the human being. On the one hand, the system of nature as we reflectively conceive of it is indexed to *us*. From a position of reflection, we can judge that we provide the final end of nature, thus organizing nature as a meaningful whole. On the other hand, and at the same time however, nature's interest in human beings is judged to be to discharge us from its influence. The system of nature as a whole is granted systematicity only insofar as it is oriented by expelling human beings from its order. In this, we are able to judge the domain of nature as a system only insofar as we take it to have the domain of freedom as its organizing aim.

The Critique of Teleological Judgment is taken in part to be a contribution to Kant's thinking about the philosophy of science. This understanding of the text – which is, of course, correct – comes to the fore in virtue of a central claim that it makes about the possible relation of mechanism to teleology. As we saw in Chapter 3, the critical turn in Kant's thinking precluded the possibility of the life sciences. Here, Kant returns to their possibility under the auspices of reflective judgment. As we shall see, his invocation of teleology in science is nuanced – we do not simply employ the principle determinatively, that is, constitutively. It functions as a heuristic, orienting principle to guide and organize proper research and explanation executed through the understanding. While he had previously denied the life sciences and affirmed physical science, Kant here is resurrecting the possibility of biology as a proper science. Recent scholarship has seen a decided uptick in engagements with the Critique of Teleological Judgment and, in particular, his concept of organicity.

Perhaps the turning point was Zuckert's sustained and serious treatment of teleology in *Kant on Beauty and Biology*; there, teleology was elevated to pride of place in interpreting the text. Since then, further extended investigations of these sections of the text can be found in Jennifer Mensch's *Kant's Organicism*, and a comprehensive collection of essays on *Kant's Theory of Biology*, edited by Ina Goy and Eric Watkins. Much of this literature, too, rightfully seeks to address how Kant's claims about the scope and limits of scientific inquiry sit within the broader framework of his project. Rarely, though, do they take the question of meaning as their point of departure. For instance, Philippe Huneman's treatment of mechanism and teleology gestures only at the end to the question of meaning.[1]

There are multiple layers to and thus varied implications for Kant's argument beyond those for the life sciences. What I will show here is that the basic impetus for each move in the argument – the need for a systematic whole and the demand we find ourselves subject to with respect to thinking that way – means that science itself becomes situated within a larger context of human inquiry and human life. Our engagement with living beings – with life – continually refers us to questions of purpose and meaning. Indeed, the driving worry of this part of the text – *contingency* – is rooted not only in an epistemological or theoretical concern but also in one that is existential and meaningful. Employing teleology with respect to individual things as well as particular empirical laws entails, for Kant, thinking the broader whole of nature teleologically, too. The argument thus culminates with Kant's discussion of culture, and the claim that we reflectively judge human beings to be the final end of nature. I thus divide the Critique of Teleological Judgment into two sections: §62–§84, and then §85 – the end of the text. Each deals, I think, with different, though inextricably linked, questions: The first part deals with ends in nature, the second with the status of its ultimate cause. These final two chapters (Chapters 6 and 7) will thus also be divided in accord with this distinction.

There are two principal, interrelated ways the topic of this chapter speaks to the interests of hope. First, in the existence of living beings, we are prompted to find that nature can be thought by us as involving causality other than the mere mechanism that stands opposed to the ends of freedom. Second, the system of nature that we are inevitably led to as a result of this observation suggests that nature is, in fact, *for us*, and for our moral vocation. While we do not come to judge that nature is amenable to

---

[1] Philippe Huneman, "Purposiveness, Necessity, and Contingency," in *Kant's Theory of Biology*, Ina Goy and Eric Watkins, eds. (Berlin: De Gruyter, 2014), 200.

taking on our ends in this latter judgment, we nevertheless learn how nature is not indifferent to, but rather for, our moral vocation. Once mere mechanism becomes circumscribed by teleology in organicity, the entire domain of nature can be seen to be circumscribed by freedom.

This chapter will unfold in four sections. Section 6.1 treats one of the key motivations for Kant's turn to teleology, namely the problem of contingency. Here, I take up how contingency is principally an issue of meaning, even though it also has bearing scientifically. In Section 6.2, I turn to Kant's justification of the use of the principle of teleology in nature. It is our encounters with organisms – living beings – out in the territory that will justify our use of it. Once we are justified in reflectively employing the principle of teleology, as Section 6.3 outlines, we are ineluctably led to think the entire system of nature in accord with ends. This leads to positing the human being, who is the only being who sets ends from itself, as the final end of nature. As the final end of nature, Kant argues, nature serves the human being by preparing us for moral life through effacing its own influence over us. Kant names this movement of the self-effacement of nature: culture. Lastly, in Section 6.4, I turn to Kant's account of the sublime. The sublime, like culture, also embodies a moment in the text where we find that rather than belonging to a larger context of nature, the natural order discharges us from itself.

6.1 Contingency

The Critique of Teleological Judgment announces itself as investigating the *objective* purposiveness of nature, of which there are two kinds: Objects may be purposive in themselves with regard to their own internal end (perfection) or with regard to their usefulness for another, external thing (utility) (KU §61). Kant introduces purposiveness in general explicitly with reference to the problem of *contingency*. The Critique of Aesthetic Judgment may be seen to address the apparent contingency of an accord between objects in the world and the faculties of human knowing through subjective purposiveness. The Critique of Teleological Judgment, by contrast, is focused on the contingency of natural forms and natural laws. The question of this section will be keyed not to the suitability of the natural order for human beings, but rather its intelligibility and orderedness.

Kant is driven by a concern for contingency at least in part because of the link between intelligibility and meaningfulness. His interest in contingency, as Zuckert emphasizes, is about the conditions that must be met for human beings to have unified experience at all – for things to make sense to us they themselves cannot be contingent.² Philosophers have long associated order, necessity in being, and goodness. This thinking begins even in Parmenides, for whom *what is* is all that there is; *what is* is necessarily, and *what is* is perfect in its completeness and orderliness. *What is not* is forbidden even to be thought.³ And what looks to us as contingent – such as change or flux – must be understood still as necessary, even if it is beyond our capacities to grasp how. The basic argument philosophers have articulated is that the meaningfulness of things depends on there being *reason* in them. The reason in things must take shape as an order, and too, as necessity. The very definition of chance or contingency is that there is no reason in it; a lack of intelligibility, then, is consanguine with meaninglessness. Philippe Huneman suggests a simple and straightforward understanding: "What is contingency? It is the possibility of not being, or of being different."⁴ In his essay "The Abyss of Contingency," Barry Allen traces the historical and perennial philosophical concern with contingency that informs Kant's own approach and emphasizes the centrality of meaning for the question. While for the Ancients that which *is* has always been, and is thus necessary and good in itself, the Medievals developed a notion of God on which the world's contingency is necessarily founded: God is a necessary being, and thus grants goodness to the world he creates. Allen turns to Hans Blumenberg's observation that once the Moderns had jettisoned God's role in obviating the radical contingency of existence, "[t]he world itself had to become the necessary being."⁵ What would it be if the world and things in it were all subject to blind chance, if the world and things in it were merely accidental? Kant's concern in the Critique of Teleological Judgment is principally about the possibility of scientific inquiry and the intelligibility of the natural order. But, as we will see, he also continually refers the problem of contingency or order back to one of the meaningfulness of things. This should be no surprise, as Kant, like those before him, holds that without order and ultimately

---

² Zuckert, *Kant on Beauty and Biology*, 31ff.
³ This same sentiment is strong in Plato, and comes out forcefully in his various myths of creation, for example, in the *Timaeus* and the *Statesman*. Indeed, even the noble lie in the Republic – which tells citizens that their childhood never happened, and they were therefore never in a state of becoming – is aimed at this Parmenidean ideal.
⁴ Huneman, "Purposiveness, Necessity, and Contingency," 199.
⁵ Hans Blumenberg, "Self-Preservation and Intertia: On the Constitution of Modern Rationality," *Contemporary German Philosophy* 3 (1983), 218; cited in Barry Allen, "The Abyss of Contingency: Purposiveness and Contingency in Kant and Darwin," *History of Philosophy Quarterly* 20:4 (2003), 373.

purpose, the world and human life are without meaning – they are merely "playthings."⁶

As we may recall, contingency was announced in the Introduction to the third *Critique* as one of its principal themes and was there contrasted with the idea of an ordered whole (KU 5:183–4). In the Critique of Teleological Judgment, Kant develops how he thinks about laws of nature and contingency; as we have already established necessity as constitutive of the laws of nature in the first *Critique*, readers may wonder what the issue is. Kant is explicit that even as laws of nature – that is, those given by the understanding – may hold necessarily, we still find contingency in the appearance of things:

> For if one adduces, e.g., the structure of a bird, the hollowness of its bones, the placement of its wings for movement and of its tail for steering, etc., one says that given the mere *nexus effectivus* in nature, without the help of a special kind of causality, namely that of ends (*nexus finalis*), this is all in the highest degree contingent: i.e., that nature, considered as mere mechanism, could have formed itself in a thousand different ways without hitting precisely upon the unity in accordance with such a rule. (KU 5:360)

Kant's point here is that we may be able to construct through mechanistic laws of nature how bones come to be hollow and how wings are able to lift a bird into the air. We can trace what kinds of things cause other things such that hollow bones become lightweight or wings give flight. But this does not account for *why* hollow bones or wings have come to be in the first place; their *existence* is contingent, even if the laws by which each one exists have necessity in their causal efficacy. The laws of aerodynamics make it necessary that pressure differentials will put something into flight. Nature could, however, through myriad possibilities of mechanistic laws, have caused one thousand other things to come to be instead of birds with hollow bones and wings. From this perspective, then, the existence of hollow bones is contingent, even if the cause and effect in the laws that gave rise to them is characterized by necessity.⁷ In the first *Critique*, Kant defines something as contingent if *we can think its nonexistence or its being*

---

⁶ In the *Idea for Universal History*, Kant argues that if human beings' capacities are not to be fully developed, they are "purposeless and wasted," meaning that nature is indulging in "childish play" (IaG). Oliver Sensen argues, "without freedom one would be a mere plaything of nature, or the means to someone else's end." Sensen, "Dignity and the Formula of Humanity," *Kant's Groundwork for the Metaphysics of Morals: A Critical Guide*, Jens Timmermann, ed. (Cambridge: Cambridge University Press, 2009), 111. The basic idea is the same: Without purpose and necessity, things would be meaningless and mere play.

⁷ It may even be too much to say all of this for Kant. Articulating the problem this way, however, allows the problem of the contingent to come out more fully.

otherwise without contradiction. The contingent still has a cause; it is not a kind of miracle. What is at stake in the contingent is whether it could have been otherwise or not at all (KrV B289ff). Here, Kant follows Leibniz, for whom facts – the way things are – are contingent. By contrast: "Truths of reasoning are necessary, and their opposite is impossible."[8] If it is merely *possible* something could have been otherwise or not have been, it is not necessary.

Further, the relation of bones to feathers and the overall functioning of the bird remains unaccounted for from the standpoint of *explanation*. Dalia Nassar argues that this aspect of contingency is a problem of underdetermination, and gets at the problem this way: "Contingency implies that there is no *a priori* legislation provided by the understanding to determine how we must judge a bird's structure."[9] Mechanism gives no place to begin our investigation of a bird. This is a basic problem of interpretation and understanding – we must have some sense of the whole of the thing in order to get at any of its parts. Mechanism is inherently limited with respect to orientation in inquiry. Even if it can to a certain extent retrospectively give a minimal causal explanation of aspects of a bird, it gives no context for getting off of the ground with questions to ask. Mechanism, it turns out, is severely curtailed in the explanatory power it can bring to bear on living beings. It is worth noting here that what may be meant by "mechanical inexplicability" is debated amongst scholars. Most notably, we find Peter McLaughlin's *Kant's Critique of Teleology in Biological Explanation*, who rejected the notion that the issue was one of causality. Hannah Ginsborg also treats the issue at length, and more recently Andrea Breitenbach has taken up the question.[10] While what exactly the failure is is less relevant for my argument than the turn it precipitates in the text, I describe the problem as one of mechanistic causality largely because, as we shall see in what follows, this is how

---

[8] Gottfried Leibniz, *Monadology*, in *Philosophical Texts* (Oxford: Oxford University Press, 1998), 272. Kant is explicit in his endorsement of the Leibniz's principle of sufficient reason that underlies this distinction, and even argues that Leibniz could only have understood it subjectively as he does, and not objectively (ÜE 8:248).

[9] Dalia Nassar, "Analogical reflection as a source for the science of life: Kant and the possibility of the biological sciences," *Studies in History and Philosophy of Science* 58 (2016), 61.

[10] Peter McLaughlin, *Kant's Critique of Teleology in Biological Explanation* (Lewiston, NY: Edwin Mellen Press, 1990); Hannah Ginsborg, "Two Kinds of Mechanical Inexplicability in Kant and Aristotle," in *The Normativity of Nature* (Oxford: Oxford University Press, 2015), 281–315; Andrea Breitenbach, "Two Views on Nature: A Solution to the Kant's Antinomy of Mechanism and Teleology," *British Journal for the History of Philosophy* 16:2 (2008), 351–369.

The Domain of Nature as System: Ends 163

Kant himself addresses it when he names the measure for the use of teleology in judging organisms.

The problem of contingency continues further up the levels of our comprehension of nature. Mechanism not only fails to account for the forms of individual things but also leaves us with contingency with respect to empirical laws. Our understanding is capable of determining particular laws of nature. Each law, however, is contingent – why there are these particular laws of nature is not explainable by mere mechanism. We are left, on this front, with a hodgepodge of empirical laws of nature, rather than a system of interrelated laws. Kant writes that

> we must think of there being in nature, with regard to its merely empirical laws, a possibility of infinitely manifold empirical laws, which as far as our insight goes are nevertheless contingent (cannot be cognized *a priori*); and with regard to them we judge the unity of nature in accordance with empirical laws and the possibility of the unity of experience ... as contingent. (KU 5:180)

The issue of contingency is thus not only about a thoroughly systematic scientific understanding of nature but also about how we have our own experience. If the things we encounter in experience are all taken by us merely to be contingent, our experience will lack any kind of interconnectedness:

> [S]ince such a unity must still necessarily be presupposed and assumed, for otherwise no thoroughgoing interconnection of empirical cognitions into a whole of experience would take place ... the power of judgment must thus assume it as an a priori principle for its own use that what is contingent for human insight into the particular (empirical) laws of nature nevertheless contains a lawful unity, not fathomable by us but still thinkable, in the combination of its manifold into one experience possible in itself. (KU 5:183)

Contingency in empirical laws means there is no coherent whole to which we can refer our individual experiences. Our lives would be constituted by one thing after another – indeed, with one thing causing what is next – with no broader principle of unity to make sense of things or how they are related to other things. Things would appear to us to happen as if by chance; indeed, they would thus be, for us, "confused." If we are unable to discover in the diversity of natural laws "an order that we can grasp," we cannot then have an "interconnected experience" (KU 5:185). It is teleology that allows us to make sense of how individual living beings come to be as well as a possible systematic relation among laws.

Indeed, the problem of contingency as Kant addresses it is centrally a problem born of an emphasis on *relation*. As Gottfried Martin points out, for the Ancient Greeks, "natural science treats of the essence and the essential qualities of living things." For modern, Newtonian science, by contrast, "Nature itself is nothing whatever but a totality of relations."[11] Then, once cognizable relations of necessity are limited to those of mere cause and effect, too, much of what we find in nature will come to appear as accident or coincidence. The bare fact of things as they are – indeed, *that* they are – is, in a way, more apparent in the context of modernity. There is no underlying sense that things are the work of God, and thus their appearance, even if determined through natural necessity and mechanism, is mere chance. In the modern frame, the existence of things – why they exist and what their purpose is – is in question.

The problem of contingency in Kant, then, is a particularly modern iteration of the Ancient, indeed, perennial issue of intelligibility and with this, meaning. It takes shape in Kant, principally, as a problem of how things are related to each other and, crucially, to an organized whole. As we have already seen in the Introduction, Kant explicitly argues that each thing is intelligible only insofar as we can situate it in the context of a larger whole and thereby also in relation to the other parts of that whole. It is because mechanism is insufficient with respect to this task of ultimate intelligibility that Kant turns to teleology.

6.2 Justifying Teleology: Organicity and Natural Ends

While the human being may have both a theoretical as well as practical need for there to be reason and ordered purpose in things, this need does not itself justify the use of teleology with respect to our investigation of nature. This portion of Kant's text will first, then, seek out a justification for the use of teleology, and only then return to investigate nature with principle in hand. The movement of the argument will thus be an initial denial of the justificatory power of invoking the principle of purposiveness in a system of nature. The principle can only be justified when we find no other means of conceiving something we encounter in nature, which happens in organisms. Now justified, we can then turn to nature as a system of ends.

---

[11] Gottfried Martin, *Kant's Metaphysics and Theory of Science* (Manchester: Manchester University Press, 1955), 91.

Kant begins examining the different kinds of purposiveness we may attribute to nature in an effort to discern which, if any, may justify the use of teleology in judgment. The measure of justification is whether or not something may be conceived as possible only as the product of a concept (KU 5:370). He begins his discussion with reference to geometric figures. While he observes that we are able to comprehend "many rules resulting from the construction of" these figures, and that these rules are useful to us for a host of things, this does not mean that such an end is therefore the ground of these rules or of the figures themselves (KU 5:364). Simply because something useful emerges from geometric figures does not mean that such usefulness is a *ground* of their existence. As James Kreines puts the objection, we have "no reason to doubt that the benefit itself is just an accidental consequent of non-teleological causes."[12] Kant will draw a similar conclusion in §63, when he turns to what he calls *relative or external purposiveness*. He begins by noting that "[e]xperience leads our power of judgment to the concept of objective and material purposiveness, i.e., to the concept of an end of nature, only if there is a relation of the cause to the effect to be judged" (KU 5:366). One way we may come to judge this is if we regard something "as an end or as a means of the purposive use of other causes" (KU 5:367). Kant names this a *relative* purposiveness because things are conceived as purposes only *in relation to* other things for which they are useful. As his example he describes the silt left by rivers, which makes land fertile for human agricultural endeavors. In the same way, grass appears to be advantageous for the animals that eat it: horses, cattle, and so forth. Kant makes two points with respect to this purposiveness, though. First, it is not a purposiveness of the things themselves, as the purpose is found in other, external things. That is, the usefulness of grass to horses is not a *cause* of grass. Second, if we conceive of the system of nature as a connection of usefulness, there would then need to be some necessary end that caps the chain of interconnection for the entire chain to be thought under these auspices. That is, only if the final end of the advantageous relations is itself a necessary end may we judge the whole set of things to be necessarily arranged the way it is. As the final end of nature's advantageous would be the human being, then only if there is necessity to our existence on the earth are we justified in judging the whole chain as being in accord with natural ends. But, he argues, there is no reason to think that "human beings have to live on the earth," and so "it

---

[12] James Kreines, "The Inexplicability of Kant's *Naturzweck*: Kant on Teleology, Explanation, and Biology," *Archiv fur Geschichte der Philosophie* 87 (2005), 278–279.

follows that relative purposiveness, although it gives hypothetical indications of natural ends, nevertheless justifies no absolute teleological judgments" (KU 5:369). As we shall see later, however, while relative purposiveness may not *justify* the use of teleology, once it is justified, we will return to what it may mean reflectively to contemplate nature as just such a system of means and ends.

Organisms, however, do justify our use of the principle of teleology with respect to nature. Kant sets out the criterion of justification for the use of the principle:

> In order to see that a thing is possible only as an end, i.e., that the causality of its origin must be sought not in the mechanism of nature, but in a cause whose productive capacity is determined by concepts, it is necessary that its form not be possible in accordance with mere natural laws, i.e., ones that can be cognized by us through the understanding, applied to objects of the senses, alone; rather even empirical cognition of their cause and effect presupposes concepts of reason. (KU 5:370)

When we are confronted with an object whose form is not able to be understood by us by way of mechanistic laws of cause and effect, we are led to take the coming into being of that form to be akin to a product of a will, that is, in accord with ends. The use of teleology as a principle is given when we can only conceive of something as being produced in accord with concepts, for the sake of some end. When we encounter living beings, we can only make sense of them by way of their teleological arrangement, their internal purposiveness. While products of art – that is, human artifacts – are quite easily conceived in accord with ends, products of nature are more complicated, as we cannot attribute a will to nature or its forms. This presents a "contradiction" that leads Kant to develop his notion of the objective purposiveness of organisms as *natural ends* (KU 5:370).

Kant takes pains in the next few sections of the text to lay out how a living being is only thought as possible in accord with concepts. He names this a *natural end*: A thing is purposive in its form, based on a concept of what it is, but without a will that arranges it thus. For us to think an object teleologically, we must conceive of it as **"cause and effect of itself"** (KU 5:371). As we do not attribute a will to nature, a natural end must be *the cause of itself* with respect to its form; its form is the effect of its own purposiveness and activity in accord with its end. Nature manifests things as causes and effects of themselves with respect to three kinds of generation: as a species, as individuals, and the parts of a creature.

Kant names a natural end an organized being (*organisirte Wesen*). More specifically, this means it is *reciprocally self-organizing*. For a thing to be self-organizing means that it alone is the cause of the relation of its parts to each other and to the whole of what it is. Reciprocity is the key causal concept Kant attributes to this activity of the organization of parts and whole. This is because "for a thing as a natural end it is requisite, first, that its parts ... are possible only in relation to the whole" (KU 5:373). A work of art – which is caused by something external to it – need not embody reciprocity in all of its parts. In human artifacts, the idea of the whole is able to bring all parts into proper relation through the activity of the will, which represents the idea of the whole to itself throughout the generation of the thing. When one produces a painting, for example, the idea of the finished product functions as an *archē* that determines each step of the process. The canvas does not stand in a reciprocally causal relation to the frame, though they are both a part of the whole. When something is a product of a will that stands outside of that thing, the parts are brought together piecemeal – with reference to the whole, but not in a mutually dependent way. Each part of the work of art depends only on the will of the artist. A natural end, by contrast, does not have an external will that combines the parts into a whole. The combination must be thought to be accomplished internal to the thing, and thus we conceive of its parts as reciprocally causal. In this, the whole is internal to each of the parts, and the parts are necessarily related to each other. Kant goes so far as to argue that "its parts reciprocally produce each other," and that "each part is conceived as if it exists only **through** all the others, thus as if existing **for the sake of the others** and on **account of** the whole, i.e., as an instrument (organ) ... that **produces** the other parts" (KU 5:373–4).

In an organism, such reciprocity defines the causal nexus by which the thing comes to be, and also persists in being. In this, in an organism, each part is constitutive of the thing in a distinct way, and is, in turn, constituted by being part of the whole. Because organisms have the capacity within themselves reciprocally to produce their own parts, they have the potential for healing and regeneration. Each part also then can influence and affect the others – the thoroughgoing relation of causality means also that the parts depend on each other absolutely. If one part fails, the other parts inevitably suffer, as does the whole. Kant contrasts this with a watch, which, when broken, requires an external will for its repair. Inversely – following Aristotle – Kant notes that a part separated from its larger organic whole is no longer genuinely what it is. Aristotle will argue that a hand cut off from the body is a hand merely homonymously – in name only. While it retains the look or shape of a hand, it performs no "handy" functions and is, in fact, no longer alive.

In individual living beings, Kant argues that mechanism thus fails to account for the form of the thing. The form can only be made sense of, Kant argues, by way of teleology. The being and functioning of an organism, he asserts, is clearly guided by a concept of the whole; and, too, as we are dealing with products of nature and not of a will, the parts must stand in relation to this whole in a causal relation of reciprocity. *It is the existence of living beings, then, that ultimately leads us to the question of the purpose or meaningfulness of things as a whole.*

Kant acknowledges that while organisms justify the use of the principle of teleology, we are unable to delineate this causality further. That is, we do not really comprehend how it works. At first reading, we may be tempted to think that Kant has revoked his prohibition on the possibility of thinking *life*, as we discussed in Chapter 3. On the contrary, Kant here directly grapples with the utter inaccessibility of the arrangement of nature to the human intellect. What he has described for us functions more akin to a distant horizon that allows closer things to come into relief; when we focus on that horizon, however, we discern nothing but an indistinguishable haze. He writes:

> An organized being is thus not a mere machine, for that has only **motive** power, while the organized being possesses in itself a **formative** power, and indeed one that it communicates to the matter, which does not have it (it organizes the latter): thus it has a self-propagating formative power, which cannot be explained through the capacity for movement alone (that is, mechanism) ... Perhaps one comes closer to this inscrutable property if one calls it an **analogue of life**: but then must either endow matter as mere matter with a property (hylozoism) that contradicts its essence, or else associate with it an alien principle standing in communion with it (a soul) ... Strictly speaking, the organization of nature is therefore not analogous with any causality that we know. (KU 5:374–5)

Kant first designates the force of organization as a formative power (*Bildungskraft*). This is simply the power to give form to the thing – to provide the material, modify it, and put it in its proper place (KU 5:377). But how this power comes into contact with and actually does the work of forming the material into its parts remains a mystery. Kant rejects the possibility that the matter itself has such force, or that living beings have independently existing souls. We are left with the claim that such force is "inscrutable" [*unerforsichlichen*]; we are not even able to inquire after it, as it exceeds our capacities for understanding. While we are justified in employing the principle of teleology reflectively and as guidance for mechanistic inquiry, Kant has not gone back on his disavowal of the possibility of life sciences altogether.

In the end, the sections devoted to proper scientific methodology in the Critique of Teleological Judgment are few, relative to the other concerns Kant addresses in this section of the text. After justifying the use of the principle of teleology, Kant takes pains to establish the limits of its use and its authority. Its use in scientific inquiry will be at once constrained and necessary.

As a principle of reflection, Kant reminds us that the purposiveness we find in nature is not constitutive of it. We cannot lay claim to *knowing* that objects we judge as natural ends are actually constituted by internal purposiveness. That is, while we find we are required to think of organisms this way, we are prohibited from attributing their existence to this form of causality in themselves. So, while "the power of judgment, as a reflecting ... power of judgment, is forced to think of another principle than that of the mechanism of nature as the ground of the possibility of certain forms in nature" it must remain a mere "guideline" or heuristic (KU 5:388;389).

The principle of purposiveness is necessary, however, for orienting mechanistic investigation. That is, it is not simply the case that we are led to think organisms purposively. In order for mechanistic inquiry to proceed, science requires the context of organicity in order even to know what to ask. Teleology is "a heuristic principle for researching the particular laws of nature"; the explanation we seek by way of mechanism must be subordinated to it. This is to say that our aerodynamic account of the lift of a bird's wing is only possible if we grasp its purpose and place in a larger organism – it is for flying and stands in a reciprocal relation with the weight of the bird's bones, for example. Kant's concept of a *Naturzweck* is such that any part of a thing may only be grasped in virtue of its relation to other parts and to the whole. His claim about the subordination of mechanistic investigation to organicity means that the mechanistic accounts of each part, or of a relation between parts, is given context and orientation by the teleological understanding of the organism. Kant writes:

> If, therefore, the investigator of nature is not to work entirely in vain, he must, in the judging of things whose concept as natural ends is indubitably established (organized beings), always base them on some original organization, which uses that mechanism itself in order to produce other organized forms or develop its own into new configurations. (KU 5:418)

Kant's suggestion is that mechanism is used in the service of producing organisms; to investigate a living being mechanistically, then, is to discern how mechanism may effect organic arrangements.[13]

6.3 From Science to Culture

Insofar as we must couch mechanistic inquiry within purposiveness, we see one of the most significant insights Kant offers about the pursuit of proper science in the Critique of Teleological Judgment. If proper science is understood by Kant as mechanism, what emerges in this part of the text is just how limited that is. On its own, mechanism cannot reveal much about the natural order. Mechanism does not yield necessity – it cannot answer why anything exists. It also cannot even begin to investigate many things without orientation from reflection first. Even science, then, is properly pursued only under the auspices of a larger context of meaning, or, purpose. That purpose is given, first, in an organized being, a *living* being.

That scientific inquiry is properly pursued by us within a larger context of meaning comes out most fully when Kant turns from individual living beings to the system of nature. Indeed, part of Kant's dismissal of external purposiveness as justificatory for the principle of teleology is what would be required to take the entire system of relations as necessary. For each thing in a chain of usefulness to be necessarily purposive and not contingently so, there must be a "cognition of the final end (*scopus*) of nature, which requires the relation of nature to something supersensible . . . for the end of the existence of nature itself must be beyond nature" (KU 5:378). Put simply, Kant is here arguing that for the entire system of nature to embody purposiveness among its constituent parts, we must be able to able to answer the question: why is there something rather than nothing? Nature's ultimate justification for its existence – that is, nature's purpose – cannot be found in nature itself. We must look elsewhere, to the supersensible even, for an ultimate purpose to nature's existence. Nature must have some higher meaning for us to understand its parts as purposively related.[14]

---

[13] There are numerous puzzles a close reading of Kant on mechanism and teleology will yield. Two authors who have treated these issues with a careful eye, in addition to others cited here, are Breitenbach and Ginsborg. See especially Breitenbach's, "Two Views on Nature: A Solution to the Kant's Antinomy of Mechanism and Teleology," and Ginsborg, chapters 11–13 in *The Normativity of Nature*.

[14] I treat this more extensively in Chapter 7.

While the usefulness of one thing for another – external purposiveness – cannot justify the use of the principle of teleology, once it is justified in organicity, we can return to nature as a system with it in hand. Indeed, Kant's argument is quite forceful: "[T]his concept [of a natural end] necessarily leads to the idea of the whole of nature as a system in accordance with the rule of ends" (KU 5:379). We make this leap, Kant holds, precisely because the introduction of purposiveness as a legitimate mode of making sense of things leads us to the very idea of the supersensible that is denied in his initial discussion of system. His claim is limited – there is no proof of God here – but significant. We are led to the ground of an organic structure as "beyond the sensible world" (KU 5:381). There is no positive claim about what the supersensible might be, only that there appears to be such a thing beyond what shows up sensibly. Nevertheless, once we accept purposiveness as a reflectively valid principle for individual living beings, we must also accept the reflective introduction of purposiveness as well as the supersensible into the system of nature. We are led to think nature as purposeful when we encounter life – that is, living beings. Once we have accepted living beings, we are ineluctably led to think the whole of nature in a radical new way.

The move that Kant makes here – from organisms to the system of nature – is one that he deems as "necessary." Eric Watkins focuses on this passage to suggest that what makes this necessary is the movement of reason toward the unconditioned.[15] But Kant seems to suggest more than the need of reason as cause for the movement. While Kant does go on in the next few lines to note the subjective principle of reason that nature does nothing in vain, he qualifies this idea as "only subjective." An organism is "an example" of a natural end; it is this, he writes, that "[calls] upon" us to "expect" that nature as a whole is organized purposively. So, it seems that the actual existence of teleological beings demands that we turn to ends in nature more broadly. Once nature appears as purposive, we necessarily seek this purposiveness more broadly in it. It is not born of a merely subjective need of reason.

Kant's basic idea here is that when we stand out in the territory and take the domain of nature as an object for us, we are inevitably led to think of it purposively. When we take the whole of nature, we find that much in the natural order can only be explained purposively, and we must therefore appeal to principles other than mechanism to offer a full accounting. The

---

[15] Eric Watkins, "Nature in General as a System of Ends," in *Kant's Theory of Biology*, Ina Goy and Eric Watkins, eds. (Berlin: de Gruyter, 2014), 117–130.

turning point in our reflection is living beings, organisms, which suggest to us the question of the purpose and then meaningfulness of nature. Why do living beings exist? With this question in hand, we will reflect on the system of nature in a dramatically different way. As we shall see, our perspective out in the territory, which is not bound by but is searching for rules for what is given, leads us to take the whole of nature not merely as purposive, but as purposive for human life. In the territory, our intellectual freedom to find new rules leads us to rethink the sphere of nature and also to bring the two domains into relation in a new way as we seek to answer the question of why living beings exist.

When we take nature to be a teleological system, we are interested in the external relations between things. The principal question we ask in this context is: Why does this thing exist? This is what distinguishes reflective inquiry from mechanistic inquiry. But this inquiry presents its own limitations. Kant lays out the thinking involved. "If one looks at the vegetable kingdom ... [we are led] to the question: Why do these creatures exist? If one answers, for the animal kingdom ... " (KU 5:426). But we are then led to ask why herbivorous creatures exist, if not for the sake of feeding the carnivorous ones. And again, what are these good for? Any inquiry about what things in nature are good for, Kant seems to think, will lead us ultimately to: "for the human being."

Kant names the human being the ultimate or last end [*letzte Zweck*] of the chain of ends. Without such an end, the plethora of means/ends relations we may find in nature would remain a cacophony of relations, going in all sorts of directions; it would be, to borrow a phrase from Pablo Muchnik, a "jungle of means."[16] The chain of ends must be closed in order for it truly to become a system; the whole thus needs its own end or purpose. For the final end to function as genuinely final, however, this end can have no further end outside of it. It must be an end in and of itself, or, it again becomes one more link in the chain of an open system. Human beings are what can provide such an end, and thus orient and give purpose to the whole. We are "the only being on earth who forms a concept of ends for" ourselves (KU 5:427). Because our existence is an end in and of itself, we are not means to any ends other than our own. Kant thus names us the "ultimate end of nature here on earth," and argues that we may reflectively judge that it is in relation to us that "all other natural things constitute a

---

[16] Muchnik uses this phrase in contrast with the kingdom of ends in his book on Kant's moral philosophy, *Kant's Theory of Evil: An Essay on the Dangers of Self-Love and Aprioricity of History* (New York: Lexington Books, 2008), 48–220.

system of ends" (KU 5:429). So, while Kant denies that our existence justifies the use of teleology, once the principle is justified through the existence of living beings, we are once again returned (albeit reflectively) to the end of nature. Nature, then, is arranged as a system of ends for us.

There are two ways Kant suggests that nature, as a system, may work as a means for us. The first way in which human beings possibly provide an end that organizes nature is through happiness. This is "the kind of end that can be satisfied by the beneficence of nature itself" (KU 5:430). Happiness is the natural end of the human being, comprised of the satisfaction of our natural inclinations and desires. Yet Kant denies that human happiness is a genuine end for nature, on three counts. First, Kant argues that the possibility of actual satisfaction of our desires seems impossible; it does not seem to be in the nature of desire ever to be fully met. Second, even if inclinations and desire did not proliferate indefinitely, our own observation of nature demonstrates that nature is indifferent to our happiness: "[I]t is so far from being the case that nature has made the human being its special favorite ... that it has rather spared him just as little as any other animal from its destructive effects, whether of pestilence, hunger, danger of flood" and so on (KU 5:430). Third, our own natural predispositions incline us, as a species, to our own wars and plagues, thereby denying happiness to ourselves. Happiness, then, is not a legitimate end of nature, and thus nothing more than a mere "link in the chain" of mechanism on this score.

While happiness cannot serve as the ultimate or last end of nature's chain of ends, Kant argues that nature does have a role to play with respect to our moral vocation. The human being, in virtue of our end setting capacity, exists as a final end, that is, an end in and of ourselves. It is with respect to this final end that we may serve as an ultimate or last end in nature's system. Our final end, of course, is the realization of our freedom in autonomous action, that is, acting in accord with the moral law. As it is completely up to us and our own freedom whether or not we realize the demand to act from duty in accord with what reason demands, we may ask what, exactly, nature may do on this front: "In order, however, to discover where in the human being we are at least to posit that ultimate end of nature, we must seek out that which nature is capable of doing in order to prepare him for what he must himself do in order to be a final end" (KU 5:431).

Culture is Kant's name for what nature can do for the human being as preparation for our moral vocation. Kant here does not have in mind our contemporary use of the term, which designates a collection of life ways, traditions, and mores of a group of people.[17] Rather, culture for Kant is a process of enculturation, becoming cultured. We can think of the agricultural or botanical use of the term, wherein we cultivate or culture a plant through pruning, feeding, watering, selecting, and so forth. Culture, for Kant, is a process or movement. Specifically, Kant defines it thus: "[T]he production of the aptitude of a rational being for any ends in general (thus those of his freedom) is **culture**" (KU 5:431). The ultimate aim of nature, then, is human enculturation, the process by which human beings become cultured. This process, moreover, is itself oriented by an aptitude for setting ends in general. Nature, then, can culture us for the sake of our ability to set and pursue ends.

How, though, does nature aim at preparing human beings to set ends? It accomplishes this through two aspects of culture: skill and discipline. Skill cultivates an "aptitude for the promotion of ends in general"; discipline, by contrast, is superior, in that it promotes "the **will** in the determination and choice of its ends" (KU 5:432). Skill, for Kant, helps to cultivate civil society, which, following Rousseau, has to do with our outward comportment toward each other. Skill is cultivated, Kant argues, in the face of inequality. Inequality runs in tandem with the pursuit of luxury, which are the sources, Kant thinks, of progress in the culture of skill. The pursuit of luxury and its twin of oppression, produce "violence … from without [and …] dissatisfaction from within" (KU 5:432). The gap between rich and poor results in violence between them: resistance to oppression and violent subordination. The gap and its resultant strife also produce inner dissatisfaction for everyone. Kant then claims that this "splendid misery" is precisely the means that nature uses to encourage us to develop new skills in living together. The violence and dissatisfaction will ultimately, he seems to think, lead us to new and better arrangements of shared life. We will seek new modes of production to meet our needs – both basic and luxurious – and will develop new forms of interaction with others that preserve peace, including the establishment of lawful relations.[18] Nature contributes to ordering our external relations with others in virtue of

---

[17] This understanding of culture comes down to us through the academic discipline of Anthropology, which was founded in part by Kant's student Herder, with whom he had stark disagreements about these matters. See John Zammito, *Kant, Herder, and the Birth of Anthropology* (Chicago, IL: University of Chicago Press, 2002), 576.

[18] I examine what this looks like from the perspective of Kant's practical philosophy in my essay, "What is Philosophical about Kant's Anthropology," *International Journal of Philosophical Studies* 25:3 (2017), 109–118.

planting in us desires for luxury and subjugation – they lead, in a kind of dialectical reversal,[19] to skills that undo the effects of these very desires.

The more important aspect of culture that Kant argues for is that of discipline. While skill, as a capacity to effect things in the world, orders our external relations, discipline works on us internally, that is, on our will. While a lawful society may be possible for a "race of devils," moral goodness requires that our moral disposition – our inner freedom – be proper. Kant also names the culture of discipline "training" [*Zucht*; literally, breeding]. The aim of nature is to liberate us from nature itself: "[T]he culture of training (discipline) is negative and consists in the liberation of the will from the despotism of desires" (KU 5:432). This despotism of desires is nothing other than the myriad natural inclinations to which we are subject as a part of the natural order. While Kant is clear that these desires are, in themselves, a good – that is, they are not the source of evil in us – they do pose a counterweight to the demands of reason in us. Kant describes these desires as a "tyranny of sensible tendencies" (KU 5:433).

Kant argues that culture can "reduce" the influence our natural desires have over us. He does not lay out systematically the process by which this is effected, however, so to get a sense for this movement, we must turn to some other texts.[20] Kant's idea of culture as a kind of self-effacement of nature's influence over us is linked with his notion of unsocial sociability. In the Fourth Proposition of the Universal History essay, Kant describes the "first true steps from crudity toward culture" (IaG 8:21). On the one hand, human beings have an inclination to be social; on the other, to "individualize" and isolate ourselves. This propensity to isolate ourselves is nothing other, he argues, than a desire to have things go our own way. The combination of unsociability and sociability leads us to feel resistance. In society, we cannot make things go our own way:

> Now it is this resistance that awakens all the powers of the human, brings him to overcome his propensity to indolence, and, driven by ambition, tyranny, and greed, to obtain for himself a rank among his fellows, whom he cannot *stand*, but also cannot *leave alone*. (IaG 8:21)

---

[19] Yirmiahu Yovel refers to this movement as nature's "dialectical self-overcoming," which brings Kant closer to his heirs in the nineteenth century. Yovel, *Kant the Philosophy of History* (Princeton, NJ: Princeton University Press, 1980), 181.
[20] For a longer account of Kant on the culture of discipline, see my "Kant and the Culture of Discipline: Rethinking the Nature of Nature," *Epoché: A Journal for the History of Philosophy* 15:1 (2010), 121–138.

Kant's implication is that our ambition – our desire to do better than and to have more than our peers – wakes us up. The idea is that while we may begin with a multitude of disordered and wild desires, our ambition will lead us to focus on pruning these desires down in order to succeed and elevate ourselves above others. Thus, a desire to excel over others will lead us to discipline ourselves in school or on the basketball court. This discipline, though, is a training of our wills that lessens the overall influence of natural desires and inclinations on us. Nature, in "willing discord" actually promotes our moral well-being (IaG 8:21). While the disciplining of our inclinations to lessen their influence over us is not enough to ensure moral goodness, it can, Kant argues, be preparatory. Once the tyranny of desires is tamed, we become open to the higher call of the demand of reason. It can "prepare humans for a sovereignty in which reason alone shall have power ... and thus allows us to feel an aptitude for higher ends" (KU 5:433–4).

Nature, through the cultures of skill and discipline, works on our wills. It aids us in the capacity to set and pursue ends in general (skill), and effaces its own influence over us through cultivation. In this, nature actually works to discharge us from participation in the natural order. As the ultimate or last end in the chain of nature, nature works to release us from her influence. This preparation for autonomous, moral willing cannot be accomplished by nature; reason alone may achieve this end. But nature stands in our way insofar as we are inextricably bound to our inclinations and desires. What nature can do, however, is temper its own influence over us, thus readying us to receive the call of reason.

The movement of the Critique of Teleological Judgment, then, is from the organism to the moral life of human beings. Living beings establish the legitimate use of the principle of teleology, thus speaking to the interests of hope for a nature that is not merely mechanistic. From here, we are led reflectively to judge that nature as a whole is for us – it promotes our moral well-being, lending even further buttressing to the hope we have that we may be able to realize the ends of freedom. We thus reconceive of nature as a system that is oriented by us, by human freedom, and our capacity to set ends in accord with the demands of the moral law. Kant's argument is, for all this, quite remarkable. When we encounter organisms out in the territory, we are given to judge that the whole of nature has human beings as its end. And, too, the way that nature is for us is precisely to discharge us from its order.

6.4 The Sublime

Kant's account of the dialectical movement of nature with respect to our moral vocation in culture is also found in his account of the sublime. While it may seem out of place to treat the sublime in the part of this book dedicated to the Critique of Teleological Judgment, I maintain that it is more closely aligned with the arguments of this text relative to those of the aesthetic.[21] This is not to dispute the placement of the Analytic of the Sublime in the text. Indeed, it is without question an issue of reflective judgment based in the aesthetic, and also embodies a subjective purposiveness. But, the beautiful, I have maintained, is what, for Kant, reminds us that we belong to a broader context of nature. Culture, and also the sublime, remind us that we do not belong to nature in a very important regard: its influence over our inner selves. And, like culture, nature here is reflectively judged as initiating a process by which we are discharged from its chain of effects. And, unlike the beautiful, which may include human-produced artworks , the sublime is keyed specifically to objects of nature. The affinity between the sublime and culture can be captured in Zammito's account of the development of the third *Critique*, which places Kant's thinking about the sublime as part of the "ethical turn" of the text.[22]

There are two significant differences between the beautiful and the sublime. First, the sublime is, strictly speaking, not a judgment that refers to natural objects themselves. Second, the character of the pleasure involved in each of them differs; the beautiful is sheer pleasure, while Kant names the pleasure in the sublime a "negative pleasure." The sublime even involves a moment of displeasure, before it culminates in respect.

A judgment of the sublime is a judgment about our own elevated position with respect to nature. As we saw in Chapters 1–5, judgments of taste disclose to us an accord between beautiful things and our faculties. The sublime, however, is discordant: It "[appears] in its form to be contrapurposive for our power of judgment" (KU 5:245). While it is

---

[21] A recent piece by John Zammito on the sublime would, though, place it more firmly with the reading I offer of the aesthetic. Zammito connects the sublime to *Lebensgefühl* and *Geistesgefühl*, and, ultimately, to metaphysics. Zammito, "The 'Sublime,' the 'Supersensible Substrate,' and 'Spirit' – Intuitions of the Ultimate in Kant's third Critique," in *Kant on Intuition: Western and Asian Perspectives on Transcendental Idealism*, Stephen Palmquist, ed. (London: Routledge, 2019), 139–158.

[22] Zammito, *Genesis of Kant's third* Critique, 276. Please see also Robert Clewis, *The Kantian Sublime and the Revelation of Freedom* (London: Cambridge University Press, 2009). This book offers a sustained account of the relation of the sublime to Kant's practical philosophy.

contrapurposive for one faculty, however, this discloses the sublimity of our own faculty of reason, which turns out to be integral to the initial moment of contrapurposiveness we feel. Thus, Kant argues, this indicates that, in fact, the sublimity is in our own minds. "We can say no more than that the object serves for the presentation of a sublimity that can be found in the mind; for what is properly sublime cannot be contained in any sensible form, but concerns only ideas of reason . . . . Thus the wide ocean, enraged by storms, cannot be called sublime" (KU 5:245). The only thing which may properly be called sublime is the human mind itself: "[T]rue sublimity must be sought only in the mind of the one who judges" (KU 5:256). We are not, then, making a judgment about nature itself; it is only by way of subreption that we call nature sublime insofar as it "serves" to draw attention to the genuinely sublime (KU 5:245). Nature is that which occasions a feeling of our own sublimity (as we will see in what follows). What we come to learn about nature – about nature in ourselves – in a judgment of the sublime, then, does not take nature as an object. At the same time, the judgment of the sublime is constituted by a consideration of nature and our place relative to it. This consideration is not about the object in nature that occasioned the judgment; rather, it is about the whole of nature itself and our participation in it.

The feeling of the sublime is embodied in a movement of two moments. While Kant distinguishes between what he calls the Mathematical and the Dynamical instantiations of the sublime, each has the same movement: "[T]he feeling of a momentary inhibition of the vital powers and the immediately following and all the more powerful outpouring of them" (KU 5:245). In each, it is the initial violence done to the imagination that gives rise to the first moment of pain. In the Mathematical Sublime, the greatness of the object resists comprehension by our imagination. Quite simply: The object is too big for us to take in as a whole. While we can "apprehend" in our imagination partial, successive representations of the object we are looking at, we are unable to combine all of these together into one representation that grasps all of the whole as well as its parts, that is, we are unable to *comprehend* the object.

There is no difficulty with apprehension because it can go on to infinity; but

> comprehension becomes ever more difficult the further apprehension advances ... For when apprehension has gone so far that the partial representations of the intuition of the senses that were apprehended first already beginning to fade in the imagination as the latter proceeds on to the apprehension of further ones, then it loses on one side as much as it gains on the other. (KU 5:252)

To demonstrate the phenomenon, the example Kant gives is the pyramids in Egypt. When we stand close to the structure, we are able to see the individual stones and their arrangement; we are unable, however, to take in the whole. When we step back to take in the whole, we lose sight of the individual stones. If we try to hold together both the representation of the whole that includes the detail of the stones, we are unable – we cannot comprehend the entirety of what we have apprehended in parts. In the face of the failure to comprehend an object that is too large for our imagination, we feel pain: "[T]here is a feeling of the inadequacy of his imagination for presenting the ideas of a whole, which the imagination reaches its maximum and, in the effort to extend it, sinks back into itself [*in sich selbst zurück sinkt*]" (KU 5:252).

Kant is explicit about the destructive character of this first moment in the Mathematical Sublime, as he will be in the Dynamical. The excessive character of the object of the sublime leads the imagination to an "abyss, in which it fears to lose itself" (KU 5:258). He goes on to argue that our "incapacity" ultimately "does violence [*Gewalt*] to the inner sense" (KU 5:257). This is why, he suggests, the sublime is contrapurposive for our faculties – the imagination breaks down in the face of objects whose excessive size resist our efforts to comprehend them.

The contrapurposiveness of the sublime for our faculties, however, turns over into a purposiveness for our recognition of reason's superiority. The failure of the imagination to comprehend the whole reveals to us the source of the demand for this comprehension in the first place. It is a "law of reason" that enjoins us to intuit the whole; we are thereby filled with respect for the very ideas of reason to which the imagination aspires (KU 5:257). Our "incapacity reveals the consciousness of an unlimited capacity" in the use of reason (KU 5:259). We thus move from a feeling of "displeasure" to "a pleasure that is thereby aroused at the same time" for the vocation of reason.

If the Mathematical Sublime draws our attention to the possibilities for *thinking* that the faculty of reason offers, the dynamically sublime speaks to our *moral vocation* specifically. In the dynamically sublime, we come to feel our capacity for dominion over nature. This emerges in our confrontation not with an object too great to comprehend, but with the violent, threatening force of nature. It must arouse fear in us, such as "threatening cliffs, thunder clouds ... volcanoes with their all-destroying violence, hurricanes with the devastation they leave behind" (KU 5:261). These events remind us of the smallness of our physical capabilities with respect to nature's force. But as we view these events from a safe vantage point, we are able, first, "to recognize our own physical powerlessness," but then come to judge this aspect of our existence as nothing. We come to regard key aspects of our natural condition – "goods, health, life" – "as trivial," and those elements of our humanity and moral vocation that give us dignity as essential. In the face of losing our natural existence, we come to judge it as worthless. We are reminded of our moral vocation and of the superiority of reason over nature in us. We see here the same movement from an initial moment of displeasure that gives way to a much more intense feeling of respect for our rational natures.

Perhaps most stark is Kant's announcement at the beginning of the chapter on the sublime where he submits that unlike the pleasure in the beautiful, which is a feeling of the "promotion of life," in the sublime we find "a momentary inhibition of the vital powers (*Lebenskräfte*) and the immediately following and all the more powerful outpouring [*Ergießung*] of them" (KU 5:245). The beautiful, as we saw in Chapters 1–5, both refers us to life as the unity of force and matter, and also embodies a feeling of life in the harmony of the faculties. The pleasure in the beautiful promotes life because it is a feeling of deep agreement between our faculties of cognition and between human beings and the way things are, and it strengthens the use of our mind. In the sublime, by contrast, we do not have a feeling of life (*Lebensgefühl*) so much as a feeling of the force that may constitute our own liveliness: Here we only feel the force of life. In his statement about the sublime, Kant seems to be playing with two notions of this force. First, our vital powers are inhibited. Here, Kant seems to be referring to the vital powers that belong to us in virtue of our biological or animal being. This is clear in the dynamically sublime, for instance, in being reminded we are no match for nature's power. But we are then referred to a more robust outpouring of vital powers. Perhaps it is better to say simply: power (in the singular). Kant has made clear that freedom is the principle of life of human beings – it is what gives us the life characteristic to us. Our genuine vital power of *reason* thus pours out once our lower faculties and desires are broken apart. Even though this is a feeling of our own principle of life in reason, however, it is not for that a feeling of life itself, as an agreement with it or as the unity of this principle of force with our material being. We feel only the force of what grants us human life to begin with.

Both instances of the sublime effectively discharge the human being from the order of nature into the order of reason. However, Kant claims that this will only be the case for someone who is already to some extent *cultured*. "Without the development of moral ideas," he writes, "that which we, prepared by culture, call sublime will appear merely repellent to the unrefined person" (KU 5:265). In the absence of such prior cultivation, a person will experience the greatness and power of nature as overwhelming and come to worship it. That is, nature will come to take the place of reason as sovereign over the human being. Kant describes the foolishness of the "devotees of the icy mountains" (KU 5:265). Culture, then, in reducing the influence of nature on our wills, can make way for us to hear the demand of reason. The sublime, to be effective, must follow on this first movement of culture wherein nature's dominion over us is lessened. The sublime, then, continues the process of drawing our attention specifically to what is superior and ultimately sovereign in us, namely reason.

Neither culture nor the sublime are able to make us moral. They are both merely preparatory for our moral endeavors. In this, both culture and the sublime are part of a natural order that appears to us – in reflection – as circumscribed by the domain of freedom. The way that nature can be judged to contribute to this end, too, is by effacing its own influence over us. Nature undoes itself with respect to our participation in it.

What emerges from Kant's writings on teleology is, one, that the natural sciences must be contextualized within a larger system of meaning. Insofar as the pursuit of science speaks to our deepest human needs to know how things are, it does so only this way. When we reflect on nature as a whole, it is not for us simply a sphere of cause and effect and other natural laws. We take nature as a whole to be directed toward something, where nothing is in vain. When we reflect on nature thus, we take nature as a whole to be oriented by the moral life of human beings. It is our existence, our possibilities for setting ends, and ultimately making a moral world, that gives any meaning to nature at all.

Our hope for reason's efficacious in the natural order is sustained in a system of nature insofar as nature appears to us as purposive for us. The mere mechanism of nature that seems at odds with our moral ends is here reconceived as part of a larger teleological whole whose end is judged to be our moral vocation itself.

7

Hope and Faith: God in the Critique of Teleological Judgment

In the final sections of the Critique of Teleological Judgment, Kant expressly addresses the interests of hope.[1] The question of hope gets addressed, here, with respect to *faith*. If hope is the interest we have in our happiness being met in a moral world, faith is what we have in the *objects* that support such hope. Faith will be conviction not only in a *meaningful order of nature* but at the same time in a *moral author of nature*. This speaks directly to Kant's claim in the Introduction that judgments of reflection will be about a supersensible ground to nature that allows it to promote the ends of freedom (KU 5:196).

Kant argues that the idea of a supreme being as author of nature arises because the idea of nature as organized in accord with ends leads to the idea of "an intentionally acting cause." We must, he writes, "raise the question of an objective ground that could have determined this productive understanding to an effect of this sort" (KU 5:434–5). The organizing end of a system nature will give us insight into the system's cause. Thus, considerations of science have led us, strikingly, to religious matters.[2] Kant spends the remaining portion of the text delineating the possibilities we have for correctly thinking about this cause, given the effects we take it to produce as well as the limits of our cognition. The orienting question of these sections, then, is: What constitutes a proper theology, as we are inevitably led to think of God as the creator of what there is? That is, *what is it in which we are meant to have faith?* Here, Kant's considerations

---

[1] It is because of the express practical implications that Zammito writes of these sections: "I wish to argue that it is precisely as he composed these sections in late summer 1789 that Kant made his "ethical turn." *The Genesis of the Third Critique*, 248.

[2] One may even argue that Kant's discussion of the possibilities of the life sciences – which is about what is internal to the domain of nature itself – is more of an interlude in the Critique of Teleological Judgment. The overriding concerns seem to be the relation of the domain of nature to the domain of freedom. In any case, it should be no surprise that science and religion are treated congruently. They are two ways we have approached the same subject matter (the origin of things), regularly leading to conflict over jurisdiction.

Hope and Faith: God in the Critique of Teleological Judgment

culminate in a new argument about what justifies faith; faith is here not something merely rational, but, rather, based on judgment about how things appear to us.

Faith is about our relationship to the unseen, to what does not appear. In the Critique of Aesthetic Judgment, Kant examined our encounters with things out in the territory – beautiful objects in nature, beautiful art, and the sublime. There, we find that judgment tries to make sense of what we cannot understand in appearance. His description of the free play of the faculties and our attempts at interpreting what is not subject to the laws of the understanding greatly expanded the range of his accounting of human life beyond knowing and doing, cognition and morality; what we found is that there is a significant expansion of meaning in our encounters with beautiful things. Moreover, these judgments referred us to what is beyond what we can know or do, indeed, sometimes even beyond the possibilities of the critical system. We were referred to things that do not of themselves appear to us, save out in the territory in an albeit refracted – or, better, reflected – way: life as unity, the sensus communis, an orderedness of appearance, nature's work through genius, and aesthetic ideas. Here in the Critique of Teleological Judgment, Kant is likewise expanding the meaningfulness of human experience out in the territory. In these final sections in particular, Kant develops a new account of our relationship to a thing we cannot see and which cannot appear to us: God. And, this account is based on what does appear to us, namely living beings. From the appearance of living beings, we judge there to be a meaningful system of nature in need of some causal agent. If the first half of the Critique of Teleological Judgment situated science in a context of *meaning* – and not merely of *knowing* – the second half reminds us of how faith, and by consequence religion, may constitute a further sphere of meaning for human life by sustaining hope.

This chapter will unfold in four sections. In Section 7.1, I will offer a kind of summary account of Kant's more general philosophical interest(s) in God, followed by his specific accounts under the auspices of theoretical and then practical reason. This background will allow us better to distinguish what is different and therefore significant about Kant's new description of theology here. In Section 7.2, I examine Kant's notion of "ethicotheology." Here, I argue that Kant's emphasis is on the *system* of freedom from the perspective of reflection. From this vantage point, we come to judge that the systems of freedom and nature mutually entail – reciprocally relate to – each other in virtue of having the same final end, a final end that includes both freedom and nature. This section ultimately concludes with the idea that for Kant, living beings allow us to judge that there is a *meaningful* order of nature. In Section 7.3, I look to the intimate connections Kant has drawn between God and life. Section 7.4 then concludes the chapter with a discussion of Kant's turn to conviction. In this, we find that we may be *convicted* about the existence of God because of the objective character of our judgment about the system of nature and the fact of freedom that stands as its final end. This is Kant's most robust statement about the character of our faith and what it is we have faith in.

7.1 Kant on God

The context for Kant's considerations of theology in the Critique of Teleological Judgment is his treatment of nature as a system. After Kant has established the legitimacy of the use of the principle of teleology in scientific inquiry, and further developed the application of the principle to the system of nature, he turns to the possible cause of creation. What is the cause of things such that they come to be teleologically? Life, or organized beings, we recall, was the impetus for justifying teleology reflectively in our investigations of nature. With this principle now in hand, we found ourselves out in the territory reflectively judging the whole of the domain of nature to be oriented by the domain of freedom, with the human being as the end of nature.

Kant comes to this because nature may only be judged to be a *system* when it is organized purposively toward some end. Crucially, Kant argues that for an end to function properly as an end of an organized system, it cannot also be a means within that system, and must thus be an *end in itself*. Kant thereby makes a distinction, we recall, between the ultimate or last end of nature, and a final end. While the ultimate end is the last in the series of nature's mechanistic ends, and thereby part of the conditioned order of things, the final end must be *unconditioned*. Culture, then, which Kant has just argued is the ultimate end of nature, may only function as the ultimate end insofar as it stands in relation to the final end. The final end refers to the free exercise of the will of human beings, and thus takes us outside of the domain of nature. This is the human being "considered as noumenon ... on the basis of its own constitution, a supersensible faculty (freedom)" (KU 5:435). In virtue of being absolutely unconditioned and an end in itself, the human being's free existence "contains the highest end itself, to which, as far as he is capable, he can subject the whole of nature" (KU 5:435). It is therefore only because of our supersensible vocation, our standing outside of nature, that we provide orientation and systematicity to nature.³ It is not only that the domain of nature is oriented by human freedom. The domain of nature admits of being a coherent system only in virtue of the moral vocation of human beings.

We conceive of purposiveness principally as *intentional*. When he introduces purposiveness in the third moment of the Critique of Aesthetic Judgment, he asserts:

> An object or a state of mind or even an action, however, even if its possibility does not necessarily presuppose the representation of an end, is called purposive merely because its possibility can only be explained and conceived by us insofar as we assume as its ground a causality in accordance with ends, i.e., a will that has arranged it so in accordance with the representation of a certain rule. (KU 5:220)

While the beautiful – in nature as well as in art – is thought by us to be a product of nature, broadly conceived,⁴ we cannot help but think of the objective purposiveness we find in living beings and then the system of nature other than as the effect of a will. Kant is clear about this in §77, where he emphasizes that it is a "special character" of our faculties such that we come to this. As Kant observes, something that is teleological is brought into being in accord not only with ends but also with the representation of ends. The end is prior to the coming into being of the thing and must therefore be intended by some will; there must be something that intends the end. As Zuckert writes, "Kant argues that purposiveness must be construed intentionally in order for it to be intelligible to us."⁵ We are thus necessarily, by our own forms of thinking, led to consider the *cause* of the whole of the system of nature, which has just been established to be – at least reflectively – teleological. For the system of nature to be made thoroughly intelligible, then, we must delineate the cause that intends a system as we have conceived it. This is how concerns pertaining to science lead us to what would otherwise be considered matters of religion.

The subject matter of these sections of the Critique of Teleological Judgment, then, is how we may think of the cause of the system of nature given how it takes shape as a whole in accord with an end. This is a subject

---

³ We see here the completion of the Copernican turn outlined in the Introduction. Even when reflecting on the whole of the system of nature, we are given to posit the human being as the telos and source of meaning for all that there is.
⁴ We can think here of Kant's discussion of genius, as described in Chapter 5. Kant's account of genius is of a nature with an intention with respect to human beings and aesthetic ideas.
⁵ Zuckert, *Kant on Beauty and Biology*, 157.

matter closely related to Kant's previous treatments of God.[6] I outline those treatments here in order to give context to and thereby distinguish his third *Critique* argument as offering an objective, rather subjective account of God's existence. First, some remarks on God in Kant's philosophy more broadly.

God is, first, how we designate what intends and thereby creates the world. But, God, for Kant, is also the name for the unity of subject and object, mind and world, freedom and nature. In the first *Critique*, reason's demand for the unconditioned leads to three ideas: the immortal soul (as the unconditioned of our subjective experience), the world (as the unconditioned whole of objects in nature), and God (the unconditioned unity of the whole of what is). In the second *Critique*, Kant develops the notion of God as a *moral author* of nature. The question of God as it is formed here at the end of the third *Critique* is keyed to how freedom and nature are related – this is what will lead to what we can say about God as the creator of the whole of what is in its unity. The supersensible destiny of the system of nature reopens for Kant the possibilities of thinking the cause of this system. We thus revisit arguments for the existence of God and what it is we may say about who or what God is. It is not possible for nature itself to produce a final end, as it must be unconditioned. The causality of such a system of nature, then, must also be thought by us with reference to nature's subordination to human freedom. Thus, "we cannot conceive of nature, in the purposive arrangements that have become known to us in it, except as a product of an intelligence to which it is subject" (KU 5:441).

Kant's interest here is in the extent to which we can determine a supersensible cause of creation as well as what our epistemic relation to it might be, namely a *theology*. His long-standing concern with proofs for the existence of God has not only to do with our propensity to arrive at the idea of God by way of theoretical reason. In addition, Kant's practical or moral commitments heighten his considerations. These practical commitments are at first glance at odds with each other. On the one hand, Kant is suspicious of theological and speculative overreach, as well as with the enthusiasm such a theology may engender. He fears that this enthusiasm can lead us astray from our true moral vocation, which is exclusively to follow the law that reason prescribes to us for its own sake. Moral

---

[6] For a full account of the different arguments Kant gives for the existence of God over the stretch of his career, see Wood's *Kant's Rational Theology* (Ithaca, NY: Cornell University Press, 1978); see also Onora O'Neill, *Kant on Reason and Religion*, in *The Tanner Lectures on Human Values* (Salt Lake City, UT: University of Utah Press, 1997), 269–308.

enthusiasm, he writes, "is such an overstepping of the bounds that practical pure reason sets to humanity," and it leads us to avoid the "discipline of a duty laid before" our eyes (KpV 5:85–6). He also notes that if we had knowledge of God's existence, our actions would never stem from duty alone, but principally from "fear, [and] only a few from hope" (KpV 5:147). On the other hand, reason is limited in the effects it has in the natural order – it stands always in relation to nature and therefore finds itself dependent upon what is beyond its purview to realize its ends. For the sake of reason's self-consistency, as well as to buttress us against despair, God is necessary for us to think it is possible to make good on reason's demands.[7] These two prongs of Kant's perpetual interest in proofs for the existence of God are united insofar as both are, first, born of the interests of reason itself, and, second, constrained by the limits of our knowledge.[8]

In Chapter 3 I highlighted Kant's early and then also continual attention to the problem of life, the inner unity of force and matter. We may here point to an analogous ongoing and abiding concern about God as what guarantees the ultimate unity of human beings and things in the world.[9] Indeed, they are analogous not only insofar as Kant occupies much of his thought with these problems; the problems themselves bear resemblance to one another. If the problem of life is about the relation of force to matter in individual beings, the problem of God is about how we can conceive an unconditioned beginning of a conditioned series, and how a being with a transcendent capacity to reason, elevating it above and placing it outside of nature, nevertheless relates to and is efficacious in nature. Both life and God denote a third thing that brings together two otherwise heterogeneous things. In the case of life, the third thing is an inner unity that is impossible for us to think. In the case of God, the third thing stands outside both of the other two things and grants them unity from without. We should recall here, too, that the mission of the *Critique of Judgment* is

---

[7] A longer account of how reason depends on something outside of it to realize its ends can be found in my *Kant on Practical Life: From Duty to History*, which emphasizes the finitude of human beings in just this way. Philip Rossi's work also emphasizes this aspect of Kant, and can be found specifically with reference to hope and faith in his "Kant as a Christian Philosopher: Hope and the Symbols of the Christian Faith," *Philosophy Today* (Spring 1981), 28ff.

[8] We see here a serious conflict: Theoretical reason seeks always to posit a God. Practical reason, though, must ensure that our concept of God is correct, on pain of undermining the moral goodness of human beings. This conflict gets resolved through a union of the two systems, as we will see further down.

[9] As early as 1763, Kant published his "The Only Possible Argument in Support of a Demonstration of the Existence of God." The different possible arguments he lays out in that text, as well as his criticisms of them, remain relatively consistent over the course of his career.

to elucidate such a third thing that can mediate between freedom and nature. Life and now God, then, are proper subject matters for *reflection*, and not, as we will see, for theoretical or practical reason. While theoretical and practical reason both have strong interests in these due to their own needs, only in reflection are they presented to us "objectively."

From the perspective of theoretical reason, we are driven to presume an intelligent designer.[10] In the first *Critique*, Kant's discussion of God takes shape in the context of his treatment of the All. While the soul or the "I myself" extends systematic unity over inner experience, and the "world" extends nature as serial, God refers to the Supreme Being that creates the All (KrV A682/B710). The All is the highest ideal of reason, the complete totality of everything that there is, standing in thoroughgoing determination with respect to everything else that there is.[11] It is the "sum total of all reality" in which each particular thing is only a negation of the interconnected and interdependent whole to which it necessarily and definitively belongs (KrV A577/B605). Kant further identifies the All as both purposive and perfect: "Complete purposive unity is perfection (absolutely considered)" (KrV A694/B722). Moreover, whereas the world-whole of the cosmological idea was merely an *object* for our thinking, the All is the unity of all that there is, encompassing the human being as well as nature. The cosmological question, recall, takes shape in part as an irresolvable antinomy between the causalities of freedom and nature. In the All, by contrast, we find one reigning causality, namely purposiveness. Kant goes so far as to identify the structure of the All with the form of reason itself:

> The greatest systematic unity, consequently, all purposive unity, is the school and even the ground of the possibility of the greatest use of human reason. Hence the idea of it is inseparably bound up with the essence of our reason. The very same idea, therefore, is legislative for us, and thus it is very natural to assume a corresponding legislative reason (*intellectus archetypus*) from which all systematic unity of nature, as the object of our reason, is to be derived. (KrVA694/B722)

Nature here is conceived by us as a perfect purposive unity, reflecting the purposive essence of human reason. Thus, nature is not merely *extended* as

---

[10] I am here skipping a detailed account of the cosmological argument – there, God is only conceived as a first cause.
[11] No doubt, the concept of the All has been present since the inception of Western metaphysics, most clearly with the Parmenidean "One." This "One" pervades the thinking of this tradition, exemplified in the emphasis on Being over becoming we find in Plato, Plotinus, Augustine, Aquinas, and so on, through Heidegger. If nothing else, the history of this thought evidences Kant's claim that reason cannot but help to come to it.

it is in the idea of the world. In the All, by contrast, the *inner determination* of nature's order is rethought.

A nature whose inner determination is thoroughly interconnected and purposive, Kant thus argues, can only have been brought about by "a unique wise and all-powerful world author" (KrV A697/B725). He names this author a "world-cause," "a substratum," "a Something," and "an intelligence" (KrV A697/B725ff). He does not here name this being "God"; in fact, he even notes that it "does matter at all whether you say, 'God has wisely willed it so' or 'Nature has wisely ordered it'" (KrV A690/B727). We should note, too, by contrast with the God of the cosmological world-whole, the intelligence here is not simply a first cause that sets a series into motion. Here, the cause is wise, all-powerful, and an enduring substratum. The intelligent designer, moreover, is only something we must presuppose for the use of our faculties with respect to nature. "Thus," he writes, "I really derive nothing from [the existence of] this being, but only from the idea of it" (KrV A701/B729). As we saw Kant argue in Chapter 6, science and scientific inquiry is only possible for human beings insofar as we posit a system of nature. And, in order for this to be fully intelligible to us, we must also presume – although only regulatively – some intelligent designer that is the substratum and cause of such a system. The God of the All is not a God that is an object for us – that is, it is not an object of faith or something that grants any meaningfulness to things. There is then no theology possible. God here, as born of reason's own need for the All, is merely an *idea of God* that gives rest to reason's search for the unconditioned in the order of nature.

Kant offers his most sustained account of God as the *moral author* of nature in the *Critique of Practical Reason*. Here, he argues that there is reason for us to assent to the existence of God from a practical point of view. In this, we go one step further than mere use of the idea of God as developed for theoretical reason. Such an endorsement of assent may seem at odds with the overall thrust of the discussions of God in the first *Critique*. There, not only does Kant equate the idea of God with a wise nature, he famously rejects proofs for the existence of God. He does this while simultaneously describing the inextricable need reason in its theoretical use nevertheless has to come to such an idea. Readers of the first *Critique* may be warranted in coming away from the text sharing Heine's sentiments that with respect to the question of God, Kant was an "arch-destroyer" and that the text "is the sword that slew deism in Germany."[12]

---

[12] Heine, *Religion and Philosophy in Germany*, 109, 107.

Kant appears, after all, to argue that the idea of God is born of reason itself. And, as we saw, goes so far as to equate God with a wise nature. In the second *Critique*, however, God returns as a possible object of faith, thus finally fulfilling Kant's promise that the first *Critique* would limit knowledge to make room for such an end.[13] Indeed, it will be from the perspective of practical reason that the question of God has real urgency:

> But one can regard the need of reason as twofold: first in its theoretical, second in its practical use. The first need I have just mentioned; but one sees very well that it is only conditioned, i.e., we must assume the existence of God *if* we *want to judge* about the first causes of everything contingent, chiefly of the order of ends which is actually present in the world. Far more important is the need of reason in its practical use, because it is unconditioned, and we are necessitated to presuppose the existence of God not only if we *want* to judge, but because we *have to judge*. (WDO 8:139)

We are required to presuppose God because of the demand to realize the highest good in the world – a demand so absolute that Kant claims that the impossibility of its realization would destroy the moral law itself. In the second *Critique*, we are led by this demand to postulate immortality and God. Here, God is not simply the first in a series of causes, as in his discussion of cosmology, nor a wise author or substratum as in relation to the All. God is now related to *goodness*; in this context God is conceived explicitly and repeatedly as the moral author of nature, and, as later in the third *Critique*, as having the final end of the human being as the end of creation. We must presuppose his existence in this context in order rationally to work for the ends that reason places on us, lest we despair over the possibility of achieving our ends.[14]

The postulate of God, however, does not itself refer to God as an object. First, as a postulate, Kant indicates that it is an indemonstrable theoretical proposition (KpV 5:122). A postulate functions as a kind of hypothesis. The interests of our practical reason make it necessary for us to assume the existence of God, which was otherwise undecidable (per the Antinomy in the first *Critique*). In this, the fact of our freedom gives rational basis to assent to the idea of God – a *Fürwahrhalten*, or a "holding for true."[15]

---

[13] Chignell disagrees with this (typical) reading of Kant in favor of a more theoretical understanding. See Chignell, "Belief in Kant," *Philosophical Review* 116:3 (2007), 335ff.

[14] For a fuller account of the relation of faith and despair, please see Addison Ellis, "The Internality of Moral Faith in Kant's Religion," *Kant Yearbook* 10:1 (2018), 1–17.

[15] For discussions of what is meant by a holding-for-true, particularly in relation to opinion and knowledge, please see: Leslie Stevenson, "Opinion, Belief or Faith, and Knowledge," *Kantian Review* 7 (2003), 72–101; Chignell, "Belief in Kant"; and Joseph Trullinger, "Kant's Two

As Philip Rossi argues, "God is affirmed as effective symbol – i.e., as moral cause beyond our human shaping – in virtue of reason's interest in the permanence of the moral order."[16] Second, while the postulate is a "presupposition," it has a "practical reference" (KpV 5:132). That is, it does not extend our cognition or determination of the idea of God. Strictly speaking, the reference or object of the postulate is the highest good, on which the necessity of belief in the existence of God is thus founded. This belief, or rational faith, is simply "the most reasonable opinion for human beings" (KpV 5:142). In all of this, then, our rational faith remains merely ideal – it is only derived from a subjective need of reason that we are given to decide in favor of one side of the Antinomy of theoretical reason.

What nature and God are under the auspices of practical reason have evolved from their articulations in the context of theoretical reason. For theoretical reason, the ideal is of a nature that is complete, perfect, and thoroughly unified and interconnected. As an All, it is essentially a One; human beings are a part of this One, and our reason reflects its ordering. God, from this perspective, is that which brings the All into being and operates as its substrate. For practical reason, God as moral author of nature designs nature either so that it is amenable to the work that human beings do to transform the natural order into a wholly rational one or gives to the forms and laws of nature an explicitly moral aim. Indeed, the question of how far Kant takes the issue of nature's *possible* conformity with the demands of freedom is an open one.[17] What is clear, however, is that the God we hold to be true for moral reasons is a God that assures the possible union of freedom and nature. The highest good for a human being is virtue (freedom) causing happiness (nature). Kant is explicit that "the best world" – which is the world in which moral goodness does, in fact, lead to happiness – is actually the "*highest derived good*" (KpV 5:125). The "*highest original good*" is "the existence of God" (KpV 5:125). So the union of freedom and nature that we seek to effect through our rational action depends, first, on a God who already instantiates this union through the authoring of a morally disposed nature.

Thus, while practical reason, in its primacy over theoretical reason, gives subjective grounds for assenting to the theoretical proposition that God exists, and, too, that we may conceive of God as a moral author of nature,

---

Touchstones for Conviction: The Incommunicable Dimension of Moral Faith," *The Review of Metaphysics* 67 (2013), 369–403.

[16] Philip Rossi, "Kant as a Christian Philosopher," 29.

[17] The question is, does nature merely allow for the possibility of taking on reason's ends (it is not impossible), or does nature ensure it is possible more actively?

it remains driven by a need originating in the subject, in reason itself. That is, the idea of God viewed from the perspectives of both theoretical and practical reason remains thoroughly subjective. It is not hard to arrive at Heine's verdict about Kant on God in this light. To articulate it in terms of the geographical metaphors, each of these views of God is made from inside one or the other of the domains of freedom or nature. This is clear even from the perspective of practical reason itself. The positing of a God as a unifier of freedom and nature via moral authorship simply looks out across the territory at nature from the perch of moral duty. It is in virtue of practical reason encountering the natural order as something other, something foreign, and thus also something obdurate that it has a need to posit God for the sake of self-consistency. It is from the domain of freedom looking outward toward a heteronomous domain of nature that we postulate the existence of God.

7.2 Theology in the Third *Critique*

The third *Critique* offers a new account of nature and God and faith, one that is not born of a subjective need or interest of reason, but is predicated on what appears to us in the territory, for us to judge. "Reflection on the laws of nature," he writes, "is directed by nature" (KU 5:180) and we are thus led to by nature to the idea of God. The theology offered here, to borrow from Kant's own description of the beautiful, is disinterested. In it, Kant demonstrates that when we reflect on the relation of the two domains from the territory, we take them to be reciprocally related and mutually conditioning. They share – are jointed together by – one final end: the moral vocation of human beings to transform the natural order into a rational whole. This final end mutually implicates both systems of freedom and nature.

Kant begins his discussion of our possibilities for thinking about the cause of nature with what he calls "physicotheology": "the attempt of reason to infer from the ends of nature ... to the supreme cause of nature and its properties" (KU 5:436). A physicotheology is not, Kant argues, properly a *theology*; it remains physical *teleology* only. While we are led to inferring a supersensible cause given the teleological structures we find in nature, we can say nothing further about this cause. But because the physical teleology does not involve a *final* end of nature, it cannot actually refer to such a cause at all. Without an unconditioned end, nature lacks a "teleological principle sufficient for cognizing all the ends together in a single system." Such a physical teleology, he writes, "certainly drives us to seek a theology, but it cannot produce one" (KU 5:440); the best it yields is a "demonology" (KU 5:444). Nature as a system of ends will necessarily lead us to the notion of a supersensible cause, but it can neither prove such a thing nor give any more determinacy to the idea. At bottom, a physicotheology cannot answer why all the things that exist, exist. And, as Wood argues, physicotheology is subject to two serious dangers: (1) It lives in the "gaps" of scientific inquiry. Were science to be able to explain everything, the argument for God would be null. (2) Theologically, it would be unorthodox in the Judeo-Christian tradition to claim that God is merely the reason for purposiveness of forms in nature, rather than the creator of the whole of existence itself.[18]

Kant is thus clear about the limits of a theoretical ground for theology. First, the press for God in this context, Kant argues, arises from the finitude of our cognitive abilities. "Given the constitution and the principles of our cognitive faculty," he writes, "we cannot conceive of nature, in the purposive arrangements that have become known to us in it, except as the product of an intelligence to which it is subject" (KU 5:441). Second, theoretical research is inherently unable to discern a final end, which would stand outside of nature. Thus, whether nature is produced entirely and thoroughgoingly in accord with such an end remains an outstanding question for theory. He thereby concludes that physical teleology is merely a "propaedeutic" for theology and, crucially, is built upon another principle (KU 5:442).

The principle upon which physical teleology is built – how it finds itself supported – is a practical one. This practical ground for a physical teleology, however, is more expansive than mere moral duty. Kant turns here to what he calls "ethicotheology," which can offer a more determinate conception of a supersensible being. Indeed, it will emerge that his ethicotheology goes further than the postulate of God which practical reason allows us to hold as true. He begins §86 with a succinct summary of what he has just established through reflection, and also treated in Chapter 5: The whole of creation and all creatures "would exist for nothing if there were not among them human beings" (KU 5:442). But Kant goes even further than this, asserting that the value [*Werth*] of creation is given only through the existence of the human being, who creates all value through the determination of the moral law in action.[19] All

---

[18] Wood, *Kant's Rational Theology*, 139.
[19] For a longer account of how the human being is the source of the good in Kant's moral philosophy, please see my *Kant on Practical Life*, 38–46.

good in the world is derived from – conditioned upon – the one unconditioned good, namely the good will (G 4:393). It is only in virtue of the human being as a moral being, he reminds us, that we can regard "the world as a whole interconnected in accordance with ends and as a system of final causes" (KU 5:444). The moral foundation of nature's systematicity is what grants further determinacy to our conception of the cause of this system and will admit of a theology. The final end of the system – which both stands outside of it as well as gives it determinacy – is what allows us to say something about its cause. The creation of the world must be accomplished by a being whose end is the very value that humans bring into being. "In this way," Kant writes, "**moral** teleology makes good the defect of **physical** teleology, and first establishes a **theology**" (KU 5:444). If physical teleology fails at theology because it only yields an intelligent cause, moral teleology succeeds because it yields a *moral author* of an entire system of nature.

At first glance, we may find that Kant seems only to be repeating what he has previously offered in his "moral theology" [*Moraltheologie*].[20] As Guyer argues, "As the conclusion of each of the three *Critiques*, Kant argues that the rationality of moral conduct requires a conception of the laws of nature as favorable for the realization of human objectives."[21] This description is correct for the first two *Critiques*, which each take the perspective of reason's interests. In this "moral theology," our practical interests are what dictate our conception of nature. So: How is the third *Critique* different? Answering this will give us an understanding of what kind of hope the third *Critique* – what nature conceived purposively by way of reflective judgment – may offer to our moral vocation. What will emerge is that under the auspices of reflection, rather than a need of reason, we can take our faithful orientation from nature itself, and not only a "felt need" of the subject.

Our first clue is Kant's introduction of a new term in this text: *Ethikotheologie*. While he had previously designated a moral theology to discuss similar themes, this is the first (and only) appearance of "ethicotheology." Remarkably, even in a footnote on the title of the

---

[20] For a succinct account of Kant's arguments for a "moral theology," please see Marie Zermatt Schutt, "Kant's Moral Theology," *British Journal for the History of Philosophy* 18:4 (2010), 611–633. Tellingly, Schutt's account does not take up the third *Critique* discussion at much length; when it does, it is not treated as adding anything distinctive to the argument Kant gives from practical reason.
[21] Guyer, "From Nature to Morality: Kant's New Argument in the Critique of Teleological Judgment," in *Kant's System of Nature and Freedom*.

section, Guyer and Matthews equate *Ethikotheologie* with Kant's moral theology, which more aptly describes his argument from morality in the *Critique of Practical Reason*.[22] Kant is very consistent in his use of the term "*Ethik*"; scholars' failures to note the difference here, then, also indicates a failure to appreciate what is significant not only about Kant's claims in the section but also about the sphere of reflection as its own, independent sphere of human life.

Ethik and its variants refer specifically to a *science* or *doctrine*. This is in contrast with words deriving from *Moral* or *Sitte*, which Kant uses quite regularly throughout his practical writings to refer to or describe the character of human activity. Human beings may act *moralisch* or *sittlich*; *ethisch* does not, for Kant, denote a species of human action or the perspective of human beings. In the Introduction to the *Groundwork*, Kant identifies ethics as one of three sciences – physics and logic completing the triptych. Ethics is here defined as part of "material philosophy, which has to do with determinate objects and the laws to which they are subject"; ethics is the science of the laws of freedom (G 4:387). First, associating a science with the *establishment of laws* is key to his conception. In the opening of the first *Critique*, he laments that metaphysics, which was once the "**queen** of all the sciences," is now in disrepute because of the myriad "controversies" and the state of undecidability with respect to its laws (KrV AiX). Metaphysics, in virtue of its lawlessness, is judged to be in a state of constant battles. These battles, on Kant's account, are all born of reason's theoretical interest in metaphysical objects. Second, these laws must be established in their systematicity for something to be considered scientific; thus, in the *Metaphysics of Morals*, ethics is defined as a system of the concepts of practical reason (MS 6:412). Karl Ameriks observes this about Kant: "[W]hat distinguishes science as such is that it is a study that has a unity of principles, rather than being a mere aggregate of claims."[23] The system of laws, too, is not born of practical reason's interest, but rather, the being of practical reason and its relation to nature. Thus, it will be by way of critique that the science of both metaphysics and ethics can be discerned. The critical method is how we complete "the inventory of all we possess through pure reason, ordered systematically" (KrV AX). What is significant about the critical method for Kant is that it is an activity

---

[22] See *Critique of the Power Judgment*, nt. 26, page 394.
[23] Karl Ameriks, "Kant on Science and Common Knowledge," in *Kant and the Sciences* (Oxford: Oxford University Press), 39.

carried out by *reflection*.²⁴ It is reflection in its transcendental application that is able to discern the source of and laws for both cognition and morality. It will likewise be reflection – albeit not transcendental – that establishes this theology as well. Nevertheless, it is only in reflection that we are able to systematize and organize laws into a coherent whole.

Kant thus argues that a theology may be based on the scientific systematization of the laws of freedom and laws of nature. This will provide a "moral proof for the existence of God."²⁵ Again, this is not based on the demand we find reason in its practical use as will places on us; rather, this system of the laws of the freedom is found through the activity of reflection. From the perspective of reflection out in the territory, *the system of ethics is inextricably bound up with the system of nature*. Reflection is out in the territory and belongs to neither domain; from here, it observes the relation – or, interrelation – of the two domains. In the Critique of Aesthetic Judgment, we had encounters in the territory that disclosed to us the possibility of a larger, more expansive system to which freedom and nature both belonged. While the Critique of Teleological Judgment does not go that far, it does exceed previous approaches to proofs of God in Kant's writings because it takes a proper view of both domains – as systems of laws – together. The ethicotheology, as Kant has it, does not belong solely to the domain of freedom. The domains appear to us as inextricably bound up with each other. As we will see, this theology derives from the inextricable relation of the two domains:

> Yet this moral teleology concerns us as beings in the world and thus as beings connected to other things in the world, upon which this very same law prescribes us to direct our judging, whether as ends or as objects in regard to which we ourselves are ends. Now from this moral teleology, which concerns the relation of our own causality to ends and even to a final end that must be aimed at by us in the world, and thus the reciprocal relation of the world to that moral end and the external possibility of its accomplishment (to which no physical teleology can guide us), there arises the necessary question of whether it compels our rational judging to go beyond the world and seek an intelligent supreme principle for that relation of nature to what is moral in us. (KU 5:447–8)

---

²⁴ See again, Westphal, "Epistemic Reflection and Cognitive Reference in Kant's Transcendental Response to Skepticism," *Kant-Studien* 94 (2003), 135–171; Lyotard, *Lessons on the Analytic of the Sublime* (Stanford, CA: Stanford University Press, 1994).
²⁵ This moral teleology, I will take pains again to note, is not a moral theology. Kant does not invoke *Moraltheologie* in §87 either.

The domains of freedom and nature thus stand in a reciprocal relation [*wechselseitige Beziehung*] with each other. This is because the final end of the two domains is identical, and, as such, each system necessarily entails the other domain with it. The final end – of both the system of nature and the system of freedom – is the highest good. The highest good, as Kant conceives it, is a moral world in which virtue causes happiness. This world is constituted by a free federation of states with republican constitutions, guaranteed cosmopolitan right, and human beings actively participating in ethical communities. That is, our final end is not simply duty, or a good will, which are both achievable autonomously and subjectively. Rather, the final end of human freedom is the transformation of the world in which we find ourselves from *what is* into *what ought to be*. Our final end necessarily involves dealing with what is exterior to our will, namely the world. Thus, the laws of freedom are here conceived with respect to the final end they entail, and, thereby, our connection to the world in which that end must be realized. The system of nature is thus necessarily brought into the domain of freedom – as moral beings, we are already bound up with and bound to the world and the things in it. From the perspective of practical reason, as we noted earlier, the sphere of nature is simply something external and heterogeneous with respect to this end. From a practical point of view, nature stands across a gulf. Here, from the perspective of reflection, the final end of human beings necessarily relates us to the domain of nature *internally*. That is, the domain of nature as the site in which our freedom must do its work internal to the domain of freedom, and part of the sphere over which its laws must legislate.

The domain of nature as a system of laws also has the final end of human beings as *its own* final end, as Chapter 6 demonstrated. In fact, we saw that nature only becomes a true system of laws insofar as it has human beings, as beings who have their own final end, as *its* final end, "For if creation has a final end at all, we cannot conceive of it except as having to correspond to the final end of morality" (KU 5:453). Nature's systematicity depends on the existence of the systematicity of freedom. When Kant claims that a physical teleology must rest on another principle – this is what he is indicating. A teleological system of nature requires a final end, and such an end is given in the system of freedom. Moreover, it is by way of the human being's place in this system that the system itself has purpose, or, rather, *meaning*. It is through human freedom that everything else in the world can acquire worth. The system of nature relates to the domain of freedom *internally*, insofar as its very organization and meaning depend on it. The end of human life is the teleological principle that organizes the natural order as a system; the laws of nature are thereby already related to the laws of freedom. In sharing an identical final end, the domains of freedom and nature mutually imply, and, indeed, reciprocally condition one another. The final end of human life serves as the *joint* end of these systems, and, as such, joins or knots them inextricably together.

Kant is clearest in these sections – §86 and §87 – that the system of nature is not simply a system of empirical laws but is something meaningful. While Kant's previous analysis of the human being as the orienting end for the system of nature was what allowed for system, he goes even further here. All good in the world is conditioned upon the one unconditioned good – the good will of the human being.[26] With nature actively organized by its contribution to the final end, nature thus becomes meaningful as part of the endeavor to bring about the good. Indeed, the good becomes the purpose of the system of nature and the reason for its being: "[T]hings in the world ... would exist for nothing if there were not among them human beings" (KU 5:442). This is a profoundly different order of nature than we have found elsewhere in Kant's system. While it does not quite instantiate the All, we can see resonances of it in the notion that the system of nature is shot through with purposiveness guided by the good. Things in nature now have a purpose, a reason for being that organizes them and thereby makes them what they are. In Kant's practical philosophy, we see how all good in the world is a product of human making, in virtue of the will standing as the source of the good. Here, we see that nature is brought under the goodness of the will not insofar as we have brought it into being, but insofar as nature stands under the will as its organizing principle nevertheless. This is a judgment of reflection, and not a judgment produced by the interest that reason has in nature being so.

The question of *why things exist* is hereby answered. Human beings exist to be good – to exercise their free, rational wills and transform the natural order into a rational whole. Nature exists for us not only as the site on which we accomplish this, but also as a contributor to this pursuit.

As we emphasized throughout, what human beings really hope for is that the world is suited for us. We hope that if we are good, we will be able to find some happiness, namely that the world will reward our moral righteousness. To find a natural order that is purposeful and meaningful, and not merely mechanistic means that we have some hope that if we are good, we will also be happy. We have some hope that the world is

---

[26] "It is impossible to think of anything at all in the world, or indeed beyond it, that could be considered good without limitation except a **good will**" (G 4:393).

receptive to the moral good, and not hostile to it, and will yield to us accordingly. What we see around us is a nature that is meaningful, which further warrants taking there to be a God that causes a such an order.

7.3 God and Life

We might now draw a clear connection between life and God in the Critique of Teleological Judgment. It is ultimately the existence of life, that there is life, that gives "proof" to the existence of God. We saw that the use of the principle of teleology is justified in virtue of our encounters with living beings. In such encounters, what appears can only be conceived purposively. Living beings have their own purpose: to live and be alive, to grow and reproduce themselves. We cannot say this of a rock. Once the existence of purposiveness in nature is granted, we may take the entire round of the natural order also to have a purpose, and thereby be made into a system of laws. The fact that there is life is inextricably linked to the judgment that things are meaningful. There must, then, be a reason for nature to be. And, when we take in the whole of nature, we find that its worth and ultimate purpose is given – perhaps even proven – by the existence of the human being, on whom all worth depends. Nature then is transformed from mere mechanism that resists the ends of freedom to something alive and purposeful for us. While we do not belong to nature in this context, as we do when it appears as beautiful, it does, now, belong to us and to the sphere of meaning.

For freedom and nature to find such mutuality, and for the system of nature now to be characterized by having a purpose, we come inevitably to the cause of such a system. Here, we find an even more intimate connection between life and God. As we noted previously, Kant turns to the question of theology because we cannot help but seek the *intentionality* that brought a purposeful thing into being. Things that are purposive cannot but be thought by us as intentional, that is, as brought into being through the representation of an end. God, therefore, is the name for the being whose will intends a system of meaningful nature whose purpose is found in the moral vocation of one of its beings. God wills a reciprocal union of freedom and nature. However, Kant also names such willful intention "life" elsewhere in his writings. First, to act not only in accord with ends, but in accord with their *representation*, is what it means to have a will. Second, this very characteristic is what constitutes the "life" of human beings. "**Life**," Kant writes, "is the faculty of a being to act in accordance with the laws of the faculty of desire. The **faculty of desire** is a being's *faculty to be by means of its representations the cause of the reality of the objects of these representations"* (KpV 5:9nt). We conceive therefore of God as a kind of primal will or life force. We further take God to be not only the author of nature, but a moral author. As the laws of nature are organized by the laws of freedom, we can judge therefore that the will of God is also governed by the laws of morality. If reason finds itself reflected in the All, it further finds itself reflected in the moral author of nature who creates the whole intentionally for the sake of the highest good. That the final end of the intertwining systems of freedom and nature is a moral end ineluctably proposes that the cause of these systems is moral, too.

This is all to say that for Kant, the association of God and life is strong. He is not, of course, a Spinozist who identifies the system of nature with God. Rather, it would seem that the underlying structural association of God, life, and the human will is ultimately why we are led from our encounters with living beings – and thinking that life is meaningful – to the notion of a moral author of nature.

We would further do well to note that despite God as a moral author of nature, God is *not the source of meaning*. Rather, for Kant, God simply is necessary to create a world in which all meaning derives from the meaningfulness of human life. Even, then, in his most robust articulation of God as a moral author of nature, the human being remains fully autonomous and fully the source of the good. God is still a derivative or buttressing concept, even if he is the giver of life.

7.4 Conviction

To what, however, does this "proof" amount? The reciprocal relation between the two systems, the subsequent meaningfulness of nature, and the positing of a will that intends this does not, of course, amount to *knowledge*. The judgment we come to is still *reflective*. This means, though, that it is not founded on a subjective need that we have. Reflection, rather, is always reflection on something given in a representation. Thus, while it is not objective in the way a cognition is, it nevertheless involves a kind of objectivity or exteriority in the judging – it is ultimately about an actual matter.

Kant thereby argues that the "proof" he has just offered of the conjoined systems of freedom and nature leads to "conviction" (KU 5:461ff). Kant has already introduced conviction in the *Critique of Pure Reason* as a species of assent, falling under the auspices of belief (or, faith, as *Glaube* may also be translated).²⁷ Kant writes:

> Taking something to be true is an occurrence in our understanding that may rest on objective grounds, but that also requires subjective causes in the mind of him who judges. If it is valid for everyone merely as long as he has reason, then its ground is objectively sufficient, and in that case taking something to be true is called **conviction**. If it has a ground only in the particular constitution of the subject, then it is called **persuasion**.

He goes on:

> The touchstone of whether taking something to be true is conviction or mere persuasion is therefore, externally, the possibility of communicating it and finding it to be valid for the reason of every human being to take it to be true; for in that case there is at least a presumption that the ground of the agreement of all judgments, regardless of the difference among the subjects, rests on the common ground, namely the object, with which they therefore all agree and through which the truth of the judgment is proved. (KrV A820–1/B848–9)

Conviction, then, is related not only to the subject but also to objects, and, crucially, is *communicable*. What is it, though, that allows for one to be *convicted* about the existence of God based on what we have outlined earlier?

First, there are clearly limits to what Kant counts as "valid for everyone merely as long as he has reason." The postulates of God and immortality in the second *Critique* were developed out of the needs of reason. Yet Kant does not argue for conviction in that context. The assent there – the holding for true – is couched as a "deciding ground" for our speculative need (KpV 5:145). Indeed, the problem he articulates in the *Critique of Practical Reason* is what gets resolved under the science of an ethicotheology; the problem is just the lack of objective sway:

> But as for the way we are to represent this possibility [of realizing the highest good], whether in accordance with the universal laws of nature without a wise author presiding over nature or only on the supposition of such an author, reason cannot decide this objectively. Now a *subjective* condition of reason enters into this. (KpV 5:145)

---

²⁷ I have in this chapter followed the convention of rendering *Glaube* as faith, and not belief, when it is pertaining to practical and/or religious matters; belief is typically reserved for theoretical matters. For a more detailed accounting of Kant's taxonomy of opinion, knowing, and believing, please see the Stevenson, Chignell, and Trullinger pieces cited in footnote 15.

In this context, it may universally be a need of reason to assent to the existence of God. However, there is nothing beyond reason's own need that gives warrant to the claim. Reason cannot, he suggests, "decide this objectively," or, we might say, with reference to anything objective.

Conviction in this context is rooted in the fact of freedom. The shared final end that entails the reciprocal relation of freedom and nature is thus based on *fact*. And, as Nuzzo observes, this is not the fact of reason to which our will is subject in the second *Critique*. Rather, this "is a discovery of the reflective faculty of judgment."[28] Freedom is thus an object for our judging. Kant writes that freedom "is the concept of the supersensible which proves its objective reality ... in nature" (KU 5:474). It is not simply a fact for our will; it is a fact of reality observed in reflection. As such a fact, then, it is able to secure the connection of the other two ideas of reason – God and immortality – to nature as well. In proving itself as real in the natural order through its causality, it thereby makes God and immortality real to us. The entire system of nature actually looks different to us. It appears now as creation (that is, created), and not merely lawful.

The further measure of conviction that Kant links with objectivity is *communicability*. This is not surprising, as our ability to communicate, and our common sense for things, coincides with objectivity for Kant.[29] Our faith in God, from the perspective of this moral proof, must be able to be communicated. That is, we can expect that any human being will also judge nature to be a meaningful system of ends, organized by the fact of human freedom, that must have been intended by a willful being. Communicability presents a clear analogy here with judgments of taste. Beauty is not something that we can prove in the manner of cognition or logic; yet we rightfully claim that things are beautiful, based on how they appear. Thus, under an ethicotheology, we can expect other human beings to observe the same thing about nature and arrive at the same judgment of it. While Kant does not say much on this front, we can surmise, I think, that as in a judgment of taste, the actual agreement or disagreement of others will not shake our conviction. Both judgments made out in the territory, then, have a distinctive kind of truthfulness and objectivity to them. Both require and indeed implore the assent of others, but neither is able to secure it. The best we can do is evaluate for ourselves whether the grounds on which our own judgments rest are those that can be shared.

---

[28] Nuzzo, *Kant and the Unity of Reason*, 368. She further notes the difference in language Kant uses. In the second *Critique*, it is a *Faktum der Vernunft*, but here it is a *Tatsache*.

[29] This was argued for in Chapter 3.

What conviction – and its objective basis – reveals is that in reflection, we find traces of the supersensible in the sensible. I have been highlighting how Kant takes the physical teleology to rest on ethicotheology. Indeed, in a remarkable final passage of the text, Kant writes:

> The fact that the rational beings in the actual world find ample material for physical teleology ... serves as the desired confirmation of the moral argument, insofar as nature is thus capable of displaying [*aufzustellen*] something analogous to the (moral) ideas of reason. For the concept of a supreme cause that has understanding ... thereby acquires sufficient reality for the reflecting power of judgment. (KU 5:479)

These are multiple remarkable conclusions Kant draws here. First, Kant here is clearly highlighting the objective character of the claims in his emphasis on "rational beings in the actual world [*der wirklichen Welt*]." The real world itself gives us the material we need for faith. Second, what we find in the real world, on account of the fact of freedom, is that the moral ideas are on display or exhibited in the natural order. That is, the natural order "puts on" something like the moral ideas for us. Third, the reflecting power of judgment, in taking account of things objectively, gives God "sufficient reality [*hinreichende Realität*]." While we still do not get knowledge of God, we have a kind of ample evidence for a faith that is convinced of his existence and role in creating a meaningful world order.

Our faith in God, then, hereby gains conviction: We are *convinced* of God's existence through our encounters with living beings while out in the territory, and our reflections on the systems of freedom and nature from this same vantage point. We are so convinced, in part, because life and the organization of nature appear to us (reflectively) as having traces of the supersensible in the sensible. Life and nature are meaningful, and not merely lawful. They exceed a merely lawful understanding of them, and their inextricable relation to human life and meaning thus confirms for us a moral author of nature. What is unseen comes then, in some way, to be seen. Perhaps more than any other place in the text, too, we find occasion for hope.

Conclusion
To See What Good Is There[1]

For what may we hope? The thesis of this book is that the third *Critique* is oriented by the problem of hope. Hope is born of the interests of reason, but these interests can only be met in a sphere of human experience not subject to or born of the demands of reason. Whatever speaks to the interests of hope must do so *disinterestedly*. What we hope for is that our wills can be efficacious, that the good we do is not in vain but can have real effects in the world. This, though, depends on something that is not subject to our wills, namely how things actually are. Will the world conform? Will nature yield? The stakes of our interest in this are high: Both reason's, self-consistency and the risk of existential despair are on the line. Kant's concern for these seems to grow as his career progresses; the third *Critique* is his most systematic treatment of the maintenance of hope in what can sometimes seem a banal or cruel world.

The third *Critique* addresses the question of our hopes for nature by describing a separate and independent sphere of human life. This sphere is not governed by the laws of either cognition or morality, but is a sphere where we must instead use our *judgment*. He names this sphere *the territory* – the land beyond jurisdiction that makes possible a transition between the lawful realms of freedom and nature. What we find out there in the territory are things we cannot understand: beautiful things and living things. These are the things that give us hope – indeed, legitimate our hope – that the world is not so bad, that maybe there is some good there, and that the demands we have to make the world better can in fact be realized by our own efforts. We need not despair, because there is beauty and because there is life. These two aspects of the text – aesthetic and teleological judgments – are held together because they share in a basic sense we find out in the territory that the world may accommodate our

---

[1] Dante opens the Inferno: "to treat the good I found there as well/I'll tell what I saw," Dante, *The Inferno* (New York: Farrar, Straus and Giroux, 1994), 5.

desire after all. This sense is occasioned by what is exterior and objective for us, most importantly.

We are inevitably led to the question of hope because of the intractable dialectic between freedom and nature. While this dialectic may express itself existentially in the human being as despair, it has deep, metaphysical, and transcendental grounds for Kant. His treatment of the problem in the third *Critique* is from this philosophical perspective. Kant is thus forced, by the structure of his own philosophical system – his commitments to the relation between reason and nature – to return to what the *Critique of Pure Reason* had ruled out. The issue of the third *Critique*, taken as how the unconditioned may relate to the conditioned, or how a free being is able to bring things into being in the natural order, is properly a metaphysical one.

This is not to say that what Kant engages in here violates the limits he laid down in the first *Critique* for the use of reason in speculation. There, reason's use was illegitimate because it exceeded anything given in an empirical representation – it sought to extend out beyond what we could experience. In the territory of judgment, by contrast, we exercise our faculties while considering what is given to us in an empirical representation. This making sense – an activity of interpretation – is our attempt to get at how things are when they are beyond what we can comprehend. In addition to introducing a third sphere of human experience, Kant thus also legitimates a third way that human beings have of thinking about and being involved with things. We can reflect on things coming into being, even though we cannot *know* them in this regard. We can have a sense of life, of the cosmos, and of the meaningfulness of the natural order. We cannot know these things as they are, but we are referred to them and we can interpret things along these lines.

What we come to when we reflect on things in the territory is, first, beauty. There are beautiful things in nature and in human culture. Beauty gives us a sense that there is a larger cosmic whole to which both nature and freedom belong; it is a cosmos to which *we* belong. Beauty also gives us the sense that we belong to a larger human community – there is a basic, shared character of being human. In all of this, too, there is something that exceeds nature and us, namely spirit, and with that, life. All of this gives us reason to hope.

There is second, life. Life, living beings, exist. We cannot conceive of such a possibility save for teleologically. There are simply things whose existence cannot be grasped except as purposive. And, we cannot help but ask *why* they exist. The marvel of life and the apparent meaningfulness of the natural order in its systematic organization give us further reason to hope. It also secures for us one of the oldest bastions of hopefulness, namely faith in God.

But while all of this speaks to the interests of hope, we do not have these experiences so that we can hope. The only way they are able to speak to the interests of hope is simply that we have them. That is to say, we would have them even if they did not speak to the interests of reason; there would still be beautiful things and living beings.

The third *Critique* thus makes a compelling case for the arts, culture, religion, and natural sciences as profound and necessary aspects to human existence. They cultivate, on Kant's account, a sense of belonging to something larger than ourselves – the human community and a cosmic order. Their existential benefit can perhaps be best understood in a section I have not treated in this book: section §59, "On beauty as a symbol of morality." In arguing that beauty symbolizes morality, Kant basically asserts that beauty *is like* the good. It is not the good, but it reminds us of it. We see this through the text at various moments. Beautiful nature reminds us of moral ideas. Life in nature *reminds us* of the meaningfulness of things. Similarly, the mode of these reminders is *like* knowledge. We are sure of our judgments of taste, and confident in our sharing of them. We are convinced of the meaningful order of nature and the existence of God; they are valid interpretations of how things are, grounded in how they appear to us. While we cannot prove the beauty of something or the value of the living being as part of the system of nature, our encounters remind us of what it is like to know something, this is what it feels like. In reminding us both of the good and of cognition, judgments out in the territory are transitional and grounding for each of those two spheres.

In Chapter 1, I highlighted the morally Copernican worldview that Kant's practical philosophy portends – there is potentially no "outside" to the demands of human freedom. Everything in life becomes subsumed under our need to bring about a rational world order. I suggested there, too, that the third *Critique* may offer a kind of relief from the potential hegemony of the practical, as here we find two crucial antidotes. First, our encounters out in the territory are of an exterior world that exceeds what we can do and know. Second, as emphasized previously, we find that the world of human morality is given a context, is situated within broader spheres of meaning. In these, Kant clearly finds beauty and living beings – both in their excessiveness – to be central and load-bearing features of human existence.

Bibliography

Allen, Barry, "The Abyss of Contingency: Purposiveness and Contingency in Kant and Darwin," *History of Philosophy Quarterly* 20:4 (2003): 373–391.
Allison, Henry, *Kant's Theory of Taste: A Reading of the Critique of Aesthetic Judgment* (Cambridge: Cambridge University Press, 2001).
Ameriks, Karl, "How to Save Kant's Deduction of Taste," *Journal of Value Inquiry* 16 (1982): 295–302.
"Kant on Science and Common Knowledge," in Eric Watkins, ed., *Kant and the Sciences* (Oxford: Oxford University Press, 2001), 31–52.
Arendt, Hannah, *Lectures on Kant's Political Philosophy* (Chicago: University of Chicago Press, 1989).
Aristotle, *Metaphysics* (Indianapolis: Hackett Publishing, 2016).
On the Soul, in W. S. Hett (trans.) *Aristotle: On the Soul, Parva Naturalia, On Breath* (Cambridge, MA: Loeb Classical Library, 1957), 2–203.
Arthos, John, "The Paradigmatic Interpenetration of Hermeneutics and Rhetoric," in Theodore George and Gert-Jan van der Heiden, eds., *The Gadamerian Mind* (London: Routledge, 2021), 400–417.
Bacon, Francis, *The New Organon* (London: Cambridge University Press, 2000).
Beiser, Frederick C., *The Genesis of Neo-Kantianism, 1796–1880* (New York: Oxford University Press, 2014).
Blumenberg, Hans, "Self-Preservation and Intertia: On the Constitution of Modern Rationality," *Contemporary German Philosophy* 3 (1983): 209–256.
Breazeale, Daniel, "'The Summit of Kantian Speculation': Fichte's Reception of the Third *Critique*," *Anuario Filosófico* 52:1 (2019): 113–144.
Breitenbach, Angela, "Two Views on Nature: A Solution to the Kant's Antinomy of Mechanism and Teleology," *British Journal for the History of Philosophy* 16:2 (2008): 351–369.
Bruno, Paul, *Kant's Concept of Genius: Its Origin and Function in the Third Critique* (New York: Continuum, 2010).
Buck, Carl Darling, *A Dictionary of Selected Synonyms in the Principal Indo-European Languages* (Chicago: University of Chicago Press, 1949).
Cassirer, H. W., *A Commentary of Kant's Critique of Judgment* (New York: Routledge, 2016).
Chignell, Andrew, "Belief in Kant," *Philosophical Review* 116:3 (2007): 323–360.

"Rational Hope, Moral Order, and the Revolution of the Will," in Eric Watkins, ed., *Divine Order, Human Order, and the Order of Nature* (London: Oxford University Press, 2013), 197–218.

"Rational Hope, Possibility, and Divine Action," in Eric Watkins, ed., *Kant's Religion within the Boundaries of Mere Reason: A Critical Guide* (Cambridge: Cambridge University Press, 2014), 98–117.

Clark, Christopher, *Iron Kingdom: The Rise and Downfall of Prussia, 1600–1947* (Cambridge, MA: Harvard University Press, 2006).

Clewis, Robert, *The Kantian Sublime and the Revelation of Freedom* (London: Cambridge University Press, 2009).

Crawford, Donald, *Kant's Aesthetic Theory* (Madison: University of Wisconsin Press, 1974).

Cureton, Adam, "Reasonable Hope in Kant's Ethics," *Kantian Review* 23:2 (2018): 181–203.

Dante, *The Inferno* (New York: Farrar, Straus and Giroux, 1994).

Debord, Charles, "*Geist* and Communication in Kant's Theory of Aesthetic Ideas," *Kantian Review* 17:2 (2012): 177–190.

Descartes, René, "Meditations on First Philosophy," in John Cottingham, Robert Stoothoff, Dugald Murdoch (trans.) *The Philosophical Writings of Descartes*, vol. 2 (London: Cambridge University Press, 1984), 1–62.

"Passions of the Soul," in John Cottingham, Robert Stoothoff, Dugald Murdoch (trans.) *The Philosophical Writings of Descartes*, vol. 1 (Cambridge: Cambridge University Press, 1985), 325–404.

"*Rules for the Direction of the Mind,*" in John Cottingham, Robert Stoothoff, Dugald Murdoch (trans.) *The Philosophical Writings of Descartes*, vol. 1 (London: Cambridge University Press, 1985), 7–78.

Edwards, Jeffrey, *Substance, Force, and the Possibility of Knowledge: On Kant's Philosophy of Material Nature* (Berkeley: University of California Press, 2000).

"One More Time: Kant's Metaphysics of Nature and the Idea of Transition," in Cinzia Ferrini, ed., *Eredita kantiane* (Rome: Bibliopolis, 2004), 155–188.

Elden, Stuart, *The Birth of Territory* (Chicago: University of Chicago Press, 2013).

Figal, Günter, *Aesthetics as Phenomenology: The Appearance of Things* (Indianapolis: Indiana University Press, 2010).

Ford, Richard T., "Law's Territory (A History of Jurisdiction)," *Michigan Law Review* 97 (1999): 843–930.

Förster, Eckart, *Kant's Final Synthesis: An Essay on the Opus postumum* (Cambridge, MA: Harvard University Press, 2000).

Friedlander, Eli, *Expressions of Judgment: As Essay on Kant's Aesthetics* (Cambridge, MA: Harvard University Press, 2015).

Funderbunk, L., "Book Review of *Kant's Concept of Teleology*," *Kant-Studien* 62:1 (1971): 137–138.

Gadamer, Hans-Georg, "Intuition and Vividness," in Robert Bernasconi, ed., *The Relevance of the Beautiful and Other Essays* (Cambridge: Cambridge University Press, 1986), 155–170.

Truth and Method (New York: Continuum Press, 1995).
Gammon, Martin, "'Exemplary Originality': Kant on Genius and Imitation," *Journal of the History of Philosophy* 35:4 (1997): 563–592.
Gasché, Rodolphe, *The Idea of Form: Rethinking Kant's Aesthetics* (Stanford: Stanford University Press, 2003).
Ginsborg, Hannah, *The Normativity of Nature: Essays on Kant's Critique of Judgment* (Oxford: Oxford University Press, 2015).
Grier, Michelle, *Kant's Doctrine of Transcendental Illusion* (Cambridge: Cambridge University Press, 2001).
Guyer, Paul, "Feeling and Freedom," in *Kant and the Experience of Freedom* (Cambridge: Cambridge University Press, 1996), 278–313.
  "From Nature to Morality: Kant's New Argument in the 'Critique of Teleological Judgment,'" in *Kant's System of Natura and Freedom: Selected Essays* (Oxford: Oxford University Press, 2005).
  ed., *Kant's Critique of the Power of Judgment: Critical Essays* (Lanham, MD: Rowman and Littlefield, 2003), 314–342.
  "The Unity of Nature and Freedom: Kant's Conception of the System of Philosophy," in *Kant's System of Nature and Freedom: Selected Essays* (Oxford: Oxford University Press, 2005), 278–313.
Hamlyn, D. W., *Aristotle's De Anima Books II and III* (Oxford: Oxford University Press, 1968).
  "'Koinē Aisthēsis," *The Monist* 52 (1968): 195–209.
Hampshire, Stuart, "The Social Spirit of Mankind," in Eckart Förster, ed., *Kant's Transcendental Deductions: The Three Critiques and the Opus postumum* (Stanford: Stanford University Press, 1989), 145–156.
Hegel, G. W. F., *Faith and Knowledge* (Albany: State University of New York Press, 1977).
Heine, Heinrich, *Religion and Philosophy in Germany* (Albany: State University of New York Press, 1986).
Henrich, Dieter, "Kant's Notion of a Deduction and the Methodological Background of the first *Critique*," in Eckart Förster, ed., *Kant's Transcendental Deductions* (Stanford: Stanford University Press, 1989), 27–46.
Hicks, R.D, "Introduction" in *Aristotle De Anima* (Cambridge: Cambridge University Press, 2015, xix–lxxxiii).
Howard, Stephen, "The Transition within the Transition: The *Übergang* from the *Selbstsetzungslehre* to the Ether Proofs in Kant's *Opus postumum*," *Kant-Studien* 110:4 (2019): 595–617.
Huneman, Phillippe, "Purposiveness, Necessity, and Contingency," in Ina Goy and Eric Watkins, eds., *Kant's Theory of Biology* (Berlin: De Gruyter, 2014), 185–202.
Iltis, Carolyn, "Leibniz and the Vis Viva Controversy," *Isis* 62:1 (1971): 21–35.
Insole, Christopher, "The Irreducible Importance of Religious Hope in Kant's Conception of the Highest Good," *Philosophy* 83 (2008): 333–351.
Kalar, Brent, "The Ethical Significance of Kant's *Sensus Communis*: From Aesthetic to Ethical Community," *Idealistic Studies* 47:1&2 (2018): 43–58.

Kemal, Salim, *Kant and Fine Art: An Essay on Kant and the Philosophy of Fine Art and Culture* (Oxford: Oxford University Press, 1986).
Kern, Andrea, "Aesthetic Self-Consciousness and *Sensus Communis*: On the Significance of Ordinary Language in Kant's Analytic of the Beautiful," *Graduate Faculty Philosophy Journal* 39:2 (2019): 451–471.
Kneller, Jane, *Kant and the Power of Imagination* (Cambridge: Cambridge University Press, 2007), cf. Chapters 2–4.
Kreines, James, "The Inexplicability of Kant's *Naturzweck*: Kant on Teleology, Explanation, and Biology," *Archiv fur Geschichte der Philosophie* 87 (2005): 270–311.
Kuehn, Manfred, "Kant's Teachers in the Exact Sciences," in Eric Watkins, ed., *Kant and the Sciences* (Oxford: Oxford University Press, 2001), 11–30.
Scottish Common Sense in Germany, 1768–1800: A Contribution to the History of Critical Philosophy (Kingston: McGill-Queen's University Press, 1987).
Leibniz, Gottfried, *De Jure Suprematu Principum Germaniae (Caeserinus Fürstenerius)*, in *The Political Writings of Leibniz* (New York: Cambridge University Press, 1972).
Monadology, in R. S. Woolhouse and Richard Francks, eds., *Philosophical Texts* (Oxford: Oxford University Press, 1998), 267–281.
Lyotard, Jean-François, "Sensus Communis," *Paragraph* 11 (1988): 1–23.
Lessons on the Analytic of the Sublime (Stanford: Stanford University Press, 1994).
The Online Lidell-Scott-Jones Greek-English Lexicon, via Thesaurus Linguae Graecae.
Makkreel, Rudolf A., *Imagination and Interpretation in Kant: The Hermeneutical Import of the Critique of Judgment* (Chicago, University of Chicago Press, 1990).
Orientation and Judgment in Hermeneutics (Chicago: University of Chicago Press, 2015).
Makkreel, Rudolf A. and Luft, Sebastian *Neo-Kantianism in Contemporary Philosophy* (Bloomington: Indiana University Press, 2010).
Malpas, Jeff and Karsten Thiel, "Kant's Geography and Reason," in Stuart Elden and Eduardo Mendieta, eds., *Reading Kant's Geography* (Albany: State University of New York Press, 2011).
Martin, Gottfried, *Kant's Metaphysics and Theory of Science* (Manchester: Manchester University Press, 1955).
McFarland, J. D., *Kant's Concept of Teleology* (Edinburgh: Edinburgh University Press, 1970).
"The Bogus Unity of the Kantian Philosophy," in François Duchesneau, Pierre Laberge & Bryan E. Morrisey, eds., *Actes du congres d'ottawa sur Kant dans les traditions Anglo-Americans et Continentales tenu du 10 au 14 octobre 1974/ Proceedings of the Ottawa Congress on Kant in the Anglo-american and Continental Traditions Held 10–14 October, 1974* (Ottawa: University of Ottawa Press, 1976), 180–196.
McLaughlin, Peter, *Kant's Critique of Teleology in Biological Explanation* (Lewiston, NY: Edwin Mellen Press, 1990).

Meerbote, Ralf, "Reflection on Beauty," in Ted Cohen and Paul Guyer, eds., *Essays in Kant's Aesthetics* (Chicago: University of Chicago Press, 1982), 55–86.
Mensch, Jennifer, *Kant's Organicism: Epigenesis and the Development of Critical Philosophy* (Chicago: University of Chicago Press, 2013).
Muchnik, Pablo, *Kant's Theory of Evil: An Essay on the Dangers of Self-Love and Aprioricity of History* (New York: Lexington Books, 2008).
Naas, Michael, *Plato and the Invention of Life* (New York: Fordham University Press, 2018).
Nassar, Dalia, "Analogical Reflection as a Source for the Science of Life: Kant and the Possibility of the Biological Sciences," *Studies in History and Philosophy of Science* 58 (2016): 57–66.
Neal, Robert J.M., "Kant's Ideality of Genius," *Kant-Studien* 103 (2012): 351–360.
Neiman, Susan, *The Unity of Reason* (Oxford: Oxford University Press, 1994).
Nuzzo, Angelica, *Kant and the Unity of Reason* (West Lafayette, IN: Purdue University Press, 2005).
  "Leben and Leib in Kant and Hegel," *Hegel-Jahrbuch* 2 (2007): 97–101.
  Ideal Embodiment (Bloomington: Indiana University Press, 2008).
O'Neill, Onora, Kant on Reason and Religion, in *The Tanner Lectures on Human Values* (Salt Lake City: University of Utah Press, 1997), 269–308.
Ostaric, Lara, "Kant on the Normativity of Creative Production," *Kantian Review* 17:1, (2012): 75–107.
Papineau, David, "The Vis Viva Controversy: Do Meanings Matter?" *Studies in History and Philosophy of Science,* 8:2 (1977): 111–142.
Parmenides, *On Nature, Early Greek Philosophy, Volume V: Western Greek Thinkers, Part 2*. Edited and translated by André Laks, Glenn W. Most. Loeb Classical Library 528. (Cambridge, MA: Harvard University Press, 2016).
Peters, F.E., *Greek Philosophical Terms: A Historical Lexicon* (New York: New York University Press, 1967).
Plato, *Theaetetus*, in John M. Cooper, ed., *Plato: Complete Works* (Indianapolis: Hackett Publishing, 1997).
Proulx, Jeremy, "Art and the Fecundity of Nature," in Stefano Bacin, Alfredo Ferrarin, Claudio La Rocca and Margit Ruffing, eds., *Kant und die Philosophie in weltbürgerlicher Absicht: Akten des XI. Internationalen Kant-Kongress* (Berlin: De Gruyter, 2013): 191–201.
Rauscher, Fred, Book review of *Kant on Beauty and Biology: An Interpretation of the Critique of Judgment*. Notre Dame Philosophical Reviews, May 7, 2009.
Reid, Thomas, *An Inquiry into the Human Mind and the Principles of Common Sense* (Edinburgh: Edinburgh University Press, 1764).
Rohlf, Michael, "The Transition from Nature to Freedom in Kant's Third Critique," *Kant-Studien* 99 (2008): 339–360.
Ross, David, "Introduction," in David Ross, ed., *Aristotle De Anima* (Oxford: Oxford University Press, 1961), 1–59.

Rossi, Philip, "*Kant as a Christian Philosopher: Hope and the Symbols of the Christian Faith*," Philosophy Today 25:1 (1981): 24–33.
Sassen, Brigitte, "Artistic Genius and the Question of Creativity," in Paul Guyer, ed., *Kant's Critique of the Power of Judgment: Critical Essays* (New York: Rowman and Littlefield, 2003).
Schaefer, John D., *Sensus Communis: Vico, Rhetoric, and the Limits of Relativism* (Durham: Duke University Press, 1990).
Schaftesbury, Anthony Ashley Cooper, *Sensus Communis: An Essay on the Freedom of Wit and Humour*, (London: Egbert Sanger, 1709).
Schelling, F. W. J., *The Philosophy of Art* (Minneapolis: University of Minnesota Press, 1989).
Schutt, Marie Zermatt, "Kant's Moral Theology," *British Journal for the History of Philosophy*, 18:4 (2010): 611–633.
Sensen, Oliver, "Dignity and the Formula of Humanity," in Jens Timmermann, ed., *Kant's Groundwork for the Metaphysics of Morals: A Critical Guide*, (Cambridge: Cambridge University Press, 2009): 102–118.
Sheehan, James, *German History 1770–1866* (Oxford: Clarendon Press, 1989).
Smith, John E., "Foreword," to Richard Kroner, *Kant's Weltanschauung: The Ethical and Religious Derivation of Kant's Worldview* (Chicago: University of Chicago Press, 1956).
Stevenson, Leslie, "Opinion, Belief or Faith, and Knowledge," *Kantian Review*, 7 (2003): 72–101.
Stoner, Samuel, "On the Primacy of the Spectator in Kant's Account of Genius," *The Review of Metaphysics* 70 (2016): 87–117.
Sweet, Kristi, "Reflection: Its Structure and Meaning inn Kant's Judgements of Taste," *Kantian Review* 14:1 (2009): 53–80.
  "Kant and the Culture of Discipline: Rethinking the Nature of Nature," *Epoché: A Journal for the History of Philosophy* 15:1 (2010): 121–138.
  Kant on Practical Life: From Duty to History (Cambridge: Cambridge University Press, 2013).
  "What Is Philosophical about Kant's Anthropology," *International Journal of Philosophical Studies* 25:3 (2017): 109–118.
Tarbet, David. W., "The Fabric of Metaphor in Kant's Critique of Pure Reason," *Journal of the History of Philosophy* 6:3 (1968): 257–270.
Terrall, Mary, "Vis Viva *Revisited*," *History of Science* xlii (2004): 189–209.
Thorndike, Oliver, *Kant's Transition Project and Late Philosophy: Connecting the Opus Postumum and the Metaphysics of Morals* (London: Bloomsbury, 2018).
Toyoda, Tetsuya, *Theory and Politics of the Law of Nations: Political Bias in International Law Discourse of German Court Councilors in the Seventeenth and Eighteenth Centuries* (Leiden: Brill Publishing, 2011).
Trullinger, Joseph, "Kant's Two Touchstones for Conviction: The Incommunicable Dimension of Moral Faith," *The Review of Metaphysics* 67 (2013): 369–403.

Tuschling, Burkhard, "The System of Transcendental Idealism: Questions Raised and Left Open in the Kritik der Urteilskraft," *The Southern Journal of Philosophy* 30 (1991): 196–210.

Watkins, Eric, "Nature in General as a System of Ends," in Ina Goy and Eric Watkins, eds., *Kant's Theory of Biology* (Berlin: de Gruyter, 2014), 117–130.

Westphal, K.R.,"Epistemic Reflection and Cognitive Reference in Kant's Transcendental Response to Skepticism," *Kant-Studien* 94 (2003): 135–171.

Wood, Allen, *Kant's Rational Theology* (Ithaca, NY: Cornell University Press, 1978).

Woolwine, Sarah, "Systematicity in the Critique of Judgment: The Emergence of a Unified Subject," *Journal of Speculative Philosophy* 25:4 (2011): 343–358.

Yovel, Yirmihau, *Kant the Philosophy of History* (Princeton, NJ: Princeton University Press, 1980).

Ypi, Lea, "The Problem of Systematic Unity in Kant's Two Definitions of Philosophy," in Stefano Bacin, Alfredo Ferrarin, Claudio La Rocca and Margit Ruffing, eds., *Kant und die Philosophie in weltbürgerlicher Absicht. Akten des XI. Internationalen Kant-Kongresses* (Berlin: De Gruyter, 2013), 773–785.

Zammito, John, *The Genesis of Kant's Critique of Judgment* (Chicago: Chicago University Press, 1992).

Kant, Herder, and the Birth of Anthropology (Chicago: University of Chicago Press, 2002).

"Kant and the Medical Faculty: One 'Conflict of the Faculties'," *Epoché: A Journal for the History of Philosophy* 22:2 (2018): 429–451.

"The 'Sublime,' the 'Supersensible Substrate,' and 'Spirit'—Intuitions of the Ultimate in Kant's third Critique," in Stephen Palmquist, ed., *Kant on Intuition: Western and Asian Perspectives on Transcendental Idealism* (London: Routledge, 2019).

Zinkin, Melissa, "Kant and the Pleasure of 'Mere Reflection'," *Inquiry* 55:5 (2012): 433–453.

"Kant's Supersensible Substratum of Humanity," in *Kant und die Philosophie in weltbürgerlicher Absicht, Akten des XI. Internationalen Kant-Kongresses*, Band 4 (Berlin: De Gruyter, 2013), 334–342.

Zuckert, Rachel, "Boring Beauty and Universal Morality: Kant on the Ideal of Beauty," *Inquiry* 48:2 (2005): 107–130.

Kant on Beauty and Biology: An Interpretation of the Critique of Judgment (Cambridge: Cambridge University Press, 2007).

"Hidden Antinomies of Practical Reason, and Kant's Religion of Hope," *Kant Yearbook* 10 (2018): 199–217.

"Is Kantian Hope a Feeling?" in Kelly Sorenson and Diane Williamson, eds., *Kant and the Faculty of Feeling* (Cambridge: Cambridge University Press, 2018), 242–259.

Index

absolute, 3, 8, 22, 102, 110, 131, 166
   a demand so, 190
   determination, 4, 92
   end of reason, 27–28
   exteriority, 75
   good, 51
   idealism, 60
   knowing, 22
   relation to ourselves, 96
   totality of conditions, 25
   unity, 83
action
   free moral, 136
   freedom in autonomous, 173
actions
   free, 131
activity
   cognitive, 124
   free human, 132
aesthetic 'should', 110
aesthetic ideas, 19, 78, 94, 98, 131–136, 140, 142–147, 149–153, 183
aesthetics, 6, 11–12, 14
   formalist, 77
   visionary, 132
Agamben, Giorgio, 86
agreeable, the, 110
All, the, 188–191
Allison, Henry, 11, 13, 64, 93, 105–106, 134
Althusius, Johannes, 42
Ameriks, Karl, 128, 195
amphiboly, 39, 63
antinomy, 190
apprehension, 178
Arendt, Hannah, 54, 106
Aristotle, 25, 75, 86, 88, 116–119, 142, 167
art, 1, 6, 8, 73, 77–78, 90, 94, 132–137, 147–150, 185
   and genius, 16, 97, 134, 138–141

beautiful, 69, 77–79, 94, 97–98, 100, 131, 133, 135–144, 146, 183
   fine, 97, 102, 132
   objects of, 137
   purpose of being, 137
   work of, 19, 78, 98, 139–142, 147, 149, 152, 167, 177
artifacts
   human, 68, 137, 166–167
arts, the, 7, 15, 142, 151, 206

beauty, 1, 8, 55, 93, 95–96, 106, 109–111, 113, 135, 152–154, 204, 206
   and teleology, 8, 20, 34, 55
   apprehension of, 135
   artistic, 8, 48, 134–135
   as its own form, 111
   as symbol of morality, 12, 206
   claim of, 109, 111
   deduction of, 115
   formal, 95
   formalist interpretation of, 94
   'free', 95
   in nature, 48, 134, 151
   merely formal purposiveness of, 96
   objective, 110–112
   standard of, 94
being
   biological or animal, 180
   free, 205
   necessary, the idea of a, 83
being in common, 105–129, 150
Beiser, Frederick C., 8–9
Beneke, Friedrich Eduard, 9
Blumenberg, Hans, 160
bodies
   inner nature of, 88
body
   human, form of a, 136
Breitenbach, Andrea, 162
Bruno, Paul, 138

Cassirer, H. W., 9, 114
causes
   final, 194
Chignell, Andrew, 32–34
civil condition, 44
Cleon, 117
cognition, 33, 40, 50, 57, 60–63, 65–66, 72, 74, 78, 124, 129, 155, 182, 191, 200, 202, 204, 206
   and moral life, 19
   and morality, 61, 70, 153, 183, 196
   context of, 65
   determinate, 63, 71, 127
   domain of, 15, 42, 47, 67, 70
   empirical, 163, 166
   experience and, 63
   faculty of, 14, 16, 36, 66, 124, 126, 128, 153, 180
   in general, 72–74, 107, 125–126
   judgments of, 64, 112–114, 126
   objects of, 37, 63
   possibility of, 72–73, 107
   possible, 40, 42, 46–47
   rational, 60
   sources of, 63
   structures of, 62
   theoretical, 28–29
Cohen, Hermann, 9
common sense, 116, 118–119, 121–122, 124, 202
communality
   barest form of, 129
concept, 23, 27, 39, 64, 67, 71, 73–74, 77–79, 85, 95–96, 98, 106–107, 111, 113, 115, 128, 138, 144–146, 150, 152, 165–167, 169–171
   empirical, 68
   of a supreme cause, 203
   of an organism, 90
   of ends, 172
   of freedom, 39, 42, 45, 49, 56
   of nature, 17, 39, 45
   of objective purposiveness, 95
   of organicity, 157
   of perfection, 96
   of territory, 6, 42–43
   of the supersensible, 202
   of the understanding, 62–63, 146
   of the whole, 168
   without the mediation of a, 128
concepts, 28, 40, 60, 65–66, 78–79, 94, 97, 106, 141, 147–148, 150, 166
   determinate, 94
   field of, 40
   mediating, 49

   of nature, 42, 46, 49, 60
   of practical reason, 195
   of reason, 79, 98, 145, 166
   of reflection, 39
   of the understanding, 21, 63, 147
cosmic, 2, 5–6, 16, 18, 32, 34, 53, 55, 81–82, 84, 88, 155, 205
Crawford, Donald, 10, 132
critique, 14, 22, 59, 62, 145, 149, 195
   of the power of judgment, 16
   of traditional metaphysics, 58
Critique of Aesthetic Judgment, 6, 12, 15, 17, 67, 109, 111, 133, 152, 154–155, 159, 183, 185, 196
Critique of Judgment, the, 1–3, 20, 27, 32, 34–35, 38, 40, 48–49, 51, 53–55, 57, 60, 62, 70, 75, 90, 93, 104–106, 126, 133, 156, 161, 177, 186–187, 190, 192, 194, 204–206
Critique of Practical Reason, the, 1, 5, 14, 24–26, 32, 92, 101, 109, 186, 189–190, 195, 201–202
Critique of Pure Reason, the, 1, 5, 19, 21, 23–24, 26, 30, 37–40, 42, 47, 57, 60, 62–63, 65, 75, 79, 89, 94, 97, 102, 106, 108–109, 123, 126, 131, 136, 144, 149, 161–162, 186, 188–190, 195, 200, 205
Critique of Taste, 14
critique of taste, a, 14
Critique of Teleological Judgment, 12, 16, 19, 154–156, 169–170, 176–177, 182–185, 196, 199
culture, 1, 19, 36, 41, 48, 119, 148, 158–159, 170, 173–175, 177, 181, 184, 205

Debord, Charles, 132
deduction, 19, 38, 106–115, 126–128, 133–134, 136, 153
   purpose of a, 108, 126
Derrida, Jacques, 86
Descartes, René, 87–88, 116, 118, 120
desire, 14, 20, 23, 28, 33, 58, 71, 101, 173, 175–176, 200, 205
   faculty of, 14, 20, 101, 200
   for metaphysical objects, 23
   for the unconditioned, 28
   nature of, 173
   rational, 23
   reason's, to know, 30
Diotima, 111
diversity
   natural, 15
Doctrine of Right, 44
domain, 17, 36, 38, 40–42, 44–47, 52, 54, 63, 67, 70, 97–98, 104, 113, 155–156, 159, 171, 181, 184, 192, 196

domains
  theoretical and practical, 13, 48, 76
Düsing, Klaus, 36
duty, 24, 52, 92, 173, 187, 197
  moral, 192–193

Edwards, Jeffrey, 84, 88
Elden, Stuart, 40
empirical, the, 9–11, 30, 68, 73, 79, 115
end
  final, 19, 157–159, 165, 170, 172–173, 183–186, 190, 192–194, 196, 200, 202
enlargement
  aesthetic, 78
  conceptual, 78, 147–148
  judgments of, 78
enliven, 19, 87, 144–145, 147
epistemology, 9, 50, 120
ethicotheology, 7, 19, 183, 193–194, 196, 201–202
exemplarity, 112, 114, 140–141
existence
  human being's free, 184
experience
  empirical stream of, 136
  formal conditions of, 66
  objective form of, in general, 56, 66
  unity of, 84, 163
expression, 32, 52, 72, 77, 98, 134, 147, 150–152

faculties
  cognitive, 71, 73, 147, 150
  free play of the, 77–78, 98, 137, 148, 154, 183
  harmony of the, 180
faculty, 12–14, 35, 41, 44, 47, 62, 117, 122–123, 127, 152, 178
  cognitive, 146, 193
  fitting, 63
  for judging, 16
  legislating, 42
  productive, 124, 138
faith, 7, 16, 60, 182–184, 189–192, 201–203, 206
feeling, 12–14, 74, 101, 112, 123, 127–129, 147–148, 150, 153, 155, 179–180
  faculty of, 14
  moral, 97
  of freedom, 146
  of life, 101, 148, 180
  of pleasure, 14, 16, 74, 111, 115, 124
  of the beautiful, 98
  of the promotion of life, 91, 180
  pathological, 100
Fichte, Johann Gottlieb, 7–8

Figal, Günter, 69, 140
finitude
  two forms of, 146
force, 18, 23, 41, 44–45, 81, 84, 87, 89, 99–103, 109, 125, 131, 136, 141, 146, 168, 179
  and matter, 18, 81–84, 87–92, 102–103, 180, 187
forces, living, 86–91
  vis viva, 86
Ford, Richard, 40
form, 68, 116, 152, 166, 178
  as effect of its own purposiveness, 166
  barest, 57, 70
  highest, 28, 56, 148
  human, 98, 149
  mere, 67–68, 140
  of being purposeful, 68
  of the object for reflection, 73
  of what appears, the, 77
  of what is beautiful, 93
  purposiveness concerning, 68
formalism, 93
formations
  free, 140
forms
  Ideal, 18
  manifold of, 77
  natural, 159
  organized, 169
Förster, Eckart, 49
freedom, 3, 5, 24, 31, 39, 42, 45, 49, 56, 59, 82, 96–100, 137–138, 144, 147–149, 154, 156, 173, 176, 185–186, 190, 197, 202, 206
  and nature, 2–3, 16–18, 20, 35–39, 46, 48–50, 76, 81–82, 89, 92, 103, 183, 186, 188
  and nature, causalities of, 188
  and nature, combination of, 36
  and nature, gulf between, 2, 40
  and nature, inner unity of, 3
  and nature, ontological unity of, 8
  and nature, problem of, 7
  and nature, spheres of, 16, 37, 46, 50
  and nature, system of, 13, 15, 19, 155, 183, 192, 200, 203
  and nature, unity of, 4, 7–10, 81–82, 85, 92–93, 101, 131, 155, 191, 199
  and rational cosmology, 58
  and reason, 138
  as a fact in nature, 19
  as an aesthetic idea, 98
  demands of, 2–3, 105, 191
  determination of the body by, 98
  domain of, 3, 15, 17–18, 42, 45, 54, 62, 66, 75, 157, 181, 184, 192, 196–198

ends of, 45, 53, 158, 176, 182, 199
excessive, 148
fact of, 184, 202–203
feeling of, 146
force of, 81, 100
inner, 175
intellectual, 172
possibility of, 4, 17, 103
sphere of, 105
system of, 155, 183, 197
work of, 3
Friedlander, Eli, 139, 148

Gadamer, Hans-Georg, 94, 107, 121
Gammon, Martin, 141
Gasché, Rodolphe, 72, 138
genius, 7, 16, 99, 105, 132, 135, 138–144, 146–148, 151–152
 and aesthetic ideas, 19, 131–132, 142, 153
 and nature, 146, 183
 art and, 97, 133–134
 gift of, 131, 145, 147
Ginsborg, Hannah, 10, 141, 162
God, 6, 31, 58–59, 120, 160, 164, 184–192, 199, 203
 and immortality, 201–202
 and life, 184, 200
 argument for, 193
 as moral author of nature, 31, 186, 189–191, 200
 as necessary being, 83, 160
 as the author of a meaningful nature, 19
 as the unconditioned, 26, 28, 186
 existence of, 1, 19, 31, 120, 184, 186, 189–191, 196, 199, 201–202, 206
 faith in, 7, 16, 202–203, 206
 idea of, 144, 186, 189, 191–192
 knowledge of, 92, 187, 203
 postulate of, 31, 190, 193
 proof of, 171
 soul and, 31
Goy, Ina, 158
Guyer, Paul, 6, 10–11, 93, 95, 126, 134, 194–195

happiness, 25, 27, 173, 182, 198
 and hope, 29
 and virtue, 25–26, 191
 cause of, 25
 freedom and, 24
 natural end of, 25, 27
harmony, 27, 61, 72, 75–76, 180
heautonomy, 47, 105
Hegel, G. W. F., 7, 22, 60
Heine, Heinrich, 8, 58, 189, 192
Henrich, Dieter, 38, 108–109

Herbart, Johann Friedrich, 9
Herz, Markus, 14
highest good, 24–27, 31, 51–52, 190–191, 197, 200–201
Hobbes, Thomas, 121
Homer, 142–143
hope, 5, 17–18, 20, 23–24, 28–35, 53, 55, 92, 130, 149, 154, 181, 187, 194, 203
 centrality of, and Kant's system, 20
 character of, 33
 formal, 34
 interests of, 70, 76, 81, 84, 103, 105, 129, 132, 153, 158, 176, 182, 204, 206
 is practical, 29
 need for, 1–2, 18, 24, 50
 problem of, 1–3, 6–7, 16–17, 56, 106, 132, 182, 204–205
 rational, 132
 reason to, 4, 76, 205
 scope, limits, and demands of, 34
 theoretical and practical simultaneity of, 29
Howard, Stephen, 84
humanity
 the idea of, 97
Hume, David, 39, 121
Huneman, Phillippe, 158, 160
hylozoism, 90, 168

idea, 7, 23, 25, 36–37, 93–99, 110, 113, 128, 144, 147, 151, 189
 as concept of reason, 96
 concrete instantiation of an, 95
 cosmological, 188
 indeterminate, of a maximum, 93
Ideal of Beauty, 7, 16, 18, 81–82, 85, 91–98, 101–103, 131, 136, 141, 153
ideas, 6, 21, 31, 59, 76, 95, 97, 99, 139, 143, 145, 151
 moral, 98, 180, 203, 206
 of metaphysical objects, 58
 rational, 79, 145
 regulative function of, 95
imagination, 77, 99, 102, 132, 144, 146–148, 154, 178–179
 and understanding, 71–73, 146–147, 150
 free play of the, 72, 77, 79, 112, 124, 137
 free use of the, 147
 giving life to concepts, 78
 productive force of the, 146
Insole, Christopher, 32
intentionality, 69, 199
interest
 empirical and intellectual, 134
 practical, 29, 194
 practical reason's, 195

interpretation, 6, 8, 12–13, 17, 20, 52, 62, 71, 77, 80, 93, 132, 140, 162, 205
intersubjectivity, 126

judgment, 17, 39, 63, 67, 73, 78–79, 105, 114, 123, 129, 134, 141
  aesthetic, 112, 114
  determinative, 112, 146
  faculty of, 18, 35, 56–57, 106, 115, 154, 202
  of taste, feeling of a, 129
  of the sublime, 177
  power of, 1, 14, 16, 36, 45–49, 60–62, 65, 67, 73, 113, 115, 126, 163, 165, 169, 177, 203
  principle of, 47, 60
  reflective, 4, 6, 10, 36, 38, 48, 56–57, 61–62, 66, 68, 76, 79, 82, 90, 157, 177, 194
  sphere of, 5, 20
  teleological, 6, 17, 157, 165–166, 204
  territory of, 2, 43, 62, 69, 205

Kalar, Brent, 110
Kern, Andrea, 110
Kneller, Jane, 132
Knichen, Andreas, 42
knowledge, 11, 22, 29, 51, 54, 58, 61, 78, 80, 89, 96, 105, 109, 114, 116–118, 120, 122, 126, 187, 190, 200, 206
  and reflection, activity of, 80
  and science, 137
  demands of, 29
  empirical, 12, 30
  jurisdiction of, 123
  moral goodness and, 121
  of God, 92, 187, 203
  of metaphysical objects, 59
Kreines, James, 165
Kroner, Richard, 9
Kuehn, Manfred, 121

lawfulness, 15, 43, 45, 70, 73
laws, 23, 43, 100, 195
  empirical, 54, 156, 158, 163, 198
  for cognition and morality, 196
  mechanistic, 57, 68, 161, 166
  natural, 1, 29–30, 75–76, 159, 161, 163, 166, 181, 191–192, 194, 196, 198, 200–201
  of causality, 21, 64
  of freedom, 45, 195–198, 200
  of morality, 24, 200
  of reason, 67
  of the faculty of desire, 101, 200
  particular, 43, 48–49, 163, 169
  possible systematic relation among, 163
  reason's, 27
  system of, 3, 15–17, 195, 197, 199

Leibniz, Gottfried Wilhelm, 42–44, 87–89, 162
life, 2–4, 7, 16, 18–19, 25–26, 29–32, 41, 48, 51–55, 61, 67, 75, 78, 81–93, 97, 99–103, 105, 118, 121–122, 128–130, 147–149, 153, 155, 157–159, 161, 168–169, 171–174, 176, 180–181, 183–184, 187, 195, 197–200, 203
  as faculty of substance, 89, 101
  as unity, 81, 183
  feeling of, 101, 148, 180
  human form of, 149
  practical, 75, 87
Locke, John, 42
logos, 74–75, 102
Luther, Martin, 119
Lyotard, JeanFrançois, 107

Malpas, Jeff, 39
Martin, Gottfried, 141, 164
Matthews, Eric, 134, 195
McLaughlin, Peter, 162
Mensch, Jennifer, 89, 158
moral law, 14, 24–25, 27, 29, 31–32, 37, 42, 52, 97, 107, 129, 173, 176, 190, 193
moral world, 24, 26, 28, 31, 52, 76, 181, 197
morality, 108, 206
  argument from, 195
  beauty as symbol of, 12, 206
  cognition and, 15, 47, 61, 70, 114, 153, 183, 196, 204
  demands of, 29
  final end of, 197
  laws of, 24, 200
  self-rewarding, 26
  sphere of, 51
Muchnik, Pablo, 172
music, 151

Nassar, Dalia, 162
Natorp, Paul, 9
nature, 3–5, 8, 16–17, 19, 22–24, 27–32, 34–35, 39, 47–48, 50, 52–53, 56, 59, 89–91, 99, 101, 131–132, 134–136, 139, 142–143, 145–146, 148–149, 152, 155, 163, 166, 168–178, 180–181, 184, 186, 189, 192–194, 198, 203, 206
  and aesthetic ideas, 152
  and art, 150
  and communicability, 149
  and freedom, 37, 81, 105
  and God, 191–192
  and happiness, 27, 173
  and moral life, 29–31
  and purposiveness, 170, 186, 193, 199
  and reason, 32, 145

and spirit, 148
and sublimity, 178
and supersensible ground of, 49
and the sublime, 178
as a system of laws, 17
as mechanical, 6, 32, 38, 57, 100, 131, 138, 153, 166, 169, 181
as object of theoretical knowledge, 29
as purposive, 38, 49, 134, 171, 199
as sum total of appearances, 82
as teleological system, 172
as teleological whole, 16
beautiful, 94, 134–135, 151, 205
beneficence of, 29, 173
concept of, 17, 39, 42, 45–46, 49, 60
corporeal, 49
cosmic sense of, 2, 6, 16, 32, 34
domain of, 17, 54, 155–156, 171, 184, 192, 197
empirical laws of, 156, 163
end of, 159, 165, 173, 184
excess of, 147
expansive, 133, 149
final end of, 157–159, 165, 192
force of, 179
influence of, 26, 31, 131, 181
intellectual interest in, 134, 151
laws of, 75, 161, 163, 169, 191–192, 194, 196, 198, 200–201
life and, 203, 206
material, 91, 100, 141, 147
objective purposiveness of, 159
objects in, 137, 183, 186
of the cosmos, 59
possibility of, 16, 31, 47, 149
product of, 73, 138, 166, 168, 185
rational, 16, 180
reason's interest in, 34
sphere of, 16, 105, 172, 197
spiritualized, 149
subjective purposiveness of, 153
system of, purpose of, 198
teleological judgments of, 157
unity of, 163, 188
whole of, 50, 82, 146, 158, 171–172, 176, 178, 184, 199
work of, 31
Neal, Robert J. M., 135
Newton, Isaac, Sir, 143
normativity, 105, 141
noumenal, the, 59, 61
Nuzzo, Angelica, 14, 100, 115, 152, 202

object
 form of, 67–69, 73, 95, 113–114
 purposiveness of the, 17, 73
 representation of, is subjectively purposive, 113
objects
 beautiful, 183
 purposive in themselves, 159
order
 comprehension of, 15
ordered, 5, 15, 23–24, 32, 56–57, 59, 68, 70, 140, 161, 164, 189, 195
ordering, 15, 56, 67, 70, 74–75, 140, 174, 191
organism, 37, 90, 167, 169, 171, 176
originality, 139–142
Ostaric, Lara, 132, 153

Parmenides, 74, 160
perfection
 as complete purposive unity, 188
 idea of, 96
philosophy
 moral, 92
 practical, 10–11, 30, 42, 87, 131, 198, 206
 theoretical and practical, 45
Plato, 51, 96, 111, 116, 142
play, 63, 71, 152
 and art, 137
 and purposiveness without a purpose, 106
 between the imagination and understanding, 77–78
 creative, of the genius, 147
 free, 71–72, 77–79, 98, 112, 124, 137, 148, 154, 183
 mere, 149
 purposive, 137
 subjective, 123, 125
pleasure, 25, 57, 70–71, 73, 77, 79, 105, 108, 111–114, 124–125, 130, 148, 154, 177, 180
 agreeable, 110
 and universality, 110
 contemplative, 65, 71, 135
 feeling of, 12, 14, 16, 74, 111, 115, 124
 ground of the, 73
 in beauty, 57, 105, 111, 153, 180
 in the good, 111
 negative, 177
 subjective, 108, 110, 114, 133
 universal, possibility of a, 108
possession
 empirical, 44
practical, 3, 11, 24, 27–29, 32, 48, 54, 66, 75, 92, 206
 and theoretical, 13, 28–29, 32–33, 39, 45, 48, 55, 76, 82, 155, 188, 192
 primacy of the, 30, 121
 social and, 107, 116, 118, 122–123, 125

purpose, 15–17, 68–69, 122, 138, 154, 164–165, 168, 172, 198
  and meaning, 158, 168
  determinate, 68
  nature's, 170
  purposive without a, 17, 56–57, 68–69, 93, 104, 140
purposiveness
  different kinds of, 165
  external, 165, 170
  formal, 16, 96
  in general, 159
  in nature, 199
  intentional, 185
  internal, 90, 166, 169
  judgments of, 77
  law of, 47
  material, 165
  mechanistic inquiry within, 170
  objective, 56, 67–69, 74, 95, 154, 159, 166, 185
  play and, 106
  principle of, 1, 12–18, 35–36, 47, 56–57, 61, 67, 128, 154, 156, 164, 169
  relative, 165
  subjective, 56–57, 70, 73, 113, 153–154, 159, 177
  without a purpose, 137

Rauscher, Fred, 12
Rawls, John, 10
reality
  empirical, 83
  objective, 113, 145, 202
reason, 5, 21–24, 27–28, 30, 32, 35, 37–39, 46, 50–51, 53, 58–59, 75–76, 83, 85, 93, 95, 100–101, 127, 139, 146, 171, 178–180, 188–190, 192, 195, 201, 205
  absolute end of, 28
  and Beauty, Ideal of, 93
  and idea of maximum, 95
  and metaphysics, demand for, 5
  and natural desires, 27
  and nature, 2, 27, 146, 205
  and the understanding, 16, 35–36, 46
  concepts of, 98, 145, 166
  demands of, 26, 32, 51, 82, 91, 146, 175, 204
  ends of, 17, 32, 37, 155
  fact of, 202
  freedom and, 42, 138
  idea of, 95, 98–99, 144–145, 178–179, 202–203
  interests of, 2, 13, 29, 187, 204, 206
  law of, 76, 179
  needs of, 30, 32, 34, 74, 82, 131, 201

  practical, 25–27, 29, 31, 187, 190, 192, 195, 197
  purview of, 4, 27, 35
  speculative, 22–23
  structure of, 50
  theoretical, 29–30, 186–189, 191
  theoretical and practical, 188, 192
  universality of, 107
reflection, 3, 47, 63, 73, 76–77, 80, 124, 148, 157, 169–170, 172, 183, 194, 196–197, 202
  activity of, 18, 47, 65–67, 71–72, 80, 196
  aesthetic judgments of, 17
  associated with possibility, 57
  concepts of, 39
  contemplative, on art, 77
  definition of, 46, 63
  disinterested, 13
  judgments of, 2–3, 5, 12–14, 17, 20, 34–38, 46–49, 54, 57, 60–62, 66–67, 69, 75, 80, 102, 104–105, 140, 182, 198
  judgments of, as heautonomous, 47–49
  objects of, 66, 73
  sphere of, 13, 195
  transcendental, 39, 196
Reid, Thomas, 121
Reinhold, Karl Leonhard, 14
representation, 129
  as purposive, 137, 150
  empirical, 35, 47, 49, 57, 60–65, 68, 76, 79–80, 113, 115, 149, 205
right, 52, 106, 109, 115, 120, 122, 127
  and civil society, 52
  and taste, judgment of, 108
  cosmopolitan, 51–52, 197
  in accord with, 108
  justify an acquired, 109
  territorial, 43
Rohlf, Michael, 36
Rossi, Philip, 191
Rousseau, Jean-Jacques, 174
rule
  form of a, 140
  objective, 94, 112

Sassen, Brigitte, 132, 146
satisfaction
  feeling of, 113
  practical and theoretical, 29
Schaefer, John D., 121
Schaftesbury, Lord (Anthony Ashley Cooper), 121
Schaper, Eva, 10
Schelling, F. W. J., 7–8
Schiller, Friedrich, 8

science
  natural, 23, 30, 48, 54, 164, 181
  Newtonian, 164
sciences
  biological, 90
  empirical, 9–10
Scylla and Charybdis, 90
sense
  common, 118–119, 121–122, 124, 202
  communal, the idea of a, 127
sensibility, 39, 117, 122
sensus communis, 7, 18, 54, 109, 113, 115–130, 133, 138, 150, 153, 183
significance
  aesthetic, 100, 144
skepticism, 19, 107, 109, 120–121, 123, 127, 150
Smith, John E., 9
Socrates, 111, 116
soul
  human, essential nature of the, 58
Spinozist, 200
spirit, 19, 89, 99–100, 102–103, 107, 131–133, 143–144, 147–150, 152, 205
  as excessiveness of nature, 147
  faculty of, the, 144
Stoicism, 118
Stoner, Samuel, 135
subjectivity, 54, 110, 132
sublime, 1, 6, 19, 159, 177–181, 183
  feeling of the, 178
sublimity
  feeling of our own, 178
substrate, 132, 191
  supersensible, the Idea of nature's, 132
substratum
  supersensible, 5, 53, 56, 149–150, 152–153
subsumption, 21, 47
supersensible, 5, 31, 37, 40, 45, 49, 53, 56–57, 76, 82, 99–100, 102, 132, 145, 148–150, 152–153, 170, 182, 184, 186, 192–193, 202–203
symbol, 12, 95, 191, 206
synthesis, 22

taste, 14, 94, 115
  and the universally communicable, 152
  judgments of, 7, 11–12, 14, 17–19, 54, 56, 65, 67–74, 77, 79–80, 85, 91–96, 98, 102–103, 106–109, 111–115, 124, 126–129, 133, 135–136, 177, 202, 206
  principle of, 94
teleology, 15, 159, 168, 181, 184
  aesthetics and, 12
  beauty and, 8, 20, 34, 55

  in judging organisms, 163
  judgments of, 14
  moral, 194, 196
  nature in, 17
  physical, 192–193, 196–197, 203
  principle of, 159, 166, 168–170, 176, 184, 199
  use of, 19, 162, 164, 166, 173
territory, 1, 3, 6–7, 16–19, 36, 40–50, 54, 58, 60–61, 65–67, 69–70, 73, 75–77, 81, 93, 102–103, 109, 113, 129, 134, 140, 153–155, 157, 159, 171–172, 176, 183–184, 192, 196, 202–203
  and domain, 38, 40–41, 46, 52
  as ground, 70
  as region of human experience, 53
  itself, appearance of the, 57
  objects in the, 53
  of judgment, 2, 35, 43, 48, 62, 69, 205
Thiel, Karsten, 39
things
  form of, 163, 168
  purposive, 166, 199, 205
thinking
  forms of, 185
  human, transcendentally a priori forms of, 50
  the faculty for, 46, 62
thought
  and being, harmony of, 61, 75
  forms of human, 58
Toyoda, Tetsuya, 43
transition, 2–3, 6, 17–18, 20, 30, 35–37, 39, 42, 45, 48–49, 70, 81, 104, 154, 204
Tuschling, Burkhard, 59

understanding
  laws of the, 2, 29, 57, 67, 183
unity, 3–4, 6, 13, 15, 18, 22–23, 30, 33, 35, 49, 73, 89, 91, 103, 117, 129, 131, 163, 188, 195
  absolute, 83
  and reason, 2, 82
  highest, 21–22
  life is, 91
  of force and matter, 84, 91, 102, 180, 187
  of imagination and understanding, 73
  of nature, 163
  of our faculties, 125
  of reason's dual interests, 29
  pattern of, 4
  subjective, 72, 124
  supersensible, 37, 57
  systematic, 8, 188
  transcendental, of apperception, 62–63, 106
  unconditioned, of the whole, 186

universality
  feeling of, 127
  form of, 24

Vico, Giambattista, 118, 120
virtue
  and happiness, analytic unity of, 25

Watkins, Eric, 158, 171
whole
  ordered, the idea of an, 161
  the idea of the, 38, 167, 171
Wieland, Christoph Martin, 143
will, 3, 24, 26–28, 31, 33, 36, 44, 46, 68, 92, 97, 103, 128, 131, 137, 146, 166–168, 175–176, 181, 184–185, 197–200, 202, 204
  activity of the, 101, 167
  and freedom, 24, 46, 101
  force of our, 100
  freedom of the, 51, 184
  good, 5, 24–25, 51, 92, 194, 197–198
  holy, 32
  of God, 200
  rational, 27, 131, 198
  unconditioned, 3, 24
Wood, Allen, 193
world, 2, 19, 21, 23–24, 26, 33–35, 51, 105, 117, 125, 129, 132, 200
  idea of the, 82, 189
  morally intelligible, 24, 26
  perfectly rational, 24
  reason's efficacy in the, 6
  sensible, 31, 45, 171
  share a, in common, 19

Zammito, John, 12, 134, 138, 177
Zinkin, Melissa, 79, 125
Zuckert, Rachel, 5, 12, 15, 33–34, 93, 132, 158–159, 185

For EU product safety concerns, contact us at Calle de José Abascal, 56–1°,
28003 Madrid, Spain or eugpsr@cambridge.org.

www.ingramcontent.com/pod-product-compliance
Ingram Content Group UK Ltd.
Pitfield, Milton Keynes, MK11 3LW, UK
UKHW020744160725
460850UK00017B/221